The Other Sid
EDEN

*The Royal Mail's commemoration
stamp issue for Eden Project,
2000.*

FootSteps Press
Kernow

The Other Side of Eden

FootSteps Press First Edition
www.footsteps.co

Typeset by Daniel Nanavati

Cover design and additional
Photographs from Bob Willingham FRPS
© Bob Willingham

Photographs from Gerald Sharp
© Gerald Sharp Photography

Photographs from Ross Hoddinott
© Ross Hoddinott

Photographs from Nicholas Grimshaw Partners (NGP)
© NGP

Photographs courtesy of Western Morning News
© Western Morning News

ISBN 978-1-908867-24-7

The Other Side Of
EDEN

JONATHAN BALL

Jonathan Ball in Mediterranean Biome at Eden - September 2006.

(Photograph by Sue Handford, Chocolate Dog Marketing Services)

Jonathan Ball is the co-founder of the Eden Project in Cornwall. An architect by training, Bard of Gorsedh Kernow, choir master, traveller, husband, father and grandfather. Inspired by his love of Cornwall and of Bude in particular, he continues to champion the early concepts of the Eden Project to deliver a building of international distinction and bring a recognised centre of world wide excellence to Cornwall.

Bodelva Pit, St.Blazey 1995

*I dedicate this book to the people of Cornwall,
and in particular those Cornishmen by whose toil,
for so little reward,
Bodelva Pit was formed*

The Commission is asking you to lift your eyes from the familiar, the mediocre, the mundane and to look to the glory of the nation. We need people like yourselves, people of vision, energy and determination, up and down the country, to create partnerships of ideas, expertise and optimism. Without your input, the celebration of the millennium in the United Kingdom will become a missed opportunity. We often talk about once in a lifetime chances. The dawn of a new millennium is a once in thirty generations event. None of us should let it pass us by. One Ethelred the Unready in our history is enough.

... Why should there not be a scientific or engineering project that becomes one of the wonders of the third millennium?

... Architects must seize the chance to house these projects with the ingenuity and style that Paxton brought to the Crystal Palace.

From a speech by the Rt.Hon. Peter Brooke, CH MP, Chairman of the Millennium Commission 22nd June 1994, paragraphs 17 and 25.

Chapters

Foreword

By *Sir David Brewer CMG JP*

As you read this book, whether you know him or not, you will learn much about the character, the passion and the commitment of Jonathan Ball, and of the essential support he received from his wife, Victoria, and all of his family.

This story, of the extraordinary events which were part of the evolution of the Eden Project, reads like a legal thriller, and it will keep your attention to the end. It has been held back for many years to ensure that, with the passing of time, no harm can come to the Project, which does so much for Cornwall.

When I am at my family home in Cornwall, I have made regular trips to the Eden Project, usually with friends who are visiting Cornwall.

Jonathan lives at Bude, on the Atlantic Coast of North Cornwall, and for many years he has been involved with the Royal National Lifeboat Institution (RNLI). He is a long-serving lifeboat man, as a member of the crew of the Bude lifeboat. There can be no greater commitment to humanity than putting out out to sea in stormy conditions to rescue people who are in distress. The characteristics exemplifying this service set the tone for this book. Reading the events that are described, there must have been several times when Jonathan was in a situation which made him wish he had a paddle!

Here, with the RNLI, the links between Jonathan in Cornwall and me in London begin to overlap, as I have a long association with the City of London Branch of the RNLI, which is involved with the Tower lifeboat station, on the Thames near Waterloo Bridge, which covers the tidal waters of the River Thames.

In the world of Architecture, which Jonathan so enjoys, and in which he reached the highest professional standards and qualifications, I think of his years as Honorary Secretary of the Royal Institute of British Architects (RIBA) and - in happier times - of the success of the Jonathan Ball Practice.

Jonathan has a great love of Cornwall. When I see him there he is very patriotic, and I know how delighted he is that, as this book is published, the Cornish people have been granted minority status under European rules for the Protection of National Minorities.

When I see him in London he is a marvellous Ambassador for Cornwall. And so it was when he had the honour of being elected the Master of his Livery Company, the Worshipful Company of Chartered Architects, in 2007. Happily that was close to the same period in which I was Lord Mayor of the City of London.

So, when you reach the last page of this book, you will read the final lines of the refrain of 'Trelawny', which Jonathan rightly describes as the undisputed anthem for Cornwall.

And, in the photograph which follows this Foreword, you can see the Author of this Book (and his wife Victoria) and the Author of the Foreword, lending voice to those lines during the Banquet of the Worshipful Company of Chartered Architects at Mansion House celebrating his Master's year!

I hope you enjoy this book.

Sir David Brewer CMG JP
Lord Lieutenant of Greater London
Lord Mayor of London 2005/6

Photographs Gerald Sharp Photography

Chapter 1

The Journey to Eden

1994   *'Hi – my name's Tim Smit. I am a palindrome and I have got a good idea for a project for the Millennium. I have spoken to the four most important people in Cornwall I know and three of them have told me to ring you.'*

'Tim, flattery will get you everywhere' was my reply – 'you have my undivided attention. When can we get together?'

Thus the incredible journey began on Friday 30th September 1994 with an afternoon phone call. It is the sort of call that sets aside any plans you might have had for the following day. Early morning Saturday saw my wife Victoria and me on the road to Mevagissey to meet Tim, for the first time, at Heligan. We listened to his ideas. He wanted to build the largest greenhouses on planet earth and create a museum of

The author and Tim Smit.
(Photograph: Charles Francis. JB archive)

plants. This would tell the story of the great plant hunters and deliver a world class building and horticultural focus for Cornwall. Tim wanted to capture the striking lunar landscape of the china clay tips which define mid Cornwall and somehow harness these features to Cornwall's future.

Timothy Bartel Smit made a very charismatic impression. He was very different to anybody I had ever met before. I sensed here was someone with an air of cultivated shambolic in his appearance, and anything but shambolic in his thoughts. His steely eyes were in conflict with a warm smile. His striking characteristic was of a mad professor, with wispy hair that merged with the rising cigar smoke to create an image similar to the occasional alto cirrus of a summer Cornish sky. A Dutch national, Tim, an archaeology graduate of

Durham University, had pitched up in Cornwall in 1987 following an All-Sorts career which had spanned archaeology, music publishing, gardening, Director of a girls' school in Ascot, and rocking and rolling his way through the music industry as a record producer and composer. With Cornishman John Nelson he had set about Heligan Gardens.

Success in life is often more a matter of chance than of ability. In this lottery of life here was a moment of meeting where fortune favoured both of us, albeit fate was to get a bit muddled along the way. Chance in the twists and turns of life offers probability of success only when industry and integrity unite in common accord. Destiny would play an uneven hand in our Eden journey together.

We spoke for six and a half hours non stop, having an admiring tour of what Tim had achieved at Heligan with his business partner John Nelson, and then brainstorming next steps. Victory would be building the largest greenhouses on planet earth in Cornwall in time to greet the Millennium: and what, for Heaven's sake, would that cost? Off the top of my head, I plucked a figure of us having to find up to perhaps £300m. Already the first hours of our discussions had moved from the perceived starting point of an architect/client relationship to one of us being 50/50 business partners sharing firstly the financial risks, and then our skills, talents, expertise, contacts and imagination in order to go further and higher. Instead of it being a project to create critical mass in marketing terms for Tim's business, the Lost Gardens of Heligan, it would be a project for the people of Cornwall for the Millennium; in fact it would go beyond that which any Cornish project had aspired to in living memory.

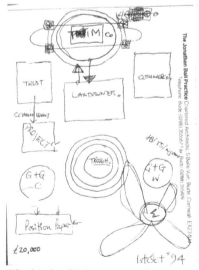

The birth of Eden postcard as sketched by the author 01/10/1994.
(JB archive)

Before the end of the first day we had so many ideas buzzing and an outline structure of how it would all work, including our business relationship, had been sketched by me on the back of a postcard. Let's call our business partnership MIMCO, I said – The Magnificent ideas for the Millennium Company. The ever astute Victoria suggested, 'even better TIMCO – The Terrific Ideas for the Millennium Company' – having already sized up Tim's belief in his aptitude for self promotion and marketing – an innate ability that had delivered to Cornwall the Lost Gardens of Heligan. What a marketing master-stroke, putting the word 'lost' into a visitor destination to encourage everyone to find it. And so it was that T replaced the crossed out M on the postcard.

We surmised there were four key task areas and we would share these equally. Tim would take ownership of leading all the procuring and delivering of the plant exhibits and also take leadership on delivery of the business case ... there was good enough reason, in that his experience to date on Heligan had confirmed to him how many gardeners per acre were needed for a large horticultural project. I would take ownership of leading the delivery of the architecture and take the lead on finding a site. I would also lead on establishing support from the great and the good both in Cornwall and London. Securing early grant aid and risking our own pump priming funding would fall equally to us both. As to personal financial risks we agreed 'a campaign of equal misery', a phrase I had borrowed from policy committee meetings at the Royal Institute of British Architects (RIBA) on which I had served for a number of years.

The author inspires early Eden supporters with a visit to Roche Rock. *(JB archive)*

A week after our meeting the first key letter was sent by Tim to Michael Galsworthy as Chairman of the Millennium Committee in Cornwall and who as High Sheriff of Cornwall had initiated the successful In Pursuit of Excellence programme, Tim and I having met Michael separately in the interim. The letter outlined Tim's original vision,

> " ... *enormous permanent structures built in the clay district enabling people to experience plants in their natural habitat, designed around a museum of gardening, explaining the history of gardening and of the great plant hunters and of their impact on the economics and demography of the world. These structures must, quite simply, be the best and a photograph of them should be internationally recognisable ... Jonathan Ball, who is joining me in advancing these ideas, is currently pursuing preliminary site appraisals in the clay district which is ideal for several reasons ...*"

The Jonathan Ball Practice had, for many years, acted for the Boscawen family, including the wholly owned Goonvean and Restowrack China Clay Company with its extensive landholding interests within the china clay district of Cornwall. It was clear to me at the outset that in negotiating with prospective landowners any project of Eden's scale and ambition would need the benefit of the mutual trust and shared intimate knowledge of working practices that flows from a long term professional relationship.

"Aaah Wilkins in all his glory" - a family and neighbours' Sunday outing to revisit the spot on a Tregothnan Open Day.

(JB archive)

Three days after our Heligan meeting I met in London with Evelyn Boscawen, son of Viscount Falmouth, whose family seat Tregothnan overlooks the majestic Carrick Roads close by where the Truro and Fal rivers meet the sea and stands sentinel over what has been one of the largest family land holdings in Cornwall since the 14th century. Tregothnan was splendidly remodelled by architect and classical scholar William Wilkins in the 1820s alongside his best known work, the National Gallery in Trafalgar Square, well before its 'carbuncle' days. Happy memories indeed of George Boscawen the 9th Viscount Falmouth conducting me around the grounds at one of our professional meetings. At the end of a delightful garden walkway we rounded a magnificent specimen rhododendron. As I stopped stood and stared at Tregothnan's exuberant front elevation, Lord Falmouth reminisced that this was the very spot where John Betjeman, on a similar conducted tour, had poetically observed ' Aaah – Wilkins in all his Glory' .

And so, within days, I was delighted to be able to let Tim know of my handshake with Evelyn Boscawen and subsequent confirmatory note to him that,

> *"... matters are now proceeding at a pace and on the understanding that the location siting will be on Tregothnan Estate/Goonvean land."*

It was this handshake that led us, soon after, to the first siting proposal for the world's largest greenhouses.

Those fond of Cornwall will know the old family estates have defined so much of the rhythm and pace of the County's evolution. Prior to the Reform Bill of 1832 Cornwall returned no fewer than 44 Members of Parliament when the whole of Scotland returned 45. Patronage, money and fiercely protected family interests prevailed. As the writings of A L Rowse point out, just some of the illustrious names returned to the Palace of Westminster to represent Cornwall included Sir Francis Drake, Sir Walter Raleigh, Sir Richard Grenville, the Trelawnys, the Boscawens, Wellington in his pre-elevation days and of course Godolphin who became Cornwall's first Prime Minister of the land. This political power accurately reflected and preserved business interests. There was order in society, with farming folk and gentry living side by side in agrarian harmony, but of course it was that which lay beneath the verdant fields that held the value. It was the owning of the mineral rights, the control of the extractive processes and the retention of these revenues not paid out as wages (particularly in the winning of China Clay) that delivered the wealth and power.

Tregothnan family history as defined by this ensured a continuity that insulated the large estates from the seasonal and economic upheavals of history delivering a timelessness reinforced by the accumulated wisdom of always retaining mineral rights regardless of any imperative to sell estate lands. All this was as much about culture as it was about economics and looking back I am sure the expansion of my architectural practice into retention by several of these Cornish estates, and some in Devon, flowed from my own empathy and understanding of where the balance between cultural and economic value lay. Even when Eden came to the substantial purchase of Bodelva Pit the mineral rights were retained by the Boscawen family – projects come and go, but rights go on for ever.

If I were to look back on one weekend in my formative years that was to forge my future most powerfully it would be about 1959 in my early years as a boarder at Truro School. My Scout master Leonard Penna, soon to become my house master and geology teacher, selected a small group of us for a hike across the moors of West Penwith and the granite uplands of the Land's End peninsula, giving me my first subliminal lesson in connecting geology, landscape and archaeology. His passion for these fabled Penwith sights was infectious and he extolled to us the immutability of granite even to weathering in this most wild of landscapes, explaining that coarse grained granite will last for ever and fine grained granite a day longer. From these granite igneous extrusions all Cornwall's mineral wealth flows.

A couple of years ahead of me at Truro School was David Penhaligon who will surely be added to the great names of Cornish Parliamentarians. He was to become the voice of Cornwall at Westminster and what a tragedy for us all when he was killed in a car crash on an early December morning 1986, en route to thanking postal workers in his constituency working overtime for Christmas tide. It was David Penhaligon who established a Cornish version of the cost benefit financial ratio. It was based on the perceived astronomical sums deployed on the County's Highways expenditure and for several years each and every item of expenditure in the County he related by quantum to equivalent yards of the Camborne by-pass. It was this Penhaligonism that was to inspire me many years later to ring up the authorities at Truro Cathedral when trying to convey to the people of Cornwall the scale of our Eden biomes.

But best of all, for me, was David's definition of an expert as, '... *someone who lives 200 miles away.*'

In my mind's eye I had the vision that a visit to Eden from London would start on platform 1 at Paddington station with the Cornish Riviera Express having a dedicated Eden coach independently liveried and possibly even with Eden team members greeting our customers and looking after them on their journey which would terminate by them stepping from the carriage directly into the Project. When the Channel Tunnel started regularly hitting the national headlines marketing images were conjured up for me, of dinner in Paris and breakfast at Eden. So a redundant china clay site, with direct access to the main line rail network, with the appropriate spectacle, but no 'visual bad neighbour' issues? A tall order indeed, but never say die. From my work with Tregothnan I knew of the clay line that linked with the main line at Par station terminating at the huge redundant Goonbarrow clay dries, an enormous building which had prompted much head scratching by Nick Jeans, Lord Falmouth's agent and myself, as to how we could find a profitable new use for this striking piece of Cornish industrial history. Added to this was, for me, the advantage that close by was Roche Rock which years before I had climbed with my A level geology group on a field trip with Leonard Penna once again sharing his Cornish passions. To this day Roche Rock remains remote and mystical. An ancient cast iron notice warns visitors brave enough to advance through bracken and an unbeaten right of way that you are on Lord Falmouth's property and to proceed with respect for this renowned Cornish antiquity. What an amazing manifestation that enshrines so much of Cornwall's spiritual essence to have as part of the garden experience for our visitors, I thought.

The location commended itself, in strategic planning terms, beyond the rail line that actually terminated at the site. The arterial A30 trunk road carries most of Cornwall's inbound and outbound visitor road traffic close by without being invasive. Of equal benefit Roche Rock is about a 20 minute drive from Cornwall's only airport at Newquay. The local planning authority at Restormel and the strategic County planning authority in Truro endorsed my assessment and we were soon able to announce not only an amazing idea with which Cornwall would hopefully greet the Millennium, but also a site full

A brooding Roche Rock with the Goonbarrow first site proposal in the distance.

(*JB archive*)

of history, and symbolism and, of equal importance, one which could handle large numbers of visitors.

With November came the vital need for project notepaper and a name. Tim readily agreed with my suggestion that we have as our holding name 'Millennium Project Cornwall UK.' The Millennium Commission held the best prospect of securing significant funding for what we hoped would be one of Britain's flagship projects and our holding name would send the strongest possible signal to the Millennium Commission. And we needed a Mission Statement. After some to-ing and fro-ing between Mevagissey and Bude we formally announced our ambition,

> *To create under one roof a range of natural plant habitats found on Planet Earth. An international resource designed for research, education and public enjoyment to herald the new Millennium, bequeathing a gift of incalculable value to those who will follow us, our hope for and belief in the future.*

First to receive this statement were the guests to our Project inaugural luncheon party held in the Belvedere, at my Bude office where I had hosted so many memorable gatherings over the years. It was a joyous occasion and is still spoken of by several in attendance who were to play a significant role in developing the project's philosophy and securing Cornwall's endorsement for the idea.

Next we needed to initiate support in London. Tim and I were all too aware that unbridled enthusiasm and commitment to an idea will only prosper if the necessary scientific gravitas underpinned the vision and we were soon to get our first lesson on the need to tread lightly on the arranged delicate flowers of vested interest in national institutions. Side by side with this was the need to have the finest creative minds of our generation engaged in realising the vision and we also soon learnt that internationally acclaimed architects and design consultants were not easily persuaded to commit unfunded resources to appraise an idea proposed on redundant china clay land at the end of the longest country road in Britain.

A next day telephone call following my first meeting with Tim was to an architect chum, Ronnie Murning, who had been closely linked with the Jonathan Ball Practice since the mid 1970's and his early architectural training days at Plymouth University. Ronnie worked with me on many projects during his time with the practice in Bude, several of which had received national design award recognition. Ronnie is defined by his evident Glaswegian characteristics. His architectural

Architect Ronnie Murning (JB archive)

talents were inevitably to take him to the other side of the River Tamar and London where his abilities and flair were soon recognised, although he returned to Bude for a further brief period with the practice in 1985 when he was made an Associate of the firm. Throughout my career I have never met anyone else who combines undiluted architectural talent with such a pragmatic, robust and forceful approach to project delivery. I was in no doubt Ronnie would be a vital contributor to any future Eden success.

Our first London dinner had to demonstrate that our ambitions were serious, achievable and demanding of support. I brought together a group of people whose influence in the fields of horticulture, project development and authority in Whitehall would likely determine whether our star could remain in the ascendency. A few days later, and amongst others I received a thank you note from the Director General of the Royal Horticultural Society describing the evening as '*one of the most memorable dinners to which I have ever had the pleasure to be invited..... and to describe your scheme as ambitious would be a gross understatement of the obvious*' . We were on our way

Our first meeting at Kew Gardens with the Director Sir Ghillean Prance did not go quite so well. Kew had its own Millennium Seed Bank Project and there was a distinct whiff of threat to this in what we were proposing. Subsequent telephone conversations between Tim and Ghillean Prance brought forth the possibility of some form of partnership which saw our first change of project name with the Regional press in the West Country trumpeting 'Kew West, Cornwall' as the banner under which we would next be advancing. Not for the last time were we to change the name above our Mission Statement on the notepaper.

Chapter   2

From the Humble to the Heroic

I had been giving a lot of thought to how we move from words to our first images on paper and having formulated my preliminary ideas asked Tim to meet me in Truro for a run through over a cup of tea, and we scheduled the meeting for Friday 2nd December 1994.

I gave him a brief, informal presentation which I entitled 'From the Humble to the Heroic'. My journey started with the famously heroic Palm House at Kew, the best recognised greenhouse worldwide, then switching back first to Tresco Abbey Gardens on the Isles of Scilly, then the Lost Gardens of Heligan, before returning to the handful of rhododendron leaves that I had collected from the hotel garden on the way in. I spoke to Tim of leaves and

The author's first presentation to Tim - the move from words to first images. (JB archive)

plants having an architecture, having a design that first gave them structural capacity, beauty and elegance, and how their form also followed function. Leaves are collectors of sunlight, energy and rain. Some leaves are designed to concentrate rainfall back to the very base of the tree or plant to which they are attached, a good example being a palm leaf that channels precious water to the very centre of the plant. Some leaves are designed to throw water off to the areas where the furthest tendrils of the tree's roots extend. I suggested Tim look at these leaves differently and by way of example I took three or four leaves, juxtaposed them into an enclosure, and asked Tim to narrow his eyes and think of them being a structure of enormous scale. My first design idea for the Visitor Entrance was a giant leaf structure arching down from the lip of the pit enabling the rain water to drain symbolically from the leaf shaped roof into the lake. Much time was devoted to exploring alternative starting points for the first visual impressions of our dream.

Meanwhile, it was the politics that prevailed. Just before Christmas Tim and I made a detailed presentation to Cornwall County Council with Peter Cocks, Chairman of the Council, the County Planning Officer along with Tim Jones representing the private sector and economic development representatives from Restormel Borough Council. Our Kew West ideas were presented as a dream alongside a begging bowl and we had much progress we could already report to the powers that be. We had a prospective site with the freeholders indicating their willingness to sell the land and also to cooperate technically with feasibility studies. We sat comfortably within strategic planning ambitions for Cornwall and Restormel Borough Council, as the local planning authority. We had already secured support of several high profile institutions and individuals at national level. Everybody had to be made aware that for a huge scheme in Cornwall to succeed, the case would have to be so compelling that the political fallout from not supporting it would be unthinkable. Certainly we were up against forces from more heavily populated areas of Britain that were better marshalled and that could only be overtaken by an idea that was so powerful that it achieved early critical mass politically and with a united voice of support from all the peoples of the far South West. And, of course, we were able to report the involvement of Quantity Surveyors of sufficient stature to establish the appropriate business and financial confidence in the Commissioners during the initial evaluation period for all projects that aspired to be one of the 12 flagship status projects for Britain.

1995   The New Year of 1995 brought enormous pressure to bring together our first submission to the Millennium Commission, which was a huge task. How on earth were we to articulate simply and concisely the length and breadth of our developing ideas? I was in no doubt that until we established some compelling images to accompany our words we would not make the progress necessary to meet the Millennium Commission's base criteria. I was also well aware that our poverty of funding did not allow my engagement of the calibre of architectural and engineering resources necessary for the delivery of a world class project. I therefore committed the resources of the Jonathan Ball Practice to this task, leading a three man team comprising myself, my senior architect Robert Harris and my senior technician Michael McMillan.

I had realised from the outset that a venture of this magnitude proposed in the rural outposts of Cornwall would need a design team of international acclaim to deliver funding credibility. In order to secure a top design team I knew we would have to develop initial concept design work as a requirement for securing a political profile sufficient to create confidence in the idea. As we had said in our presentation to Cornwall County Council we, and Cornwall, needed a proposal that made us as immediately recognisable internationally as the Sydney Opera House.

My early December presentation to Tim with my handful of leaves was a meeting he was to refer to a number of times over the coming months, as first

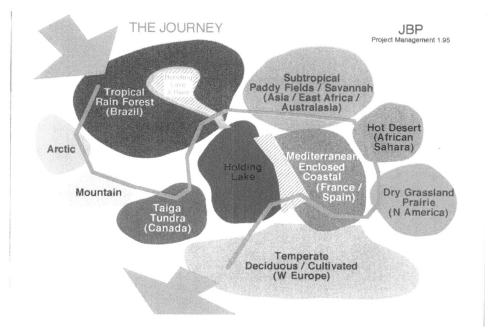

Jonathan Ball Practice January 1995. First study of the visitor journey and experience. The Bude design team took immense pride in seeing the final Eden architecture so closely reflecting this first study. (JB archive)

thumbnail sketches emerged.

These first steps in Eden's architecture were moments in time I will always cherish, not in any proprietorial sense, but in that destiny had favourably marked out my circumstances and purpose, and equipped and prepared me for the part I was to play in the task. My seven years' professional training at the Architectural Association (AA) had coincided with the flourishing of Archigram, a group of architects led by Peter Cook who became a powerful and prescient architectural phenomenon of the 1960s, a storm force 10 surging at the future. They were a new energy force equipping architectural students of my generation for innovating the future by free thinking, majoring on the need to think globally when launching on a career rooted in social engineering, and charged with the task of transforming the prospects for increasingly mobile populations.

The God of our choice in all this was the American polymath Buckminster Fuller, affectionately known as 'Bucky'. His publications such as 'Operating Manual for Spaceship Earth' gave birth to a new vocabulary which in turn spawned a new age of thinking. My Tutor at the AA, Archigram's Ron Herron, was my passport to this new world which was light years ahead of my accumulated life experience at this time.

My year 2 of AA studies had seen me struggling, with my Head of School Bill Allen eloquently noting ... 'bags of enthusiasm and full of good ideas but

The US geodesic dome Pavilion at the World Expo Montreal 1967 designed by R Buckminster Fuller, photograph by the author. *(JB archive)*

his progress has been somewhat hampered by his basic inability to draw ... .' To my rescue came Ron Herron, securing for me a trip to Expo 67 in Montreal where I was blown away by the originality of Bucky's US Pavilion, a stunning 75 metre geodesic dome, a symbol of a future pregnant with possibility. A sphere is the most efficient way of enclosing space. Bucky's brilliant, innovatory thinking, mathematically based in relation to the geometry of curved surfaces, delivered new opportunities for lightweight structures to enclose space at a scale beyond the dreams of our forebears. Pure genius.

The Eden Project is probably one of the most prominent geodesic structures in the world. Symbolically it is Cornwall's Eiffel Tower, its Taj Mahal, its Sydney Opera House. That Eden is so much more than this is due in no small measure to the insights and influence of Bucky, and Eden's prominence in both physical manifestation and cultural expression connecting firmly back to the US Pavilion at Expo 67 which launched these amazing ideas to admiring populations and dazzled architectural students. But I am ahead of myself. Our first task was to establish the scale and form of that which we needed to enclose.

Robert, Michael and I set about the process by defining the complete range of climatic types as set out in the nearest reference book, which, in the pre-Google era was the Reader's Digest Atlas of the World. Well known Cornish geologist Courtenay Smale, who was employed by the Boscawen family, suggested I get in touch with Haydn Scholes from CSMA, a company spawned out of the world renowned Camborne School of Mines, who was operating a geothermal government research contract known locally as "The Hot Rocks project". This was a European funded proposal to research geothermal heat sourced by boring through the edge of the earth's crust. Along with solar power this offered exciting prospects for our greenhouses to achieve a zero energy audit. I went to meet Haydn at Rosemanowes quarry, near Helston and it was clear from the outset than an holistic approach would be necessary. The sooner we secured scientific gravitas, and Cornwall specific science at that, the better this would validate the all too important first diagrams and images we were plucking out of our imagination in Bude and upon which the Project's dreams would likely sink or swim.

This first meeting established several key pointers signposting our future. Significantly, for my purpose, Haydn said we needed a lake in the middle which would become a heat store - establish a big lake and your main renewable issues will be solved, he said. It also became clear to me from this first meeting, a point stressed by Haydn, that politicians only finance what they can understand and that all our early work should focus on simple, easy to read and easy to interpret diagrams that conveyed in the simplest possible way what the project was all about. We would be taking excess heat in the summer and giving it back in the winter. We would be harnessing Cornwall's unique geology. We would be the first to have several branches of science all holding hands. I left the quarry with my head buzzing to return for a further meeting shortly after, to have Tim engage with the ideas.

In Peter Thoday and Philip Macmillan Browse Tim had his two key plant lieutenants, both of whom had helped deliver the Heligan garden success for Tim and John Nelson and had planted in Tim the seeds of what came next, encouraging him to dream big dreams which had resulted in our first telephone conversation. From my very first meeting with Tim we had established the concept that our story was a journey and our first images had to convey this essence. Of course, the use of the word 'journey' came from Tim's original starting point for the Project which was to tell the story of the great plant hunters in history and how their journeying back to Cornwall had created the Cornish garden tradition. Both Peter and Philip now contributed to our emerging preliminary design brief which then allowed us to consider our first site-specific working diagrams on paper. In Bude we had made the decision that we should commit to a computer-based design process as this would facilitate easy exchange of ideas and coordination with other consultants later in the development of the Project when resources allowed. Our fledgling computer technology was commensurate with the level of investment the scale and character of our Practice allowed. Here was another very simple reason why high profile international projects remain almost exclusively the province of world class design practices which have a deeper resource base in talent and technology.

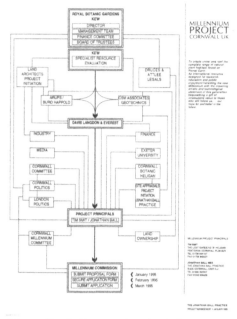

The author's first master sheet, January 1995, for the organisation to deliver the first Millennium Submission. *(JB archive)*

I created a master sheet of project communication and the overall management necessary, in my view, to deliver the Millennium submission and sketched this out on 11th January 1995. This diagram became part of the formal project management issue of mid January 1995 and delivered logic and organisation to what was a confused array of loose collaborative arrangements and allowed everybody to understand where we needed to go, how we were going to get there, and how Tim Smit and I were in charge of respective elements in leading the process. This diagram combined with the sketch study of our first site adjacent to Roche Rock and we called these diagrams The Journey – a series of images showing the sequence of spaces and the scale of the spaces relative to each habitat which is where Peter Thoday in particular, and Philip Macmillan Browse delivered valuable input and briefing, their expertise being brought to bear throughout the design and evolution of Eden.

One of our first computer generated forms looked at a concentric ziggurat as a piece of graphics to convey the essence of the idea, a journey through the various habitats of planet Earth. Concurrently with this we developed our 'journey bubbles' (page 11), an association diagram which linked spaces sequentially in order to tell the story. These bubbles became a key image for the development of the Project. The primary elements were overall plan layout and proportional scale of

The Journey

The Ziggurat January 1995. A preliminary study by the Jonathan Ball Practice as to how to convey the essence of a journey.

(JB archive)

one habitat in relation to the other, with the lake as thermal heat store with some thought as to how the visitor moved through the overall experience. All this came together in graphical form and was signed off horticulturally by Peter and Philip. It was to be of immense pride to the Bude office that some seven years later Nicholas Grimshaw's Eden was to open with a plan layout and visitor flow that so closely mirrored our initial designs in Bude in both scheme layout and proportionality.

The first sketch studies site-specific to Roche Rock comprised diagrammatic interlocking geodesic domes which reflected the relative size for each habitat as advised by Peter and Philip and how these habitats needed to connect in visitor flow. We had a cursory look at the scale of existing geodesic domes and also the largest known inflatable structures in the world at the time. Having completed these initial design studies, we went back to CSMA for further discussions about securing a

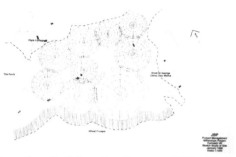

Jonathan Ball Practice, January 1995. First ideas for interlocking biomes. The first study for the Roche Rock site. (JB archive)

zero energy audit which of course would substantially impact on operating costs and would be attractive in our Business Case development. Their suggestion was that we concentrate on solar ahead of, or possibly even instead of, geothermal. Their European grant funded work was still at a research and development stage, so our prospects of having it signed off as part of our Business Case by rigorous Whitehall interrogation were slim. As it turned out Tim and I were roundly defeated in our core renewable energy ambitions. In order for us to secure finally what the number crunchers termed ' financial close', it was demanded of us that town gas be our prime energy source, the point being that if the renewable technology failed the plants would die and the entire Project would be consigned to the compost heap of history. This was to be one of the few occasions when 'the men in grey suits', as Tim referred to them, were to win the day.

Sine wave, Jonathan Ball Practice, December 1994. (JB archive)

Accordingly, we had further design meetings in Bude and came up with what we called the 'Stack Effect Profile' which in turn led our design thinking to the idea of a 'Sine Wave' form - a mathematical curve - which could be designed as one vast solar collector. Out of this thinking came the idea for a single picture to catch the public imagination.

In London Ronnie Murning was working with Richard Baldwin, then a rising star within Davis Langdon, internationally renowned Quantity Surveyors and Project Cost Consultants. On Tim's suggestion we engaged a City of London law firm founded in the mid 18th century and which by 1945

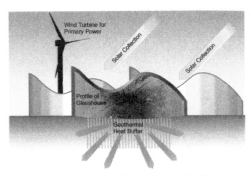

Renewable energies diagram, including geothermals, following meeting with CSMA. Jonathan Ball Practice, December 1994. *(JB archive)*

was known as Druces & Attlee when Henry Attlee, the father of the Labour Prime Minister Clement Attlee, was a partner. They acted for Tim at Heligan and his other personal and business interests and for us they were to provide advice on corporate governance, on the formation of a Trust, advice on the legals which attached to any submission to the Millennium Commission, and not least to protect the two co-founders' positions as by now the project was consuming not just our every working hour, but our every waking hour. In the Jonathan Ball Practice unfunded resources were gushing out like air from a burst inner tube.

First and foremost for me this was to be a project for the people of Cornwall and all early advice reinforced my instinct that the imperative was to take Cornwall with us on every step of our journey. Not only was it essential to demonstrate this to the Millennium Commission, but also given the pure scale and ambition, unless it was clearly signalled this was a Millennium project for Cornwall and the people of Cornwall, it would surely run out of steam sooner rather than later. The public authorities, led by Restormel Borough Council, the first to go out on a limb and vote us £25,000 project initiation funding, were soon behind us and our regional newspaper The Western Morning News became a day one champion for our cause. Suddenly there was also national media interest and a big Sunday feature promoted our project with a large photograph of Tim sitting on top of Roche Rock puffing away at his cigar. '*Sorry,*' said Tim, '*I forgot to mention to you the Sunday Telegraph were coming down for a major interview!*'

As far as the Millennium Commission was concerned, I had been able to bring a goodly measure of knowledge and background information to our first ever meeting at Heligan the previous September. Following my election in 1981 to the Council of my professional body, the Royal Institute of British Architects (RIBA) to represent the far south west, 1994 found me in my third term as the RIBA Honorary Secretary. For me this was one of the best member appointments, overseeing the constitutional running of the organisation, sitting on the right hand of the President at all meetings of Council and being able to alight on anything or everything that came to the RIBA by way of statutory consultation or any matters involving the built environment. On my first day in this post back in 1987 I had visited the various departments of the RIBA to introduce myself including the Professional Conduct and Discipline Department. This was run by the RIBA in-house lawyer, Robert. I breezed in

THE MILLENNIUM COMMISSION

A STRATEGY FOR
SUPPORTING
MILLENNIUM PROJECTS

JONATHAN BALL MBE
THE JONATHAN BALL PRACTICE
BUDE, CORNWALL EX23 8JJ
TEL (0288) 356557 FAX 356926

A SPEECH BY
THE RT HON PETER BROOKE CH MP
CHAIRMAN OF THE
MILLENNIUM COMMISSION

22 JUNE 1994

*The original photocopied introduction
from Rt.Hon Sir Peter Brooke calling for
Millennium Projects.* (JB archive)

and asked in a jocular manner how things were going for the legal eagle in Conduct and Discipline. *'Jonathan,'* came the sepulchral answer, *'shit creek is wider than you think!'*

The Millennium Commission had issued their Strategy for supporting Millennium Projects in June 1994 and I had read the documents received at the RIBA with great interest. I wrote to my local town Council in Bude saying here was an opportunity perhaps to secure a significant commission for public art and it would be the early bird that caught the worm. This idea took hold and with the tenacity of a number of local people it inspired the Bude Light, which was to become the Millennium Project for my home town.

The first Chairman of the Millennium Commission, Secretary of State Peter Brooke, set out ambitious ideas and, perhaps unusually for our nation, an ambitious funding commitment to support and encourage grand projects and bemoaned the lack of vision in this country. *'Are you ready to face this challenge'* was his invocation *'have you the vision to transform the face of our nation in the year 2000?' The Commission is asking you to lift your eyes from the familiar, the mediocre, the mundane and to look to the glory of the Nation. We need people like yourselves, people of vision, energy and determination to create partnerships of ideas, expertise and optimism. Without your input the celebration of the Millennium will become a missed opportunity. The dawn of a new Millennium is a once in 30 generations event. One Ethelred the Unready in our history is enough,'* he reminded us!

Our first pre qualification application to the Millennium Commission was despatched from Bude on 21st March 1995, retaining the Millennium Project Cornwall UK name and receiving acknowledgement

E D E N ! The
P r o j e c t
The Proposal
Volume 1
THE EDEN TRUST
December 1995

Eden Project Millennium Commission submission, volume 1 1995. (JB archive)

17

shortly thereafter confirming safe project receipt of what the Millennium Commission termed 'biodiversity glass structure' and assigning a case officer. The run up to our first submission had indeed been hectic. We knew that we had to pass certain milestones if we were to be taken seriously. Quite simply, in political terms there are not a lot of votes in Cornwall. If Cornwall was going to secure one of the 12 Landmark Projects, each of which the Millennium Commission had indicated would receive up to £50m on a matched funding basis, I knew we had to have a serious design team signed up behind the vision in time for our first submission at the end of April.

I agreed with Ronnie Murning the key to this was the cost consultants and quantity surveyors Davis Langdon, who would in turn provide confidence for internationally acclaimed architects, engineers and environmental consultants to come on board. The partner we were dealing with, Richard Baldwin, had been to see me in Bude and had also attended and clearly loved the energy that came out of that first dinner at my London Club. Richard was full of enthusiasm for the project, but sceptical about our capacity to pull it off making the good point that all the other landmark project submissions were coming from either national institutions, such as the Royal Botanic Gardens Kew, major City conurbations, or publicly funded regional development bodies, all with deep pockets, publicly funded and with heavy political support and endorsement already in the bag. So why should they take two blokes from Cornwall with a good idea seriously?

He had a point, but so did we and that was that Tim and I had travelled to London for a meeting with the Millennium Commission and had been informed that of the 1,600+ pre-qualification expressions of interest only six had received our level of interview. Yes, Richard would be delighted to accept my invitation to act for the project formally and, yes, he thought my dream team proposal of Nicholas Grimshaw and Partners as architects, Anthony Hunt Associates as engineers with Arup Associates for environmental advice and economic planning, was a winning combination. As it was to turn out both Nicholas Grimshaw and Anthony Hunt were big fans of Buckminster Fuller and of an age to have come firmly under his influence during their own student days. However, Richard cautioned, based on previous experience and current protocols attaching to the other known Millennium Landmark Project contenders,

> " ... *go away and find a financial commitment of £750,000, Jonathan, to get the design team to sign up and mobilise resources to deliver the feasibility work and outline design to deliver the dream. And please remember this: the best creative minds are already not available, so you have next to no chance of getting people to work for nothing.*"

At this hour of our lives Tim and I would have been hard pressed to muster £7500, let alone £750,000, so I said to Richard, '*OK, regardless of what you say, if I can get my first team choice of Nicholas Grimshaw and Partners and Anthony Hunt Associates to work for nothing through the first phase will Davis Langdon come on board?'* Yes they would, but don't kid yourself. Nick Grimshaw and I were both AA alumni and had found ourselves chatting at a Royal Garden Party a few years previously whilst both representing the RIBA. First, however, I spoke to Tony Hunt who loved the idea, but flagged up caution about clay tips and clay pits and their stability and structural capacity for projects of the scale we envisaged.

Tony Hunt and I had first met spending the day together at London's Festival Hall on the South Bank judging a design competition, the two other judges both being called Peter Murray, one the editor of the RIBA Journal and the other a well known disc jockey. Yes, he would be prepared to come on board gratis for the first phase if I could persuade Nicholas Grimshaw & Partners and also Davis Langdon, but he thought this was highly unlikely. I then rang Andrew Whalley the partner at Nicholas Grimshaw & Partners to have a similar conversation and received a similar response. I put the phone down, punched the air, had a cup of tea and then made three phone calls all within five minutes to Tony Hunt, Richard Baldwin and Andrew Whalley to confirm full team agreement that each were coming on board at the initial stages with no remuneration to each organisation provided the same applied to the other two. I captured what, for me was a euphoric moment by sending a confirmatory fax to Andrew Whalley welcoming Grimshaw's as our new lead consultants to the project and commending Andrew 'to keep a copy of this fax to show your grandchildren the day the eighth wonder of the world was begun.'

The design judges at the London Festival Hall 1983. l - r: Tony Hunt, Peter Murray (RIBA editor) Jonathan Ball, Nigel Verbeek and Peter Murray (disc jockey.)   *(JB archive)*

The author's fax to Andrew Whalley launching the famous line 'The eighth Wonder of the World', on the appointment of Nicholas Grimshaw Architects at the end of April 1995.   *(JB archive)*

Chapter 3

Bodelva

Our Bude drawings were ready just in time for the first proposal deadline to the Millennium Commission. Tim was very excited and complimentary, praising the Sine Wave as,

> " ... a science fiction confection that conveyed perfectly the radical change we intended to make to traditional conservatories."

I cautioned Tim that this was an image plucked off the top of our heads without any site-specific studies or any essential input from engineers or environmental consultants. Notwithstanding all this, we did have an image to capture the public imagination and one that was suitable for publication. Within a few weeks, we achieved just that and Building Magazine, the most authoritative journal covering the whole construction industry, ran a feature article on 12th May 1995 covering the most eye catching of the big ideas for the Millennium and led a several page article with us under the headline,

> "To be or not to be? ... Whether 'tis nobler to help build the largest greenhouse in the world, or to finance a new community centre, is the question."

Our image led the article and was described as the 'shimmering wave form structures by the Jonathan Ball Practice in Cornwall for the world's largest collection of greenhouses.' In Bude we were thrilled and raised a glass. At Heligan Tim was delighted and christened the image the 'Cobra's Head'.

The first of what would be many white heat project days dawned a fine late April morning with the sun streaming propitiously into the Bude Belvedere. Tim arrived early from Heligan, just over an hour's drive from Bude and we had a brain storming session for most of the day with my Practice colleagues Robert and Michael working alongside us, bringing together the report and the final imaging. All the collective wisdom from the many who by now were kindly disposed towards the project was distilled, but unknown to us one piece of the jigsaw was missing and it needed one of my guests from one of our lunches, my chum Henry Boettinger from Crackington Haven, who had kindly come in to lend an extra pair of hands on the day, to enlighten us. You seem in control, said Henry, what I will do is go back to Crackington and put together a small piece that connects you to the 'wonder of the Millennium'. Soon after this my fax machine rattled into life and out came a single sheet of A4 headed, 'The Springs of Inspiration'. It brought all activity in the office to a halt in our own wonderment at Henry's prose and his capturing of the essence and putting it in context of what the Millennium Commission were trying to achieve. It was the antithesis to the adage that a picture says 1,000 words.

We re-jigged our application submission to lead with Henry's opening paragraph, being the first words to be read by the Millennium Commission,

"The concept of the Millennium is rooted in recognition of that significant midnight when we look backward to the past and forward to the future, simultaneously. Its social value lies in concentrating our minds on past achievements, present problems and future possibilities. Any project designed to mark this transition should excite interest, understanding and involvement in shaping a desirable future ..."

We selected our fittest and fastest pigeon and from Bude was despatched the submission, Millennium Project Cornwall UK, within the end of April deadline and confirming our world class design team were now signed up. We had done it and with a huge sigh of relief I took time off the following day to go and conduct some of the pub singing for the Padstow 'Obby 'Oss May Day celebrations.

Cornish community pub singing is in my soul and it was about this time that the Bude Lifeboat Singers for whom I had been choirmaster – using this word in its loosest interpretation – since 1967 decided we would call it a day as a formal group. We numbered 12 which included three rich bass voices, but alas in short order one died and another moved to Malvern. A get together with singing chums from Falmouth was planned for a June Sunday evening after Nankersey, our favourite Cornish Male Voice Choir had given a concert in Bude.

Choirmaster of Bude Lifeboat singers since 1967, here conducting on the Atlantic Wall, Isles of Scilly, in a prized t-shirt recovered from the wreck of the Cita.

(JB archive)

It was because of this gathering that Tim agreed to the revision of our travel arrangements for an important Eden presentation we were to make in Brussels, set up by the Cornwall and Devon European Liaison Office. Tim and I had thus taken the Sunday night sleeper to London and had hunted out a coffee on Waterloo station before joining the Monday morning Eurostar when Tim exclaimed, 'God I have forgotten my passport'. 'No Worries,' I said, 'we're all Europeans nowadays'. Our paperwork included the invitation for Tim and I to present to a group of European Commissioners and Tim had his driving licence and other personal ID evidence. The UK passport control were happy for us proceed and said they would ring ahead to our colleagues in Brussels to say it was OK.

It was anything but OK when we were met by two beefy Belgian gendarmes who escorted us directly from the Arrivals platform through subterranean concrete tunnels with air conditioning ducts to a hostile bunker where Tim, a Dutch national, was intimidatingly questioned, changing desperately from English into Flemish in a vain attempt to counter the aggressive body language. To no avail. He was placed in the slammer whilst I was despatched to make the presentation alone and was told be sure to collect Tim in good time for our evening homeward departure.

My presentation was fine, but there is no doubt the absence of Tim's sprinkling of stardust diminished the overall impact. Back to the station, I collected Tim who was physically escorted by the gendarmes onto our London bound Eurostar and kept in close surveillance until we pulled out of the station.

It was a shameful episode; whatever we in Britain were paying into Europe was too much, judged on this evidence! Tim had been unjustifiably locked up for the day, not even allowed to smoke and his only contact with the outside world had been an early afternoon delivery of a modest cheese sandwich and a glass of water, followed by a second visit to charge him for the pleasure. Subsequently European funds played a significant part in match funding the Millennium Award, but added to our tears, sweat and toil in achieving these aims should be recorded the laying down of Tim's dignity and liberty in our just cause.

The 14th of June had been a good day in London for Tim and me. Our meeting at Grimshaw's offices had gone well, with Nick Grimshaw himself in attendance and we scampered to catch the early evening train back to Cornwall with spirits high. We had evolved a system for our many London visits; Tim would drive from Mevagissey to Exeter and I would drive from Bude to Exeter which would allow us meeting time together on the outward and return train journeys. I think we were between Westbury and Taunton when the mobile rang and Sue from Radio Cornwall told us the Millennium Commission list for projects to go forward had been released to the BBC and we were not on it. Disbelief was soon despatched by despair. With so much hope and so much hype and with Cornwall holding its breath, what next? My first thoughts were the prospect of what I was going to be saying to my bank manager. Tim's first thoughts were emphatically expressed ...'We'll lie. We tell' em we have got through and we'll blag it out'.

2 Little Smith Street, London SW1P 3DH
TELEPHONE: 0171 340 2001 · FAX: 0171 340 2000

Messrs Tim Smit & Jonathan Ball
Millennium Project Cornwall UK
The Jonathan Ball Practice
5, Belle Vue, Bude
Cornwall EX23 8JJ

13 June 1995

UPR Number: MC/W/478

Dear Mr Smit and Mr Ball

MILLENNIUM PROJECT, CORNWALL

Thank you for your application for Millennium Commission funds for the Millennium Project, Cornwall. The Commission received 550 full applications in its first applications round, with almost £6 billion sought in grants, significantly more than the Commission can distribute. We have appraised all applications to identify those which meet our criteria and have the highest potential impact as national, regional or local millennium projects. The quality of the projects put forward, and the innovation and enthusiasm of applicants, has impressed us all.

The Commission has now selected the applications to go forward to the next, detailed, appraisal stage, from which the successful projects will be selected. The Commission was not satisfied from the application you submitted that your project is, in principle, financially and technically viable, and it has not therefore been selected for further examination.

You are welcome to make a more detailed application for this project, or to submit other project proposals to us. If you wish to do so, please register on 0171 340 2030 for our next set of Proposal guidelines, to be launched in September. As you know, the Millennium Commission will not fund the costs of an application; support for feasibility studies is available from the Commission in exceptional circumstances, but applicants are expected to pass the first stage of the full application process under their own steam.

We are grateful to all those who clearly committed time and resources to your scheme for their enthusiasm and imagination. We do hope that the momentum you have built up, and the partnership support you have identified, can help your project or a part of it progress, even if Millennium Commission funds are not available.

On Thursday 15 June the Commission will be publishing a full list of all proposals and applications received in this first applications round, identifying those selected for more detailed review, and we will forward a copy of this list to you for information, as soon as it is available.

Yours sincerely

Jennifer A Page

JENNIFER A PAGE
Chief Executive

The Millennium Commission rejection letter 13th June 1995. (JB archive)

Sleep did not come easily and I was at my office desk by 6am the following day to prepare the master plan of who we had to speak to and in what order and what we were going to say about how we were to go forward. Thankfully the Millennium Commission rejection letter had arrived in Bude by first post and confirmed,

" ... the Commission has now selected the applications to go forward to the next appraisal stage and yours has not been selected for further examination."

The letter went on to give us an olive branch of inviting us to make a more detailed application for the Project and, if we so wished, then to register for the next proposal guidelines to be launched in September 1995.

By the time the media started its onslaught we had between us made numerous phone calls to reassure the core team and our message went out that we had been asked to make a more detailed application. The day was spent nurturing the media, me taking a 20 minute studio interview live on Radio Cornwall followed by BBC television at Roche Rock and Tim similarly covering Pirate FM Radio and Westcountry television. The Western Morning News carried Millennium matters as its Leader noting that,

" ... the only two high profile West Country projects had failed at the first hurdle this year. The Kew of the West Project, an imaginative and attractive plan, was incomplete but the Plymouth Aquarium was judged not sufficiently distinctive,"

Four days later came one of those events that make you tingle. I was already up and down between Cornwall and London like a yo-yo as RIBA Honorary Secretary and also on the Executive Committee of my Pall Mall club, the Athenaeum. Dinner, after our 19th June 1995 June Executive Committee, found me sitting next to Sir Ralph Riley. We had become good friends on the Committee and enjoyed each other's company. Sir Ralph had established himself as a true leader in the plant sciences and his Cambridge Professorship gave him huge international authority and respect. Over dinner I told him of our ambitions and by coffee we were exploring ideas of mutual interest and ideas that might help shape the future. Sir Ralph told me about the work of the Rockefeller Foundation where he chaired the Committee on Rice and about The 2020 Vision Programme to feed 8 billion people by 2020.

I could not contain my excitement. Here it was. The journey that started with Tim's idea for the largest greenhouses on planet Earth, to house a museum of gardening and tell the story of the great plant hunters had, nine months later, found me talking to probably the best man in Britain to help us articulate and redefine what our Project's philosophy should be to make it relevant to the future of mankind. It was all about land use in the next millennium, how we were to feed the expanding world's population and raising the public consciousness in respect of good husbandry of the planet and the relationship between plants and mankind. For the second time in a week, I couldn't sleep, but this time for the right reasons. The following morning I rang Tim to say I had the answer to that which had been eluding us. My conversations with Sir Ralph had finally cracked it. Tim agreed, describing my conversation as the missing piece of the jigsaw.

Dinner, after our 19th June 1995 Executive Committee. Menu card annotated front & back.

(JB archive)

I was able to set up and host a lunch in early July in order for Tim to meet Sir Ralph at our Club and for the three of us to have a further exchange of ideas, an occasion that helped refine and capture what we were all about. What Tim was much later to describe as 'the big fat idea' had finally crystallised. Sir Ralph was captivated with our ideas and enthusiasm and he soon accepted my invitation to become a Founding Trustee of the Eden Trust. History should record Sir Ralph's defining contribution to the way Eden's ethos emerged. When he died in 1999 Sir Alcon Copisarow, our first Chairman of the Eden Trustees, and I travelled to Cambridge for his funeral and heard eminent scientists deliver eulogies on how Sir Ralph, through his work at the Rothampstead Research Station, had single-handedly increased the capacity for Planet Earth to feed itself. What a man.

Early July also saw us with the need to firm up on our name. I wrote to Henry. What did he think of our favourite at this moment, 'The Eden Project,' as we did not want the Western Morning News to continue running with us as 'Kew of the West.'

The name had come out of a brainstorming session when Tim and I had written down famous gardens we had heard of in history. We agreed it was important to retain the word Project from my original holding name. Having checked with Henry who cautioned we needed to be comfortable with its Christian connotation, the Eden name was signed off in time to sit on the front page of the draft legal documents Druces & Attlee had prepared to incorporate The Eden Project, a limited company that would sit under the Eden Trust and drive the project forward commercially.

Our design team had now sprung into action and all early thoughts and eyes were on Waterloo International Railway Terminus which had recently been completed to acclaim with Grimshaws as architects and Anthony Hunt as engineers. This project cost £150m and had been delivered within 30 months and this was a good way, at the early stage, of painting pictures to the Millennium Commission and others as to similar scale, costs and delivery time. So, our next discussions would ask them to look at Waterloo International and then carry in their minds that if we were to get the go-ahead in the spring of 1996 we could commence on site 12 months later and deliver The Eden Project for Britain in time for the Millennium.

Both Sir Richard Carew Pole Bt, patriarch of one of the great families of Cornwall, and Sir Alcon Copisarow, recent past Chairman of the Athenaeum, had accepted invitations to become Trustees in time for the end of April Millennium Commission submission. By the end of July I was delighted that both Sir Ralph Riley and Sir Alan Donald, a career diplomat who had recently retired as British Ambassador to China, had also accepted my invitation to act as our Trustees. We brought them all together for the first time at Grimshaws offices in London at the end of July along with other design team members, the Chief Government Officer for the South West, and Ronnie Murning.

Ronnie's commitment to design excellence has always been uncompromising and courageous, with a reluctance to compromise on any point of quality. This commanding aura often found itself at odds with client, funder, or other design team member, but if I was to choose one name that should stand centre stage to take the bow on the successful delivery of one of Britain's most famous Millennium construction projects and the only one to be delivered on time and within budget, then it would be Ronnie. Certainly Tim Smit took a lot of convincing that my insistence on having Ronnie as one of the key players was a good idea. Tim enjoyed widespread deference and always cultivated a somewhat messianic persona. This was completely wasted on Ronnie who was soon to take every opportunity to demolish Tim's hubristic excesses. Tim had agreed to Ronnie attending this key design meeting on the basis of a promise from Ronnie that he wouldn't say one word.

The one word on my mind was, I think, that this was the first occasion when the word gravitas could properly be applied: the prestigious offices of an international design firm, an impressive presentation that included Mark Bostock from Arup Economics who was to prove a true friend of the Project, and a distinguished Trustee audience who were prepared to commit their formidable reputations and track records to our cause. Over tea we were able to reflect on the substantial progress made and we collated all the positive comments and also the notes of caution. Sir Alan Donald's distinguished diplomatic career had taken him to some far flung geography and he reminded us that he had plodded around lots of rain forests in his time and had found each and every one of them beastly places to be in and how were we going to cope with this? And so the month ended on a high for the Project and a high for Henry from Crackington who became runner up in the final of the BBC's Mastermind competition!

At the time I was working with Tregothnan's agent, Nick Jeans and Dr Bill Rickatson who headed the Goonvean organisation to ensure that our ideas for the Roche Rock site and refurbishing the Carbis Dry redundant buildings as a visitor centre were compatible with the extractive business operations of Hathe Tregothnan Estate and the Goonvean Company. Preliminary transport studies and site appraisals progressed and this involved entering into discussions with English China Clay. We had not closed our eyes to the fact that our site appraisals might result in our need to look elsewhere. We had made early decisions that the project would be seen as a landscape insertion, rather than as a building. The site certainly had spirit; well exposed to the elements, with significant interventions by mankind, the nearby monument of Roche Rock evoking memory of the past combining with the heroic sense of scale from the nearby clay pits and clay tips representing mankind's present preoccupation.

The show stopper was not long in coming. Our environmental appraisals by Alistair Guthrie at Arups identified that the working clay pits and tips to the south and west of our site sat between us and the prevailing southwest weather. The strong winds would pick up clay dust and deposit it upon our giant structures which would be a disaster for light transference and establishing the environment within which our plant exhibits would flourish. In the immortal words of Tim Smit, we would end up with the world's largest collection of twigs.

But all was not lost. We had both English China Clay and Tregothnan and Goonvean and Rostowrack China Clay Co. Ltd reviewing alternative site possibilities and I attended a meeting with Colin Griffin, the County Planner in Truro, to get some aerial photographs and discuss the County's present and future road distribution plans that might assist in site identification.

Bodelva Pit had not long been part of the Goonvean/Tregothnan empire and it immediately presented itself as having a micro climate far better suited to our needs. What we lost from the Roche Rock site being good on infrastructure and rail network links, we gained in the planning and environmental sense with the opportunity to create our own magical kingdom away from the public gaze and with a wonderful sense of place and enclosure. The land agent at Tregothnan urged me to curb Tim's proprietorial inclinations for him to proclaim to the world each positive step on our journey and we had considerable trouble in keeping our new site intentions private.

Lady Donald, Sir Alan Donald, Victoria Ball, and Ronnie Murning at Bodelva. Photograph by the author. (JB archive)

The same week the Millennium Commission wrote to me with the new submission proposal form giving us 30th November 1995 as the deadline for detailed applications and we called an early design team meeting in London to discuss and decide on our tactics. We had eight weeks to further our site discussions and statutory authority negotiations through to a position statement. This would sit alongside our business plan to date which incorporated design proposals, the finalising of our management team, evidence of funding prospects and local public support and our first outline programme through to the Millennium. And, of course, we needed this time to get our national political relationships in better repair.

The Chief Executive of the Millennium Commission was Jennie Page. Jennie had been presented with an RIBA Honorary Fellowship at the Royal Gold Medal celebrations in June 1995 and as Honorary Secretary I had read out all Citations.

Jennie was thrilled to bits with her Honorary Fellowship and we had a long chat over drinks after her presentation. *'This means more to me that my CBE,'* was her opening remark and the conversation soon passed to Eden and to where it sat alongside the multitude of submissions.

Jennie was, to say the least, robust in her approach to these matters … *I'm not about to take on any white elephants*, she said, *and I'm fed up with whingers … some of the worst are local government, they expect their share …regardless of the merit of their ideas or the quality of their architecture, but I'm not having it … and believe me there's no hijack from the Secretary of State or the Cabinet. But Jonathan, you must show me wide public support for Eden as I'm certainly not having projects fronted by a few of the great and the good telling the public what is good for them. I am keeping the public concern for wider environmental issues in the front of my mind, but people must feel they are part of the project.*

A couple of months later we had met again at the inauguration of the incoming RIBA President. I was able to demonstrate considerable progress.

Bodelva Pit when acquired. Photograph by the author. (JB archive)

Jennie was preoccupied with the concept of 'not proven' across all the submissions that came before her. *'Simply put, it breaks down Jonathan into who are you trying to kid, and get your act together.'* Eden sat firmly in the latter category. I was left in no doubt that, notwithstanding the fantastic progress and endorsements we had secured, the clear message was *get your act together*.

This was shortly followed by Nick Grimshaw having a long telephone discussion with Jennie. The wow factor had finally got through and there was a sense within the team of the project being believable for the first time with Nick's reinforcement saying the Eden Project was the most exciting set of ideas in his office.

There were two additional complications. The Millennium Commission required all projects above a certain quantum, to be subject to bids to comply with European competition requirements for publicly funded projects under what was termed OJEC procedures. Moreover, no Millennium funding was available during the feasibility stage of projects and the Commission expected all schemes submitted to be developed up to full RIBA scheme design stage without the risk averse Commission bearing any of the cost. Somehow I needed to secure agreement that, with regard to the Eden Project, if the design team was working for us at risk, then they should not have to enter any OJEC competitive bid arrangement at a future date for the next stage of their own project designs. I had a plan.

I went to see the RIBA President, Frank Duffy, declared my personal interest but explained that this regulation was causing endless problems, not only to his Honorary Secretary, but also for our RIBA members and allied professions working on Millennium project design proposals. Why should top design practices commit to advancing world class ideas with which Britain would celebrate the Millennium, sending signals to the world about the vitality and creativity of our nation, if at later stages of project development they would have to re-tender for their own work? The President already knew the

Millennium Commission was implacably opposed to taking any risks. Surely, I said, the RIBA should be making the appropriate representations to overcome what was fast becoming a hindrance that would stifle national creativity at the very moment when the nation needed it to flourish and with such strong and evocative exhortations coming from the Secretary of State, Peter Brooke. RIBA Presidential protestations to the Millennium Commission soon followed, with significant success.

Tim had been working with Druces & Attlee on the corporate governance development which was to enable our first meeting of the Trustees on 15th January 1996 when the Trust Deed was signed. Mark Bostock of Arup Economics had been drafting proposals for the management structure for the project and the relationship between the Trust and the Eden Management Company, who owned what and where the equity lay. Additionally, how all this might fit with the broad concept was exercising all our minds as here was a project that would essentially be in public ownership, whilst the legitimate expectations of the two co-founders who dreamed it up and shouldered the entrepreneurial risk from the beginning had to be protected.

Mark had put his finger on what he saw as the four key issues.

The ultimate owner must be the Eden Trust, the charitable entity, owning the site and recipient of all public sector funding from the Millennium Commission, the European Union and other public sources.

The the day to day management of the business had to be undertaken by a private sector driven company with some involvement of the Trust, probably as lead shareholder.

Both Tim and I had to be properly rewarded for our up-front costs and all our sweat equity and risk.

Any structure we came up with had to be attractive to raising debt funding.

All this had to come together elegantly alongside other work areas for the Millennium Commission submission that was now just a few weeks away. All the team members worked tirelessly to this end. With the submission preparation came the launch of our new logo under the Eden Project name with a palm leaf above and the new notepaper retaining our original mission statement below. Tim and I continued to sit as Project Principals and below that was the Eden Trust with our Trustees.

The submission to the Millennium Commission comprised three volumes:

- Volume One: *The Proposal* which contained the full physical representations including outline design drawings and our philosophy, description of exhibition themes and issues, and our engineering, environmental, management structure and preliminary transport proposals.

- Volume Two: *The Business Case* which covered the projected visitor numbers and footfall and management implementation proposals.

- Volume Three: *Letters of Support and Endorsement.*

Endell Street Model. Image from page 15, Millennium Commission Submission 1995. (NGP)

We were unveiling for the first time the design team's architectural and engineering response. The international terminal at Waterloo was highlighted as being a similar type of scheme that celebrates the successful fusion of architectural and engineering ambition. The biome architecture was explained as structuring the building as an exoskeleton, a term more usually used to describe the protective or supporting structure covering the outside of the body of many animals, with a soft clear membrane suspended beneath the lightweight taut steel structure which was a double bow string. The envelope would be formed from ETFE Foil, a transparent film formed into a three layer pneumatic pillow and the structure would snake around the north face of the clay pit.

The proposal was elegant and inescapably similar to the international terminal at Waterloo. This volume of exciting images ended with, '... *and finally... The Springs of Inspiration* ...' by Henry (see over). Our submission went in and on 8th November I received a letter from the Millennium Commission confirming the Eden Project satisfied all eligibility criteria for Millennium Projects and we would be invited to seminars and workshops during January 1996.

Image from page 17, Millennium Commission Submission 1995. (NGP)

The Springs of Inspiration

The concept of the Millennium is rooted in recognition of that significant midnight when we look backward to the past and forward to the future, simultaneously. Its social value lies in concentrating our minds on past achievements, present problems and future possibilities. Any project designed to mark this transition should excite interest, understanding and involvement in shaping a desirable future. The Eden Project aims at this ideal. Looking back a hundred (or two hundred) years, we can see that human effort, ingenuity and science were all devoted to improving the standard of living for expanding populations. This was done primarily by exploiting natural resources which, until recently, were considered practically unlimited and free to use without harm. Expanding knowledge and experiments; communication, transport, medical and chemical technologies; and searches for new varieties of plants, metals and other materials were so effectively applied that we are now facing limits to growth, and hazards to life. Widespread awareness of this unprecedented problem has evoked a wide spectrum of social and political movements to express their anxieties. Yet, intuitive interventions and spurious knowledge can cause more harm than good. Without sound understanding of various environments and ecosystems, and how they support and influence one another, well-intentioned efforts will be perverse. But, to acquire such understanding of several environments of the globe would take many lifetimes and decades of arduous travels.

The Eden Project aims to set up in one place authentic examples and experiences of the world's major environments, which can be visited for a day, or studied by scholars for years. It will provide a centre for scientists worldwide, for experiments and forums focussed on environmental issues, and a unique educational facility.

The Eden Project is not a static monument, though its architecture will be spectacular. It will grow in an open-ended way, coupling public concerns to purposeful action, soundly based. Its range of publications will appeal to the child of six and to the most esoteric scientists. It will evolve in ways congruent with the fears, hopes, opportunities and knowledge of all humankind. The criterion of its success will not be the magnificence of its buildings or gardens, impressive as they will be. Instead, in another hundred years, the world will look back and say that this Project is the symbol of mankind's shift from exploitation to conservation; from fear to hope; from isolated fanatical efforts to genuine humanitarian science and engineering. In short The Eden Project will have made a progressive difference to our world's evolution.

Henry Boettinger

Chapter   4

Kernow bys Vyken

(Cornwall for Ever)

1996   Much of January was taken up with preparation for our press launch. With a crunching financial shortfall we had made the decision to invest what meagre resources we had in a model of the proposal by professional model makers who worked closely with the design team and we made visits to check their progress in Endell Street in London's Covent Garden. Their studio was less than 100 metres from where 30 years previously I had attended tutorials with my AA tutor Ron Herron in Archigram's offices, their practice premises having formerly been a photographer's studio. Ron had chosen the Arabian Nights room as his

Endell Street Model. Image from page 23, Millennium Commission Submission. (NGP)

office with dark walls and ceiling, stars shining out and Mr Man in the Moon with a beaming smile looking down on us. Ron had died relatively young and in my mind I felt I had him smiling down from the Heavens with a guiding, approving presence as I once again strolled down Endell Street. This was shortly to be enhanced when Tim, on Ronnie Murning's advice, engaged Eden with the Imagination Organisation, the brand communication experts who had been retained for the Millennium Dome. Many meetings and presentations followed at their offices in Store Street, a building that was widely acclaimed in the architectural profession as being one of Ron Herron's best.

The advice to put our money into a model was well judged. It delivered to the project a highly photogenic image to which the media could each send their own photographer in whatever setting for the model suited them best and from whatever angle. It also gave Tim and me a focal point of interest for

Sir Ralph Riley has the honour of unveiling first project model. Photograph by the author.   *(JB archive)*

the many public meetings we were to attend.

We met to take advice and agree on our public launch and publicity strategy and it was resolved no formal press launch would be held in Cornwall. We would prepare all publication, TV and radio coverage but have it embargoed until 25th January and then would hold the launch event on that day in London, targeting the national architectural press who in turn would hand onward for wider national coverage respecting the embargo. I had to accept the professional advice, but as the Cornish co-founder was adamant there would be a Kernow bys Vyken (Cornwall for Ever) moment in London, so I approached my local town council in Bude and borrowed their large black and white cross flag of St Piran, the Patron Saint of tinners and the flag that symbolises Cornwall as a Celtic nation and the rallying point for all fervour and passion.

Because we had no money I had twisted a few arms at the RIBA to have a free room for our launch and luckily we were still in the days when these requests could have a positive outcome. The launch, in the RIBA's South Room, was a triumph and the evening saw a significant turn out. I opened the batting, followed by Tim and then Nick Grimshaw and we invited Sir Ralph Riley to unveil the model which until that point had been obscured having been clothed in the livery of the flag of St Piran. It was a lovely moment. Amongst a full gathering of international media were Pravda, together with press representatives from Japan, Taiwan and Germany. They all had the same question: what was the flag that covered the model prior to unveiling? I was able to return to Cornwall full of pride and a little boastful that I had brought a new dimension to waving the flag for Cornwall in London.

We had been very well received at a national level, being variously described as 'the West Country's biggest and most exciting plan to celebrate the Millennium', 'A brilliant concept', 'The most imaginative inspiration', 'A brilliant tourist attraction', '....a turning point in Cornwall's history...'. I noted in my diary 'all in all a splendid day', and we celebrated the remains of a long evening at a curry house. I returned from London first thing the following morning having been stopped on Paddington Station by my MP, Paul Tyler showing me the wonderful coverage in The Times. We had secured most of the page 5 Home News and I arrived back in Cornwall to the phones ringing.

Tim and Paul Travers, a friend from his rock 'n roll music days whom Tim had appointed to the team to help with PR and marketing, had done a great job bringing together the names and addresses of all local residents for issuing an invitation to those most affected by our ambitions for Bodelva Pit. We were all aware that we might well be in the process of securing the world's adulation, but without the support of the residents of Bodelva and Tregrehan behind us we were going nowhere. I had secured the enthusiastic support of a Bude chum, Bill Kneebone, who was connected with the Mid Cornwall Advertiser, a monthly newspaper which enjoyed much greater influence than might be suggested by its name. It enjoyed strong editorial content and was delivered into virtually every household in the District of Restormel, the local Council whose leap of faith to support us in the early days was to be rewarded so many times over.

We had booked Trethurgy Village Hall. What a night. They came in their droves, the curious, the sceptical and the concerned and they all listened intently. Hands made rough from the winning of china clay stroked chins thoughtfully. Hearts that yearned for days they knew would not come again sought cultural comfort. Heads searched for prospects for their grandchildren to have a future within the area they loved so well whose reliance on white water streams was at its end. A community whose given purpose for coming together generations ago was to win China clay now wanted a glimpse of a viable, credible future. A surprising number of them brought small children to the presentation.

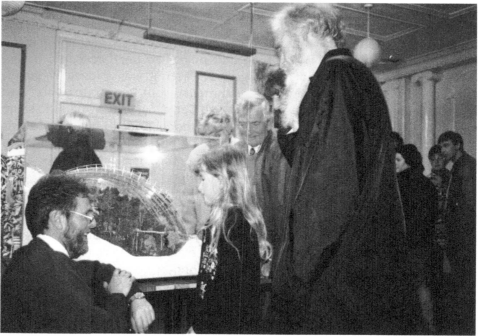

The Mid Cornwall Advertiser 15/02/1996. Bude Architect Jonathan Ball and a principal behind the Eden Project discusses the model with Jasmine Bradfield of St.Stevens School who gave the project 10 out of 10 and one day hopes to work there.   *(JB archive)*

The sense of belonging was palpable and if ever proof positive was needed of how geology inspires, shapes and forms communities and so much else, here it was. I opened the standing room only meeting by saying that our press launch in London the previous night had been wonderfully received but now it was the people who would be most directly involved who should see the model and have a chance to discuss the project before the rest of Cornwall. None of the great and the good have been invited, not one member of the chain gang, I said, save your local Restormel Councillor Neal Barnes of the Crinnis Ward who would have the honour of sweeping away the Bude Town Council's flag of St Piran covering the model. Tim's eloquence shone through in our joint fielding of the barrage of questions fired at us for well over an hour. Tim ended our presentation with a quote from Sir Ghillean Prance, Director of the Royal Botanic Gardens at Kew,

" ... it seems to me to be one of the most exciting of all the Millennium projects I have heard ... this is a project which you should consider really seriously, what an amazing thing to convert an abandoned landscape that is symbolic of destruction into something so creative and imaginative as the Eden Project."

'There were more than 100 people from Bodelva and Tregrehan who agreed with him.', was the way the local reporter from the Mid Cornwall Advertiser ended his extensive piece.

One of the issues Tim and I faced was how to convey the scale of what was firmly in our minds. I had an idea. I rang up Truro Cathedral and my diary note confirms an amusing conversation. Truro Cathedral is 300 ft long, 110 ft wide, the height of the tower is 180 ft and to the top of the spire it's 244 ft, the Cathedral coincidentally being 244 miles from London. Bingo. We had it and were able to describe our main biome structure as being capable of accommodating 13 Truro Cathedrals. That caught the imagination.

The first meeting of our Trustees had identified the need for specialist expertise in finance and business. I approached Ian Hay Davison who, amongst his many prestigious City appointments, had been Deputy Chairman and Chief Executive of Lloyds of London and was currently Chairman of Storehouse Plc and the National Mortgage Bank. We had been on regular walking holidays together and he readily agreed to become a Trustee.

It was a period of great excitement with strong international coverage and support mounting by the day. This was of some relief given Tim's and my continued personal financial exposure, but we were comforted by Sir Alcon who had made plain as Chairman of the Trustees that both Tim and I needed to be properly rewarded describing us as 'both necessary, neither sufficient'.

I have always enjoyed a strong sense of history and sense of belonging, I'm sure this is part inherited and part by my own experience during my formative years of interface with the ferociously caring and Cornish-centric Ball family. Being the youngest of the youngest of split generations excites interest in learning from the past and the epic Ball family palace of memories is inescapable and enthralling. Ingrained in our psyche is maintaining the close knit relationships from the large Launceston family, keeping in touch and looking after one another, what one of my many far-flung cousins always described as 'keeping the faith'.

The international media coverage had attracted a nice invitation for me to present the Eden Project at a lecture at the University of California, Los Angeles (UCLA) which brought a welcome short break for Victoria and me, staying in Malibu with my cousin Don and catching up on family news over glasses of wine on his front veranda. My father Christopher Edward Ball had been born in 1902 into a large Cornish family, the youngest of 11 with several of his siblings having joined the Cornish Diaspora to far flung Dominions in hope and expectation of better opportunities than the modest prospects prevailing in Cornwall at the end of the 19th Century. Don's father, my uncle Bill Ball had landed in Montreal, Canada in December 1912. This Cornishman served King and country, having signed his Attestation Papers in Winnipeg Manitoba on 7th February 1916 joining the 37th Overseas Battery of the Canadian Field Artillery. He saw action at Ypres, the Somme and Passchendaele and at Vimy Ridge, described by him in his precious wartime journal as 'the valley of sorrows' and was fortunate indeed not to be counted amongst the 10.600 Canadian casualties of that engagement described by many as being defining in the emergence of Canadian nationhood.

Bill went on to be a successful furrier to the Hollywood stars yet unable to defeat the magnetic pull of Cornwall where he returned to die in the last months of his life, and is buried in Devoran churchyard. An extraordinary trophy of World War 1, a bell from the Carillon from the top of Vimy Ridge, hung poignantly alongside us on the verandah.

Eden's progress was being intently followed in Malibu. My cousin as the American born son of a native Cornishman sharing his ingrained memories of witnessing something of a wistful recollection on the part of his father, something Don labelled, 'the long sadness.'

"The ken of an early Cornish life in which all was simple and well known, the people warm and wonderful... the mother left behind in the middle teens of life. All that was unhappy, forgotten. The economic short fall, forgotten in the expanded vision of new lands. A mixed up version of loneliness too soon and comfort too little ... things to be fixed with a trip home, someday perhaps."

That my cousin, at his most pensive, had been so imbued with his father's thraldom for the land of his birth was both moving and humbling, underlining the importance for Eden to succeed, creating opportunities for the next generation of Cornish young people. Uncle Bill had been just another name in the Cornish Diaspora as, at the turn of the 20th century, each Cornish family, without opportunity and born of necessity, lost their sons to other parts of the world, losing skills won at the expense of the community.

I am the youngest of three siblings, but the only one to be born in Bude. Brother Chris was born in 1937 and my sister Jenny five years later in 1942, both being born in Plymouth which, during the war was not a good place to be. Dad, as a Special Constable, at 40 years of age considered too old for call up in the early war years, experienced and saw things that, to my knowledge, he spoke of only once. As a Special he was recruited to back up the hard pressed Plymouth Constabulary who, throughout the Blitz survived only by their wits and their local knowledge and it was a combination of these, and an allotment hedge, that was to save Dad's life and in turn to give me mine.

On night patrol with a wily, experienced Regular and sticking to soft landscaped pathways, they were visiting and reassuring the occupants of the public air raid shelters when a bomb landed adjacent to their route through a vegetable patch blowing the allotment hedge in on top of them. Having dug themselves out they faced the grim task of revisiting the public shelter that had taken a direct hit just a few minutes after their inspection. Armed with a galvanised bucket and a spade Dad had to collect up the remains of a young Plymouth boy of similar age to Chris and wearing the identical pyjamas to those worn by him when Dad had kissed him goodnight before going out on the patrol.

West gets lucky

Millennium Joy. Front page news, 26th April 1996.　　*(Western Morning News)*

This story of my Dad's life being saved by the allotment hedge in the Plymouth Blitz is still retold in family conversations in Malibu. Together we gazed at the Carillon Bell, symbolic of the equal good fortune enjoyed by Dad's elder brother Bill Ball having left behind so many of his comrades a World War earlier buried beneath the green fields of France and Belgium.

Returning from California I received a letter from Millennium Commission CEO Jennie Page on 24th April 1996 confirming that ours was amongst the applications selected by the Commission to go forward to the detailed appraisal stage from which the successful Millennium projects for Britain would be chosen. This was

'Mr Cock-up is not at home', prepared by the author 22nd May 1996.   (JB archive)

closely followed by confirmation we were to get a visitation in Cornwall at the end of May from the Commission Officers who would also be bringing a representative of their professional advisers, KPMG. For the second time in four months the Western Morning News devoted the entire front page to the Project and had donated a bottle of Australian fizzy to enable a photo of Tim and I celebrating 'Millennium Joy' at being on the final shortlist, and two more inside pages covered how our dream edged closer to reality.

Ian Hay Davison had swung into action by arranging meetings in the City of London with prospective funders which would sharpen up our progress in this area in time for the visit to Cornwall from the Millennium Commission. The second half of May was spent in hectic preparation and the advance planning all came together by 22nd May when I was able to issue our whole team with the, 'Mr Cock-up is not At Home' Action Sheet. A delightful Bell Tent had been scrounged and erected on Flora's Green, Heligan next to the magnificent specimen rhododendron which had become the favourite backdrop for photo-shoots. Our Eden team of 18 assembled for the eve of visit briefing, first looking at Bodelva Pit and then travelling to the Lost Gardens of Heligan for Philip Macmillan Browse to give us a presentation on horticulture/botanical progress, followed by a delightful picnic prepared in Bude by Victoria to save money. Running orders were discussed and conviviality and conversation lasted well beyond daylight hours.

The following morning we arrived at the gate to Bodelva Pit to be greeted by BBC television and BBC Radio Cornwall together with a lady protestor who lived close by noisily accusing Tim of all sorts of misdemeanours. The visit went well and the business success of the Lost

A Co-founders Picnic. From left: Andrew Walley (NGP) Tim Smit, David Kirkland (NGP), Ronnie Murning (architect), Victoria Ball, the author.   (JB archive)

Bodelva Pit taken from the south above the mica dam 1996.　　　　　　(NGP)

Gardens of Heligan was used by Tim to prop up a business case proposition which inevitably and understandably had a long way to go.

We ended up on Flora's Green in the bell tent where Sir Alan Donald stole the show. Not a word on rainforests being beastly places, but a tour de force from a seasoned top diplomat who had spent 30 years overseas looking into Britain with the eyes of those from around the world looking at Britain. He reminded us there are areas where Britain still remains pre eminent and held in the highest regard, particularly in science and in recognition that the British are a very innovative race. It is with this world perspective in mind he suggested, the Eden Project magnificently captures all these elements and will powerfully express to the rest of the world how Britain is still capturing the high ground in these important areas of human endeavour. He ended by saying he had asked himself on several occasions recently, whatever was he doing being involved with the Eden Project? Now he was able to stand in front of us all and say that today had given him his answer.

It was that sort of speech that everybody remembers and we emerged from the bell tent to the botanical splendours of Flora's Green uplifted and full of purpose in a united desire to make the project fly. On the green I chatted to Bill Alexander, deputy Director of Projects for the Millennium Commission, who having reminded me that of course he was a civil servant and his own views were not much taken into account, gave his personal view that he thought the project was fabulous. The biggest problem you have got now Jonathan, is keeping up with the Millennium Commission's demands and a detailed schedule of their requirements should soon arrive in the post.

The summer passed in a frenzied haze assembling the Millennium Commission's Detailed Appraisal Reviews (DAR), with many boring compliance issues sitting alongside the excitement of being part of a world class design team in full flow, bringing together an overall master plan and following this up with scheme design studies for the buildings. Four divergent criteria were identified: to optimise solar orientation in order to achieve maximum horticultural benefit for each biome, to work in harmony with the natural beauty of Bodelva Pit, to accommodate future substantial growth and of course to create a complete architectural statement for the opening of the project.

The business plan was also developing apace and here Tim had introduced Rolf Munding, a successful businessman friend of his who had recently relocated to Cornwall. Rolf gave us some short, sharp lessons in how we prepare ourselves for joining a different world which I had certainly hitherto never inhabited. I was swimming out of my pleasant Bude goldfish bowl into a shark infested ocean. I had somewhat mistakenly thought that whilst I always admitted to a certain Cornish naivety my family upbringing and running a successful professional practice had given me a certain self belief that I could count myself as a member of the wide awake club and that I had not come down with the last shower of rain. It was becoming all too apparent to me, however, that here was emerging a project of international scale and significance. The capacity for me to be chewed up and spat out loomed large.

Bodelva 'the cliff', 1996.   *(NGP)*

Rolf Munding's entrepreneurial skills and commercial achievements were well known, what was less well known was he had spent his university days at Durham with Tim. It was after our first meeting that Rolf took me on one side to warn me that being in business partnership with Tim Smit would soon be challenging. Attached to these wise words of warning Rolf told me that Tim's nickname at Durham was 'High Rise' on account of Tim having a reputation for telling 'tall stories'. Not for the first time I had been warned, Tim could not and should not be trusted.

Tim and I reported back to our Trustees on 13th June 1996 that our meeting in Cornwall with the Commission's officers had gone well, but the Commissioners would now need to be satisfied the project would be run as a hard nosed business and Jennie Page, the Chief Executive, sought urgent satisfaction the project would be well managed and the right organisational structure put in place. Tim was also able to report that European Structural funding of approaching £3m had been provisionally approved and our joint efforts in advancing planning consent discussions were going well. At each monthly meeting of the Eden Trust we reported back steady progress and Derek Johnson, by then Project Manager appointed within Davis Langdon management, brought additional rigour to the way all information was assembled and set demanding timetables for delivery of objectives.

Already there were pressures emerging and at the July meeting of the Trust extensive consideration was given to corporate structure taking into account the need to secure the right balance between the views expressed by Tim and myself against the need to establish the corporate structure which would satisfy both the Millennium Commission and the funding institutions. The monthly trust meetings became the milestones for delivery of tasks and reporting all progress. I was delighted to tell the Trust the Eden Project had been selected by the British Council to represent Great Britain at the Venice Architecture Biennale in the coming September which was a moment of particular satisfaction amidst the walking through treacle of the Millennium Commission's DAR.

With Rolf Munding's caution ringing in my ears I raised the issue of intellectual property and its protection at the October meeting of the Trust much to the relief of Mike Jane, my bank manager. As to the registration of the Eden name and logo, this was in continuing discussion with lawyers but the Trustees resolved this was a birthright issue for the two project Principals. Certainly the culture of cooperation was changing between the two co-founders and I had to sit down with Tim and spell out what I and others were finding, that in one breath he wanted to be proprietorial and in charge of everything, but in the next breath he expected others to do everything even when he told them only at short notice and without conveying the necessary information or encouragement. He could not have it both ways.

Whilst frank, our discussions were most cordial, as ever. We remained in sacred agreement that TIMCO was owned 50/50 by us as the risk taking originators which should be the home for the registered intellectual property with us having equal liability and opportunity. The licence to use our intellectual property could be granted to the Trust on whatever terms, possibly royalty, but any negotiation would have to pass muster with public and private sector funders and sponsors. Tim was less than happy about the current chains of command and did not like the concept of having to report back to the Trustees for ratification. He seemed to be having difficulty in accepting it was the Eden Trust which was the applicant to the Millennium Commission. Nevertheless, in the main, daily excitements drowned drudgery.

Tim wrote to the acclaimed creative guru Rolf Ardell confirming the appointment of his firm 'Imagination' to act as lead communications consultants for our project. All agreed this was a big step forward and the addition of Imagination to our design team would assist us in conceiving a unique and compelling destination marketing concept for the Eden Project around the big idea that had finally come through courtesy of Sir Ralph Riley. This also, of course, was the start of our journey for building the Eden destination brand.

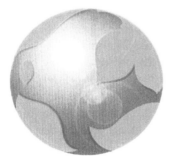

Rolf Munding's logo design, used on one of Eden's first leaflets.   *(JB archive)*

Rolf Munding suddenly arrived with logo designs via one of his business interests and we all liked the image of the globe with leaves replacing land masses and I was happy to confirm my agreement, but only on the basis TIMCO had 100% copyright ownership. Alongside this were further discussions with our lawyers Druces & Attlee who identified at this time that from here onwards Tim and I were likely to be inundated with offers of help and support such as Rolf's logo initiative. For me urgent action was needed on making sure TIMCO was legally inalienable – this was necessary in order to satisfy Mike Jane my bank manager. I was more than a little surprised that Tim seemed disinclined to give this issue the urgency it clearly demanded.

I was now approaching the completion of two years of unpaid exposure with more than four-fifths of my entire earnings capacity and livelihood having been committed to Eden, fee earning time that would otherwise have gone to my practice which, in turn, was putting its future in peril. The campaign of equal misery was no longer equal. The huge publicity bandwagon was rolling at Heligan and the turnstiles were spinning. In Bude it was the reverse, ' ... Jonathan's far too busy with his wonderful project to worry about my commissions ...' A note to Mike Jane, my bank manager confirming another increase to my personal overdraft facility followed the embarrassing moment of Victoria having her payment card rejected at the supermarket checkout.

Tim and I had arranged to meet with City of London bankers and I arrived at the meeting to find Tim had in fact remained in Cornwall and sent Rolf Munding to attend on his behalf. He had not told me. Difficult discussions followed with the design team and with the prospective funders. How we brought all this information together for the next meeting with the Trustees was clearly going to be problematic. Project procurement at the best of times can have a demanding gestation period, but Tim was of a mind that was making a difficult job impossible. We had a long conversation and I spent some time trying to persuade him out of his mindset that the Trustees were a collection of the great and the good which he could keep in a cupboard to which he held the key and only unlock the door and wheel them out when he wanted them. The temperature that was being raised minute by minute was reaching a high intensity.

A meeting was convened in Exeter with Mark Williamson of Ernst and Young who were developing the business case and also to secure TIMCO's rights within the document. All was going well until we reached a page in the draft which incorporated the words, 'The Trustees will control ...' and the meeting ground to a halt.

With the swan paddling like crazy under the water, we constructed a glide a few days later for a visit to the project by Doug Weston of the Millennium Team who was Chief of Projects and one below Jennie Page. His arrival at Heligan in bright September sunshine soon found the three of us having morning coffee under the trees and the conversation was very much within the business case remit that Tim had led since he and I had first sat under the same tree two years previously. We were delighted to be able to report the success of this visit to the September Trustees meeting and after two more weeks of treacle trampling it was a joy to me to depart for Italy to represent Eden at the VI Architecture Biennale in what was my first ever visit to Venice.

This visit had necessarily accelerated debate on the legal issues surrounding the Eden logo as Grimshaw's needed it for the British exhibit. I spoke to Druces & Attlee and was a little curious about parts of my conversation with Toby Stroh which left me enquiring of him was I speaking privately to my own legal advisor. Toby replied positively and he went on to confirm that Tim and I personally needed to own the rights so that we could then licence them onwards on terms still needing to be negotiated

The first Venice Biennale took place in 1895 and over one hundred years later it prospers as one of the most famous international gatherings for contemporary art and architecture. It was a fabulous stage on which to launch Cornwall's Eden Project internationally. The Biennale is a waterside parkland with some 30 national pavilions, the oldest of which, the British Pavilion, was acquired in 1909. It stands on the only hill in Venice, but still only 5 or 6 metres above sea level. The story goes it is built on what remained of the Campanile di San Marco which spectacularly collapsed at the turn of the century – mercifully without loss of life, save for the Curator's cat. It was a fine historical setting for the theme 'Sensing the Future'. For Cornwall and the Eden Project to be the exhibit selected by the British Council to represent Britain's view of tomorrow in this famed garden of cultural superabundance gave me a song in my heart.

Opposite:
The author and Nicholas Grimshaw, client and architect. Eden was selected as the British exhibit at the Venice vi Architecture Biennale 1996 entitled, 'Sensing the Future'.
(JB archive)

Chapter 5

The Eighth Wonder of the World

A letter arrived from the Millennium Commission on 22nd October 1996 confirming the Commissioners viewed the project as,

> *"... innovative and exciting and hope it will be possible to provide Millennium funding for the scheme ..."*

delivering another front page from the Western Morning News with the heading 'Eden Poised for Funding Victory'. Having appointed Truro based Deborah Clark to lead and control our media strategy, we had her warning that we were on a roller coaster gathering momentum which was as a result increasingly hard to control. Both Tim and I as Project Principals must be clear as to why this control was necessary, she cautioned that the information needed to remain in our ownership. 'It's a little like seduction' said Deborah with a flirtatious glint, 'if you give everything at once first, there's nothing left for later'.

The following Sunday 27th October 1996 was not a good day. Chums had rung early to say congratulations about the huge spread in the Sunday Times. 'Eh?' Tim had broken ranks again. Under the Banner Headline, 'Lottery Millions to Build New Eden', were our precious, unpublished Grimshaw images and an ego fest of,

> *"For Tim Smit who devised the scheme it will fulfil a childhood dream ... Smit approached the same team of architects that designed Waterloo ... Bodelva, the site chosen by Smit ... I realised how many species were becoming extinct, I decided we had to save some of them."*

Deborah was furious, not least because she was getting slaughtered by all her professional media contacts who thought she was in cahoots with Tim and had sanctioned his behaviour. More worryingly, she thought Tim's bid for individual glory could well turn the tide against the project and she had already that morning had conversations with others who felt the whole team effort had been hijacked by Tim's arrogance.

Mark Bostock of Arup Economics rang from London very cross and saying Tim was an extremely silly man – harsh words indeed, from so measured and consummate a professional about one of his clients. Mark thought the Millennium Commission would be wholly disapproving. Before the end of the day I had taken phone calls from very upset Trustees and Ronnie Murning, who by now was leading Design and Development, describing it as deceitful and devious of Tim and that this was no rush of blood to the head, but a premeditated and carefully planned strategy for personal glory.

There was a lot of frost on the course and Tim knew it. At the November meeting of the Trustees Sir Alcon reported with regret the resignation letter from Ian Hay Davison. Ian had accepted the Chairmanship of the Council of the Royal College of Art which demanded his resignation from a number of other interests including the Eden Project. He also let it be known, informally, he was no longer prepared to have his name attached to Tim's conduct.

1997   The New Year allowed us to review our progress with the Canadian Imperial Bank of Commerce (CIBC) Wood Gundy, our financial advisers who had yet to come up with the solutions we needed for the Millennium Commission. The selection process had now reduced the contractors under consideration to Tarmac and McAlpines. We had created autumn headlines with the news that Sir Robert McAlpine and Alfred McAlpine had teamed up to bid for Eden, their first major building joint venture since their parent company had split up in 1940. The headline read: '£75m bid unites McAlpines' and this prompted a moment's reflection for us both, not only as to satisfaction that we were hitting the construction industry radar at this level, but a cautionary comment from Tim's father who wryly warned us as individuals that we lived in a world where people were killed for £5,000 and to be aware of the potential hazards we might face when people are chasing £75m.

We hoped to secure our outline planning consent in February, but the corporate governance structure was still lagging behind. Sir Alcon was delighted with the progress we had made since the autumn but sagely observed the need to address our weakness urgently rather than dwell on our strengths.

The publication of Tim's book on Heligan Gardens brought with it renewed media attention which in turn fuelled Tim's ego. My bank manager, Mike Jane, had just read me the Riot Act. He had been closely involved since Tim and I first became partners nearly two and a half years previously and, for him, Tim's practice of claiming more of the Eden credit than was due to him, was now positively harmful to me. It was very good news for Tim Smit and for his own business interests at Heligan but in Mike's view the media coverage was now creating a wholly unreasonable imbalance in the public perception of the way the Eden risks were being carried.

All the pieces of the jigsaw were coming together in support of the

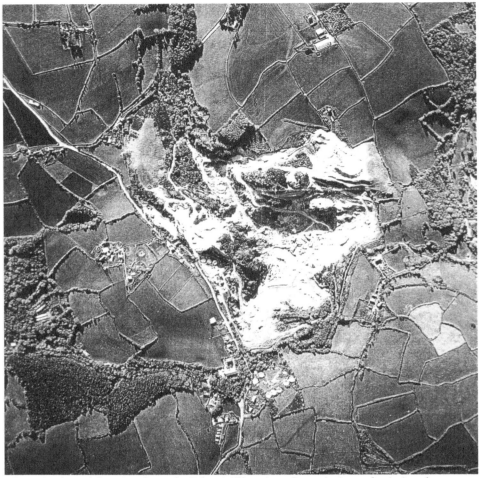

The unbuilt Bodelva site, from the Eden Millennium Commission submission document.
(Courtesy Cornwall Council Planning Department)

detailed appraisal requirements from the Millennium Commission. Jennie Page had left as CEO to oversee the Millennium Dome, a move which she would live to regret, and Acting CEO Michael O'Connor wrote congratulating Eden on progress made. With our two short-listed contractors, Tarmac and McAlpines we were focused on our need to secure a meaningful guaranteed maximum price (GMP) tender that had to align with the maximum capital expenditure (Capex) in the business case for the Millennium Commission which of course had to include all other non construction capitalised costs.

Eden was now a deliverable project with the operations management front runner being Gardner Merchant represented by Evelyn Thurlby, soon to jump ship and join us on the encouragement of Tim. The Millennium Commission was only willing to sign off visitor numbers to a maximum of 750,000 paying visitors per annum. This figure was based on the fact that, at the time the largest paying visitor destination in Cornwall, Land's End, attracted 650,000 visitors a year. The main capital outlay in terms of road infrastructure, buildings and other fixed assets, the Capex, had to be at a level to accommodate the maximum visitor numbers the Millennium Commission would accept. In turn the operating costs of maintaining the infrastructure, turnstiles, staff numbers, etc., the Opex, was similarly fixed. As we later discovered Eden was to attract 1.96m visitors in the first year. No wonder the car parking, access roads and visitor handling arrangements creaked when they had been designed for a footfall of 750,000

In the end everything that had gone before would hang by the thread of a single proposition: how many visitors would Eden attract, how much would they pay to enter and how much would they spend on site? It was as simple as that. The signing off by the Millennium Commission of 750,000 visitors a year determined the recast Capex.

Our £105m project proposals came under the spotlight at the February meeting of Restormel Council as Local Planning Authority. Of course the presumption was in favour of support for a project that offered so much to the area, but Development Committee Chairman George Down was making it very clear this would be no rubber stamping exercise. We had mustered a petition with over 1,100 signatures in support of the project in addition to 10 strong letters of support and some 25 letters of objection with particular anxieties being expressed about the transport and access implications. The economic and regenerative prospects on offer unquestionably outweighed the disadvantages and to our objectors we sought to offer comfort with our four pronged 'dilute and dispersal' strategy brought together by our traffic consultants, Arups.

In advance of this another public meeting had been called and in anticipation of a big turn out the venue was Penrice School, St Austell. In Cornwall evening public meetings in the depths of winter do not attract a large audience but the fire officer closed the door when we had 500 packed into the school hall. Restormel Chairman of Planning, George Down chaired proceedings from the hall stage and Tim masterfully articulated our case and paraphrased the words of Secretary of State Peter Brooke whose first invocation back in 1994 to lift our eyes above the mundane had got us into all this trouble in the first place. Tim pleaded with the audience not to reduce concerns to the parochial level, '... *we are talking here about the future of Cornwall.*' The Deputy Grand Bard of the Cornish Gorsedh, John Bolitho who had travelled from Bude to St Austell in my support, chose his moment from the body of the Hall to deliver an impassioned plea for the future of our grandchildren, ending his stirring words by saying that every single person in the hall should rejoice that here was a vision offering so much to the immediate area that otherwise had so little.

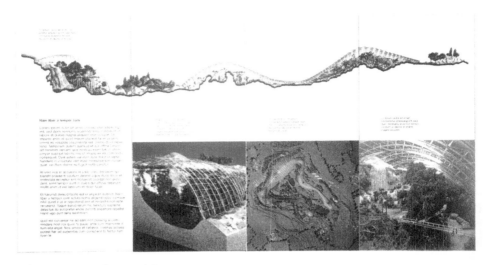

Early promotional material. (*JB archive*)

Now just more than two and a half years into our partnership it was interesting to reflect that we had remained substantially true to our first day breakdown of how the key tasks would divide. I had led on architecture, site selection, planning and project initiation which was now going into its more complex stage of detailed design led by my appointee Ronnie Murning. Tim had led on horticulture and the business plan. Certainly securing support and influence from what we called the great and the good had mainly fallen to me. There were certain areas that overlapped and involved us both: in the areas where I majored, the required action was taken on an inclusive basis: in the areas where Tim led or there was overlap it gradually became apparent to many Tim was looking to no-one's advantage but his own.

We were nearly there and it was time to talk about how, philosophically, we would launch the public announcement that we had secured the Millennium Award. It would be the culmination and high spot of more than two and a half years' work together which had involved our every waking hour, and must, in every sense, be a celebration of achievement thus far; Tim and I shoulder to shoulder as joint Project Principals warmly endorsing the support and hard work of the entire project team. But papering over the cracks was increasingly more challenging; there had been some polarisation, Tim to Canadian Imperial Bank of Commerce, Wood Gundy and me to the Trustees.

We were not yet safe however and the personal risks and exposure to both Tim, who had pledged Heligan's assets, and me, remained huge. My practice overdraft was more than the gross annual billings of the firm and I had an undertaking with Mike, my bank manager, that should the Millennium Commission say no to Eden, as it had done to more than 90% of all the projects presented to it, our family home would be sold to cover my indebtedness. The projects approved by the Millennium Commission, and those rejected by them had taken on a distinct political tinge and whilst we had a fabulous idea there were slick lobbying machines better positioned than ours, with access and ability to influence the political environment which was about to change radically.

Approaching the finishing tape involved securing a letter from CIBC Wood Gundy, our financial advisers, confirming the project met the conditions precedent for the Millennium Commission conditional grant. This grant would be for half the total project cost, the remaining match funding being secured once the landmark project public announcement was made. The Commissioners set 1st December 1997 as the first date for financial close, that is when all match funding had been secured, the moment when the conditional award went unconditional which released the Millennium Commission's multi millions across the River Tamar.

Tim felt there was a need to go under cover in order to get the required CIBC letter. There had been a quantum change of climate with the CIBC relationship following Eden's base case being established and Tim's book on Heligan and the TV series launch. I had made it clear to Tim that I wanted to be in on the CIBC key meetings, as co-founder and with my family home on the line. Tim misled me as to the date for a key meeting and when I insisted on travelling from Bude to Heligan on 7th April 1997 with the express purpose of us preparing for this meeting that would likely determine our positive future, I was dismayed to be told on arrival the meeting had already taken place without me.

Just down the road from Heligan Gardens is the Crown Inn at St Ewe where we had spent many happy hours mingling pints with lofty thoughts. Let's go for a pint, I said and we conducted an informal partners' meeting which started with me warmly congratulating Tim on the achievement that his book on Heligan in the third week since its launch was now the number one best seller in Britain. For someone who had never written a book before this was quite an accolade. Tim responded by saying for him, the best thing about our two and a half year Eden journey together had been meeting me.

It was only after raising the right elbow on the second pint of Guinness that I asked Tim, in the spirit of the moment, what it was that he really wanted. To him power and profile was much more important than money but he was also gracious enough to acknowledge that money follows power and profile and more money, in turn, delivers more power. He wanted the status of Acting Chief Executive Officer until such time as we put a professional in place after which time he wanted to be Chairman of the Project. Given Tim had been leading the negotiations with CIBC, of course they had been happy to recommend this in the draft of their confirmatory letter and Tim had been mightily peeved that the March 1997 meeting of the Eden Trustees had not been prepared to endorse this CIBC recommendation. It would not deliver the

Millennium Commission's stipulation of strong professional management and financial accountability, they said.

So what did I want? As the 50/50 originator and risk taker I also wanted the commensurate profile and respect, but I did not crave celebrity and would not be an impediment to Tim's power hungry ambitions to achieve this. I did not want to disturb all that was most precious to me in my family life in Bude, but in return what I required from him was an absolute and unequivocal undertaking to forever respect and always acknowledge my equal claim to everything we had achieved together.

Which brought us nicely to the issue of the moment. I am not a threat, Tim. We have walked through the fire together. We have shared unbelievable risks together, some would say insane personal financial risks, given that we had agreed from the outset Eden was for public, rather than personal benefit. Why, oh why, did you mislead me about the date for this crucial meeting? A tale of two emotions played out on his face, the smile was warm, but the gaze steely, tempered by an uncharacteristic hint of the confiding. Tim had nowhere to go ' if you really want to know, the truth is, I didn't want you there.' Why ever not?' 'Because I do not like other people around me when I'm telling lies'. In this admission everything was laid bare; the strength of our personal relationship and its weaknesses in one confession. Tim was prisoner of a higher order of self belief and he would do whatever he felt was necessary to reach his goals in pursuit of personal glory.

These actions ran contrary to my rule of life where the concept of probity prevails and my deeply held family values honed by my Cornish Methodist boarding school upbringing dictated my day to day conduct in commercial and professional dealings and in spite of all that was to unfold it still does. What I felt most important was that probity was the concrete and reinforcing steel of Eden's foundations. If you absent probity, virtue and solid goodness applied to all concerns of life where truth and goodness are called into question, what is left? Tim as a Dutch national had always acknowledged and relied upon me to shake the hand of my fellow Cornishman, look him in the eye and ask for his trust. He was now trespassing on an area where my views were non-negotiable. In my opinion if we did not discharge the trust that had been placed in us by others our core project values would be lost and it would be a breach of honour which could only be followed by the ill opinion of our many supporters. But it was much more than this. From inception our Eden dream was held out to all as setting a straight and undeviating course, ignoring all temptation in the delivery of an absolute integrity of belief. As Ronnie Murning was making plain at every opportunity, Tim's hubristic need to be regarded as the unchallenged project leader over rode and compromised all our claims to intellectual integrity. The patience of the Trustees was near extinguished and this created a personal difficulty for me as, with one arguable exception, they had all been appointed by me and it was my reputation and relationship with them that was thus at stake. They had not signed up to this absence of deference and took a dim view each time Tim threatened to drive his tanks onto the lawn.

The final submission had been made to the Millennium Commission in early April and it had been made clear to us we should not expect an answer until after the General Election.

The sense of anticipation that precedes any General Election was palpable and the political parties were turning all their efforts and attention on those parts of the country most likely to win seats, the large metropolitan areas and increasingly urban Britain – not rural outposts where the approaching Labour tsunami had little or no prospects. In respect of my own Cornwall North constituency a constant in people's minds is that the Labour candidate has lost their deposit in every General Election in living memory

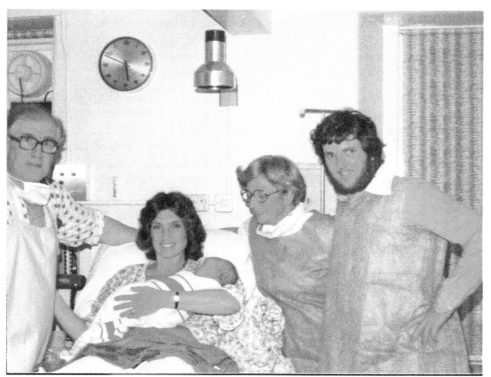

Victoria with her father Dr Anthony Blood, still in his pyjamas, having just delivered his grand-daughter Morwenna. (JB archive)

The 1st of May always finds me with a happy personal dilemma. Our younger daughter Morwenna was born at dawn on 1st May 1979 in Stratton Cottage Hospital with my GP father in law, Dr Anthony Blood who specialised in obstetrics, delivering his own granddaughter and delivering to me truly one of the most magical moments of my life. Victoria and I had come to the hospital from our then Stratton cottage, Chy an Eglos (house beside the church in the Cornish language) with midwife Mary Hooper, leaving our three year old daughter Jemima Veryan in the excited hands of our neighbours Tony and Annie.

My father in law had risen from his bed, his house being close by the hospital, put on his dressing gown and slippers and walked to join us and I was obliged to turn on the lights as we entered the Cottage Hospital. He took off his dressing gown and put on a theatre apron. He removed his slippers and replaced them with a pair of white theatre boots into which he tucked his pyjamas and Morwenna Victoria Ball entered the world just as a blackbird was announcing dawn in the front garden area of the cottage hospital to the good people of Stratton. It doesn't get better than that.

However, since the time when my memory didn't run to the contrary, as an Atlantic Coast Cornishman, I had always attended the Padstow 'Obby 'Oss celebrations on May Day and the juggling of these competing emotional tugs over the past three decades has delivered its own amusing moments, not least many years ago when Victoria first brought into common usage her description of me as being 'an and, rather than an or, person'.

May Day 1997 had further call on my state of equilibrium, it being the General Election Day that would unquestionably influence Eden's prospects. The dawn of New Labour broke on 2 May 1997. The people had spoken and put their trust in Tony Blair to sweep away what the victors termed Conservative sleaze and deliver a prosperous era of Cool Britannia. There was no glass ceiling to the optimism. The Eden Project was in harmony with the prevalent mood of renewal, recycling and ethical living. The fledgling New Labour members of Parliament were hungry for the chance to swim with the tide of corporate and individual efforts to maintain and nurture our fragile planet. Their, and our, moment was upon us.

The mid May meeting of RIBA Council found me on the crack of dawn London train from the west country. We knew the anticipated positive news would come shortly. Tim was already in London on a book signing and had set up a working lunch with Evelyn Thurlby of Gardner Merchant at Liberty's restaurant which was operated by her firm. My day at RIBA Council was soon disturbed by two messages being passed into me in close succession, one to ring Tim urgently and one from Victoria in similar vein, her having just taken a call from Sir Alcon and wanting to be the first to tell me the good news. I scribbled a note of apology to the President on my immediate left and departed the chamber swiftly in time to join Tim at Liberty's.

Evelyn was chain smoking and drinking fizzy water and somewhat sycophantic towards Tim whose mood I shared - one of quiet satisfaction rather than euphoria, rooted in the recognition that there was still an enormous amount of work to be done. It was clear Evelyn would give her notice in to

"Founders ecstatic as 'mind-boggling' Eden project wins £37m backing." WMN front page 24th May 1997.   *(Western Morning News)*

Gardner Merchant tomorrow 'if Tim would give her the Eden CEO job', but meanwhile was on secondment to Eden to develop the operational elements of the business plan and secure the all important letter from CIBC.

I returned to Bude and we had a celebratory glass of fizzy with Celia and Bill Kneebone whose stalwart companionship had much assisted in cementing our local support base. By the end of the evening it had extended to a small circle of friends, all sworn to secrecy but it was nice that some of the Bude chums knew before anybody else. A strict press embargo was imposed until Friday 12 noon 23rd May.

Thursday passed in a daze of frantic activity. I was down at Heligan before 07.30 as the Millennium Commission had a TV crew there and wanted to put their micromanaged piece in the can and control exactly what was said for the Friday lunchtime release of the embargo. Tim and I had agreed the shoulder to shoulder 50/50 bit, but because Tim is Tim it didn't quite pan out that way. The first shot put in the can was Tim in the Heligan jungle, *'I am Tim Smit of the Eden Project ... we don't have any titles or things like that connected with this project...'* said Tim in an episode straight out of Orwell's Animal Farm, knowing the Heligan backdrop would say it all for him. Next was me with Bodelva Pit as backdrop and I said *'I am Jonathan Ball and I am joint project principal with Tim Smit of the Eden project'* and followed this with our rehearsed piece that 'Britain is Back'.

Sir Alcon arrived on the Friday morning flight with the Millennium Commissioners and Ronnie Murning. Sir Alan Donald, Victoria's uncle, was due to arrive in Bude and be our overnight house guest as we didn't even have the budget for hotel accommodation for Trustees. Having spent most of the day scampering around telling key individuals on a strict embargo basis I drove back to Bude in time to pick up the lobsters I had ordered from local fisherman Tim Marshall who was a friend of long standing. His long service on the crew of Bude Lifeboat was equal to mine and just as we had faced many huge seas together we had stood side by side to receive our RNLI crew long service awards from the Director of the Institution just before the start of the 1989 summer season. A charming evening with Sir Alan followed with a celebratory

The author, Heather Couper and Tim Smit. May 24th 1997.   (*Western Morning News*)

treat of lobster and Sancerre, a lengthy amble through the politics of where it's all going and then off to bed. Tomorrow was going to be quite a day.

The big day dawned with uneven weather but with the prospect that it would probably stay dry. I was on the road early and Victoria drove down with Sir Alan mid morning. Victoria and our elder daughter Jemima had pulled out all the stops to produce more magnificent food for the occasion; yet again our hospitality budget was non existent. The marquee had been erected on Flora's Green which was the right place despite the Trustees' concerns that it was a Heligan publicity hijack. Hordes of journalists were arriving and we were giving end to end interviews in a carnival atmosphere. Heather Couper the Millennium Commissioner whose joyful task it was to make the announcement arrived all smiles and very upbeat. We moved into the marquee in front of the back drop constructed by the Millennium Commission officers with Sir Alcon chairing the morning with his usual charm. Heather Couper said wonderful things about the project and after a few words from Tim and then me singling out the Trustees for special praise, Sir Alcon concluded the short formalities with the words ...'hats off today, coats off tomorrow!'

We crossed to Bodelva Pit for more photo calls where I hailed Eden as 'The Eighth Wonder of the World', the phrase first used in my fax to Andrew Whalley of Nicholas Grimshaw and Partners 15 months previously on the day our design team committed to the dream. Another front page on the Western Morning News, Tim and I with ear-to-ear smiles under the headline 'Welcome to the Eighth Wonder of the World'. There was no shortage of superlatives, but the day probably went to Heather Couper with her 'mega brilliant' description.

As the Scientist Commissioner she was ebullient and informally advanced the view that Eden would re-write the whole way science is communicated and, ' *… I am not allowed to say this, Jonathan, but the Millennium Commissioners are united – this is the best project Britain's got… .*' The Western Morning News who had so championed our crusade noted that for project founders, Tim Smit and Jonathan Ball, the announcement vindicated their vision and tenacity in creating the world's largest botanical gardens in the heart of Cornwall.

The national press went potty and the Mid Cornwall Advertiser ran a lovely piece capturing the moment when smiles jostled with relief. They went on to note that the Millennium Commission's announcement was in the same month as Cornwall marched on London to commemorate the 500th anniversary of the peasant uprising led by An Gof and Thomas Flamank to highlight Cornwall's problems, and this had a certain poignancy. The message from Cornwall 500 years on is still one of low prosperity and low resourcing, but perhaps Eden could be a symbolic focus for regeneration.

> *"No doubt the leaders of the Keskerdh Kernow March on London have put some thought to the message they will deliver this time round,"* mused the writer. *"Can I just share a thought with them … please don't be too uppity – we haven't received the cheque from the Millennium Commission yet."*

Chapter 6

Up Shit Creek

The euphoria of what had been achieved for Cornwall by us all coming together in common conviction soon evaporated, to be replaced with communal condemnation of Tim who was preoccupied not at looking to Eden's next steps, but to his own. His every other utterance in public had been about pulling together and team work, no discomfort was ever displayed by him of his counterfeit position. Tim went into overdrive on his first person singular media avidity and mobilised the adulation as a battering ram against the Trustees and the Eden team who were thoroughly fed up with his tantrums, particularly Kary Lescure the talented administrator who had been seconded to the project from the Directors' office at Cornwall College to act as Tim's PA and bring much needed discipline to our management. The ever elegant Sir Alcon captured the moment by proclaiming that we needed to establish a strategy to capitalise on his strengths and to remove the opportunity for Tim to demonstrate publicly his weaknesses.

The author and other members of Bude Lifeboat Crew launching on exercise with Courtmacsherry Lifeboat crew, West Cork1992 on Solent class Lifeboat R. Hope Roberts in her last year of service. At the time she was the oldest lifeboat in the RNLI fleet. Following the tragic loss of the Watson class Penlee Lifeboat Solomon Browne on 19th December 1981, the RNLI fulfilled its pledge to have an all fast fleet by 1993, the R Hope Roberts being the last of the old classes of lifeboat with a maximum capability of up to 9 knots. Courtmacsherry station has a long and proud history with its Lifeboat notably launching on service to the wreck of the Lusitania on 7th May 1915. (for reference see Home from the Sea, the story of Courtmacsherry Lifeboat 1825-1995 by Mícheál Hurley.) (JB archive)

Tim threatened that if he couldn't be Acting Chief Executive he was off and came to me in damage limitation mode after Sir Alcon had let me know Tim had indicated to him privately he didn't even particularly want me as a Director of the project. Above all else loyalty to my friends and colleagues, and they, in turn, to me, means everything. Taking a lifeboat out through a big sea together is only achieved by unqualified trust, team work and knowing you can rely absolutely on each other. Tim would not have passed muster as a lifeboatman. He was displaying a loyalty where proximity was in direct proportion to his assessment of current usefulness. In his mind that which only I could have done, had been achieved.

Bill Allen, inspirational head of A A School. *(JB archive)*

When, in quiet reflective moments, I look back upon my life beyond parental values there are a small number of people I have met along life's journey that have influenced my views above all others. One of them was my Head of School at the Architectural Association, Bill Allen who was a guiding star through my professional career to his life's end and had, along with Maxwell Hutchinson, proposed me for membership of the Athenaeum. Bill had ended his inaugural address to the AA when appointed Head of School in 1962 with the words:

"And finally, deepest of all but always present as our most powerful driving force is our realisation that after the gift of life, which is mankind's first gift, is the living of it, and that it is our proud privilege and humble duty to design for this."

I had these words framed alongside my desk for most of my professional career as a constant reminder to my purpose. Bill, along with Sir Richard Acland established in me a sense of right and wrong carved in Cornish granite. What was now happening beyond the substantive Eden issues was a titanic clash of core values between Tim and me.

My first post qualification employment after graduating from the AA in 1972 had been working in Exeter for Lady Anne Acland, also an AA alumnus and a member of the Acland family that had once owned half of Bude. With this job came the tenancy of a granny annexe on the Killerton Estate, the Acland family home and with it an undertaking the landlord would keep the grass cut on my private lawn. This was a duty Sir Richard conscientiously discharged throughout the spring and summer and usually at about 6 am in the morning. Sir Richard Thomas Dyke Acland 15th Bt and I soon became friends, not least through our shared love of Bude and I look back with great affection on this time sharing his company. Sir Richard had formed and led his own Common Wealth Party in Parliament until it was swamped by the 1945 Labour landslide. In matters moral and ethical to my mind he was a Colossus, campaigning for a new public morality and he sacrificed his political career in 1955 by resigning his seat over the H Bomb.

When it was time for me to move on to Bristol to woo my sweetheart Victoria Blood his parting words of friendship in wishing me well in my career were, '*Jonathan, please always remember, that which is morally wrong can never be politically right*'. A quarter of a century later these words came flooding back, strengthening my resolve in my Eden battles with Tim, the Secretary of State, and the Millennium Commission, words that remain an ever present echo jogging fond memories of a man who epitomised decency and integrity. Sir Richard Acland would certainly have given Tim short shrift, no concept of Common Wealth here for Tim.

After some 15 months in Bristol, we had taken the first opportunity to scamper back across to the right side of the River Tamar to Bude. I set up the Jonathan Ball Practice, in the autumn of 1974 having fixed my professional plate at the bottom of some outside steps leading to two pleasant, south facing rooms close by Summerleaze beach Bude, a short dash from the Lifeboat Station and overlooking the River Neet with Nanny Moore's Bridge linking across to the Shalder Hills where I had received my primary education.

The Jonathan Ball practice extended premises in 1994 with first floor Belvedere.
(JB archive)

The Trustees remained firmly supportive noting my continuing capacity to add value, my input of ideas, contacts, promotion of the project and identifying sponsor opportunities, not least as I had successfully obtained a letter of commitment from one of my practice clients of a donation of £500,000 which brought comfort to the Millennium Commission.

Even Peter Thoday, one of Tim's most loyal advocates whose work on the Victorian Kitchen Garden had contributed most of all to the Heligan success and, in turn, Tim's media profile, was critical of Tim's behaviour in frustrating the implementation of proper corporate governance. He made his views known not only, I believe, in attempting to bring unity where there was none, but also to send a signal to Tim that Peter's friendship could not be relied upon if Tim crossed his own integrity lines. But he did so with great thought and sense of purpose. Tim was a natural born challenger, he said, challenging the Establishment, challenging convention, challenging ideas for tomorrow and in these areas, as all agreed, he was brilliant. However, when an organisation needs a Chairman or a CEO these are not qualities you look for when making such important appointments at such a defining moment in the life of the project.

The crisis point had been reached. Tim was not prepared to be answerable to a CEO and did not want Sir Alcon as non Executive Chairman of the project in addition to being a Trustee. If Tim could not be CEO then he wanted to be Chairman with the new CEO answerable to him and not to the Trustees, as recipients of all public funds. For their part Sir Alcon and the Trustees were not prepared to have Tim as CEO, preferring one with a strong track record and the right credentials primarily to perform the required function of Accounting Officer to the Trustees and beyond for the substantial public funds. All these shenanigans were being driven by a single force: Tim knew, the Eden team knew, Cornwall knew, the Millennium Commission knew and New Labour knew the significance of what we had all come up with and its capacity for delivering power and glory. In the supercharged atmosphere of these times memories were shortening that in fact there were two of us who had conceived and then taken the entrepreneurial risk to get Eden to this point.

Robert Harris and Michael McMillan, whose early input to the project established the first Eden images. In the 1980s a prerequisite to joining the Jonathan Ball Practice was circus skills. The practice had eight jugglers, a fire eater and two unicyclists. Unicyclist Michael often came to work on this unusual mode of transport.
(JB archive)

As the Project's potential grew, so did the demands which proved a hideous assault on what was left of my personal well being and equilibrium. The Practice was in crisis; both Robert and Michael, two of my three most senior colleagues of long standing who had made their own unsung creative contributions to Eden's progress, had not unreasonably had enough. With my blessing they departed Bude to set up in practice in mid Devon.

Ordinarily the managing of this departure would have set aside all other current worries but our family survival, including the retaining of our family home, was completely dependent on internal Eden politics being played out an hour away at Heligan Gardens by those who had been closest to me for approaching three years.

In the January of 1997 Ernst and Young had produced the Project structure enshrining the intellectual property (IP) within TIMCO with the **1997**

Trustees confirming the intellectual property rights belonging to myself and Tim for which we would secure a small shareholding and a small IP Royalty. The next day Druces & Attlee, our lawyers advised the Trust not to adopt the Ernst and Young proposals; they evidently saw no conflict in advising the Trust contrary to the interests of the two co-founders. Here was Druces & Attlee acting for Tim in his personal business interests at Heligan and elsewhere, acting for Tim and myself in protecting our interests as co founders of the project and on whose instruction they had prepared the Eden Trust Deed and created Eden Project Limited, the commercial vehicle that sat underneath the Trust. I wondered if this moment clarified why the legal enshrinement of TIMCO, the entity confirming and protecting Tim and I as 50/50 equal co-founders, was being frustrated by Tim. He wanted the world to believe that it was he, and he alone, who had led us to this point.

They were now also acting for the Eden Trustees and were formally appointed by them on 23 April 1997, and shortly afterwards I received a fax from Sir Alcon confirming on Druces & Attlee's advice all IP rights are now assets of the Project and Tim and Jonathan should submit alternative benefit proposals. But the IP belonged to us. How could it suddenly be an asset belonging to the Project, and if, by Druces & Attlee's legal wizardry the Project did now own the IP, where did that leave the Co Founders who were relying on Druces & Attlee's advice for protection of our own interests. Any remaining comfort I had that fairness and decency would prevail was extinguished in an early April personal phone call from Mark Williamson of Ernst and Young telling me I was very exposed legally and would be shafted unless I was able to sort out the legals asap.

On 1st July the Millennium Commission confirmed terms and a condition precedent of their award was that all IP must be vested with the recipient, the Eden Trust, for all time and not sold or licensed. But this was not in line with our final submission documents to the Millennium Commission from which the Award flowed. A phone call from Jonathan Johns of Ernst and Young confirmed his view that as a direct result of Tim's prevarication and frustrating the process we were now too late for protecting that which was properly ours – the IP for all that we had created. On 3rd July the Trustees ran up the white flag; Tim had battered his way to their confirming his appointment as Acting CEO.

Two decades of cumulative business experience heading a successful professional practice in Cornwall had neither prepared nor equipped me for the ferocity of what now followed. With Tim's encouragement Evelyn Thurlby submitted her application for the post of CEO as advertised by the Trustees, confirming Sir Alcon would be non Executive Chairman of the Board with the newly appointed CEO accountable to the Trustees and the Board, the Trustees also confirming short listing to be undertaken by Sir Alcon, Tim and myself. Evelyn was soon shortlisted with four other able candidates. Her final

The author and Victoria on a fundraising event aboard the St Mary's Isles of Scilly Severn Class lifeboat, The Whiteheads.

(JB archive)

interview and appointment took place in early August with me absent from the interview panel and Tim driving the process. Tim had another duck in place.

For years as a family we had spent summer holiday time together on the Isles of Scilly every August. This year foreshortened and cash constrained, it was never more needed. Victoria, described by Sir Alan Donald as a paragon of beauty and duty, was ever loyal, but described herself as feeling sick with worry to the bottom of her stomach. What had I done? The Practice was in freefall, we stood the very real prospect of losing our family home, and I felt I had squandered the future well being of my family. All that had been the last three years of my Eden life and the 23 years of professional practice was in crisis. The end of the holiday saw me confronting two stark alternatives: fight or flight. The decision made itself. With family bonds equal in strength to the granite bedrock of Scilly under our feet I returned refreshed and with renewed resolve to face danger's hour, fortified with the warm support of many who were soon to display true loyalty and selflessness in the stormy times ahead.

I was also soon to get the strong sense that it was the people of Cornwall who would also rally to my cause albeit there remained at this time a relatively small circle of those who knew much of what was going on. Cornwall was doing handstands at the news of Eden securing Millennium landmark project status for Britain - why wasn't I? My Irish chum Majella observed I was going around with a face the length of a wet week. In a few short August weeks Evelyn's view of me had changed dramatically.

As a paid employee her demeanour and conduct towards me from day one was as much an anxiety as it was a puzzle. In short order it felt like a declaration of war against me, one of the two co-founders; Tim's prospects were going due north and mine apparently due south. This was a partiality I neither welcomed nor understood; as to the answer why, I was obliged to wait six years and four months to the Queen's Bench Division, The Royal Courts of Justice and Day 11 of Ball v Druces & Attlee with Evelyn in the witness box being questioned by the High Court Judge, Mr Justice Nelson.

What extraordinary times. Evelyn's taking against me simply made no sense in terms of her CEO task achievement and corporate governance, in matching of resources to goals and in the discharge of her duties to the Board and to the Trustees. The absence of equity in her actions and propositions not only parted company with common sense, but as it was to transpire, her own future. I had returned from the Isles of Scilly with a single mindedness in pursuing my own legitimate expectations. I was one of Eden's two originators and risk takers and if Evelyn was attempting to deny me a continuing key role in its development my reaction was that of an elephant parted from its calf against its will – I would do all in my power to protect the Eden we had conceived and my own continuing part in it. If it was going to be the law of the jungle, so be it. In her honeymoon partiality towards Tim, Evelyn had not appreciated she was riding on the back of a crocodile and it would only be a matter of time before the crocodile was, in turn, to bite her. But for now there were more pressing Green Team imperatives to address. The plants needed to play catch up with the project design and development which had established an impressive momentum under Ronnie Murning's forceful directing.

Tim and Philip Macmillan Browse had an idea. We needed a nursery that would grow the plants and have them ready to populate our biomes when completed. The project needed to buy Watering Lane Nurseries, just down the road from Heligan which, they said, was ideal for the purpose. There was logic in the proposition and good sense in the follow up suggestion by others that the McAlpine's joint venture team, now appointed our contractors, purchase the nurseries as part of their 'hurt money' as the asset could then be ring fenced against that element of their risk. An offer, based on independent valuation, was made to the proprietor Roger Noyce, who for some time had been a business partner with Tim at Heligan, but it was declined.

Shortly afterwards Eden was informed that Watering Lane Nurseries had been acquired by Heligan Gardens on behalf of Eden, but for a figure well in excess of the McAlpine's independent valuation. The Eden Trustees reluctantly agreed to pay an annual rent of £24,000 to Heligan Gardens.

This new project facility was soon put to good use. With Roger Noyce vacating his pleasant bungalow, the core asset, we now had a base camp for the Green Team. The building was soon re-arranged for its new purpose. The sitting room became the Board Room for Eden Project Limited and the Trustees to meet, the dining room became a meeting room where the Green Team philosophies could evolve alongside the advancing architectural solutions and the bedrooms for staff accommodation which was, given its remote location, essential for on site security. On Evelyn's decree this was now the hub for all Eden activity and a garden shed was erected close to the front entrance to give her authority and privacy as Head Girl. We soon christened it the Wendy Hut.

Beyond the bungalow all we had acquired was some land with poly tunnels and propositions were made to Restormel Borough Council and the Rural Development Commission for their investment of further public funds to adapt and improve Watering Lane for its new mission. This they did. It was to become an impressive set up and along with subsequent investments the Project established purpose-designed propagation greenhouses and a phytosanitary facility that allowed us to place in quarantine the plants we were assembling from overseas in full compliance with the Ministry of Agriculture, Fisheries and Food (MAFF) and other statutory requirements. It also gave confidence to all stakeholders and Philip Macmillan Browse regularly assisted in winning sceptical hearts and minds with his conducted tours, not least by pointing out the plant world was controlled by mother nature and the seasons, unlike the Mandarins and the bankers who would turn funding taps on and off at a moment's notice. This latter task, the challenge of taking on the financial establishment and the politicians in the development of our business plan, was one Tim greatly enjoyed.

The dichotomy of the moment for the project was on the one hand Tim's rock 'n roll showmanship and marketing chutzpah which brilliantly conveyed the boldness and audacity of our ideas, giving us the edge over others; whilst his morally bankrupt methods were destroying our ethical edge and with it the ability to deliver the team's integrity of belief. Deborah Clark, in directing our public relations, was to describe our Eden core philosophy as being, *'the last sound bite that came into Tim Smit's head when in front of the TV cameras.'*

The dichotomy of the moment for me was Tim's congenial behaviour in all our face to face exchanges whilst privately seeking exclusivity in his own advantage. Recognising I was way out of my league, I sought advice from Ian Hay Davison whose vast experience had prompted his own early resignation as a Trustee. His response was characteristically swift and robust and within two days I found myself sitting across the desk of three partners of the City of London law firm Field, Fisher Waterhouse who headed up Intellectual Property Rights and Merchandising, Branding and Trade Mark Registration. They listened intently, reviewed the paperwork and within the first few moments of them delivering a summary of their advice, memories came flooding back of the conversation on my first day as the Honorary Secretary of the Royal Institute of British Architects. Shit creek was wider than I thought.

The review was frightening. There were no intellectual property rights pertaining to the concept and we, the co-founders, did not have any security or legal rights in the project or its name as it was currently structured. There was certainly moral obligation on the Trustees to repay us for our investment to date, but this would continue to get weaker. The proposed management structure as set out in the application for funding to the Millennium Commission did provide for certain rewards, but they had not been properly defined by Druces & Attlee. It was clear the Trust would need to seek sponsorship for the project and in order to do so would need to license the name and logo of the project, the trade marks, to third parties and both Tim and I as originators of the project and its name needed first to have our rights therein legally secure, a position that had been accepted in principle but there was no legal agreement in place.

I explained Druces & Attlee had advised that it was not necessary to register the name of the project. *'They would say that wouldn't they. Which of their several clients with divergent interests were they going to advise as owners of the marks'*, commented the Field, Fisher Waterhouse partners incredulously. They advised my entitlement to be the absolute return of all my disbursements that I had incurred to date, nearly a six figure sum which was crippling my Practice, the reimbursement of all my time costs, to be repaid on an agreed formula and some founder shares with specific rights attached thereto, together with being appointed to the Board of Eden Project Limited in the capacity of an Executive Director on a remunerated fixed term contract.

In having regard for my parlous situation they advised prompt action to strengthen my capacity to defend myself legally against inequitable conduct. Tim was reneging on his obligations to me but I had no wish to renege on my obligations to him nor, indeed, to the Trustees whose continuing goodwill I enjoyed.

> *"In order to continue displaying utmost good faith, what you do Jonathan is this,"* they advised, *"before you leave our offices this morning, you make the application to register the name, The Eden Project, which belongs to you and Tim. The registration application should proceed in your name on behalf of you and Tim, on behalf of the Eden Project. Thus Tim, who is reneging on you, cannot secure his own equal legitimate interest other than through you and in turn you remain true to the concept that this always was a public project for the benefit of Cornwall and beyond, but the Trustees must in turn be true to you in the process. It also provides for you a last bat and long stop position to take to your bank manager to secure your family home and provide good prospects for recovery of your costs to date and something for your trouble. Any application for trademark registration is advertised with a period for challenge but most importantly the act of making the application cannot be leap-frogged by any other party whose way forward is to challenge the application and then come into negotiation for terms. Should it be that those forces against you succeed in making you history so far as Eden is concerned they will challenge the application and we will negotiate with them recovery of your financial position in order for them to take full legal ownership of the marks and all your accumulated IP. In that event, Jonathan, take the money and get on with the rest of your life – it's not a fair world, but you are not the first person to have this happen to them and you surely won't be the last."*

Feeling more world weary than relieved, I immediately went to meet Sir Alcon and explained fully what I had done and upon what basis, leaving him in no doubt Field, Fisher Waterhouse felt, contrary to the advice being given by Druces & Attlee, that application to register the marks was essential. In this matter, I had acted entirely in line with the Minuted Resolutions of the Eden Trustees. I also immediately rang Tim but this was at a time when he was not returning my calls. Further meetings with Evelyn Thurlby and with the Millennium Commission followed with Evelyn being advised by Druces & Attlee.

Tim meanwhile had already come into a three day a week Executive Director's role with the Eden Project at a full time equivalent £100,000 salary; Evelyn had no Executive Director's remunerated role for me. Evelyn was unhappy with the concept of Tim and I having licensing rights in the name and logo of the project and I pointed out her hostile view ran contrary to the various agreements with the Trustees protecting the birthright position for Tim and I as co-founders. Both the Trustees and Evelyn had required a joint submission from Tim and me as to the future. Tim refused. I was asking for no more than fair settlement for the past and a decent run at the future. With the assistance of Field, Fisher Waterhouse I accordingly submitted an independent proposal only for Evelyn then to show it to Tim in advance of his submission which was so constructed to respond to points I had made and to my disadvantage.

Already some key personalities in the business community of Cornwall and Devon were sensing all was not well. The Chairman of the Devon and Cornwall private sector steering group, Tim Jones, recommended a conversation with Evelyn was needed, with the suggestion that her marginalisation of me was a high risk strategy to her. He counselled me to continue behaving entirely in accordance with the minuted resolutions of the Trustees and to give whatever undertakings the Trustees required for the Project's success subject only to the Trustees sticking to those resolutions that protected my birthright position. The advice from Field, Fisher Waterhouse was that I should expect a challenge sooner rather than later and in that event I would be left with little alternative, for my own integrity, than to take a negotiated settlement and become history.

The next meeting with Mike Jane, my bank manager, was much happier in consequence of the Field, Fisher Waterhouse intervention, itself the initiative of Ian Hay Davison, who was to remain a constant friend throughout some torrid years for my family. With my legal parachute in place my overdraft arrangements, whilst kept in strict control could, for the time being, now extend to cover Field, Fisher Waterhouse fees and meant my absence of positive cash flow was no longer critical. Deflecting all discouragements I was able to maintain my culture and presence within Eden and negotiate with Evelyn various new ideas and initiatives to help drive the project forward on whatever terms I could obtain.

Chapter 7

I Only Came Here to Build a Bridge...

I thought long and hard about where I could best add value to the Project's forward momentum but in a semi-detached manner insofar as I could go away, put my ideas and implementation strategies together and achieve a progress that could not be defeated by Executive marginalisation from Evelyn and Tim. I needed to protect my huge existing investment in Eden, financial, intellectual and emotional, but needed to be cautious in establishing programmes that delivered overpowering validation of my Eden co-founder position and status, as set out in the Millennium submission. One of my supporters had cautioned that Tim and Evelyn had a vested interest in my failing. Beware, I was told, the pincer movement of risking further substantial time and funds in advance of reimbursement and reward against achieving measurable success, which would inevitably be viewed by Tim as a threat.

To be fair Evelyn was certainly gracious about the way my enthusiasm remained undiminished and in time came to understand how passionate I was for the full realisation of our Eden dream. Eden, after all, now enshrined even more of my personal philosophy of having a project firmly looking to the future. Tim's original idea, as set out in his first letter on our joint behalf to Michael Galsworthy, the High Sheriff of Cornwall, was for a museum of gardening, a more retrospective project telling the story of the great plant hunters augmenting Heligan, a project that looked to the past, a concept quietly dropped by Tim, not the big fat idea he was later to claim as his own. But to Tim these things mattered not. Magnetic of personality, careless of the truth, Tim thundered on.

In consultation with chums I formulated in my mind three programmes – one that focused on marketing; one firmly fixed on global aspiration and status (after all, this was a flagship project for Britain at the turn of the Millennium) and one firmly rooted at the unglamorous end of fundraising. It would be my happy trinity of initiatives that served a number of project imperatives of the moment and offered protection to my personal investments to date and prospects for my future.

Where Tim and I remained in total accord was in our whole Eden approach which was the commitment to doing things differently. Eden was all about thinking big and catching the eye and what better starting point from an international marketing perspective, I thought, than to explore the possibility of Eden having its own postage stamp. There could arguably be no finer promotional and marketing initiative and, as far as I knew, no one had ever before been proactive in securing a Royal Mail postage stamp for an emerging capital project.

So I had the idea. What did I know? I knew roughly how stamp collectors worked, I knew all about Stanley Gibbons, but I also knew an expert in this field who was postage stamp correspondent for The Times. What did I need to do to secure a Royal Mail stamp issue and what if we explored the idea of other countries coming into collaborative arrangements with their own postage stamp issues. I went to see my contact at The Times who introduced me to the head man of the Crown Agents Stamp Bureau who act as agents to 49 national postal administrations.

Eye-catching. The author ensured a little piece of the westcountry winged its way around the world in the form of a commemoration of Eden stamp.

(Western Morning News)

Our first discussions were fascinating. What a great idea for the Eden Project. The Millennium is a big opportunity in the stamp world and the Royal Mail was already minded to have an issue in 2000 to mark the Millennium. With regard to many of the small Dependencies represented by the Crown Agents, stamp issues played a significant part in the GDP of the country delivering vital foreign revenue and most of these Dependencies had an indigenous ecology of interest and relevance to Eden's story.

And so I set in train the masterminding of a world wide stamp issue and enlisted support and assistance from Derek Miller, one of Britain's leading stamp designers to create imaginative concepts for submission to the Royal Mail and also the Crown Agents. These designs secured wide media coverage and established a momentum that finally delivered the Royal Mail's issue of the striking Eden first class stamp with a run of 75 million, shooting the Project's name and philosophy to all corners of planet Earth on 1st August 2000.

Sitting alongside this I was progressing a fundraising idea that was far less romantic. The previous October (1997) I had been a guest at a dinner given by a Cornish law firm and had sat next to a major client of theirs involved in landfill. Over dinner my companion explained all about the new landfill tax credit scheme and a new regulator, Entrust, who confirm whether or not tax credits comply with eligible criteria on any one scheme. Basically here was a great opportunity for Eden. I immediately set off for London for a meeting with the Chief Executive of Entrust to open discussions on whether Eden might qualify for enrolment as an environmental body within the requirement of the Landfill Tax Regulations 1996, a scheme that allowed landfill operators to claim credit against landfill tax payments if they made a voluntary contribution to an approved environmental scheme. In its first year of operation nationally it had thrown up revenues in excess of £80m that could be claimed against tax and it was estimated at the inception of the scheme that the top 50 landfill companies in Britain would each have about £800,000 of tax credits to give away on a year on year basis. I had stumbled across a nascent goldmine – where there's muck, there's brass – here, more like gold bars and this became part three of my happy trinity with indeed good prospects of early reward as landfill operators enjoyed this opportunity on a use-it-or-lose-it basis and were unable to carry credits forward to the following year. There was an enormous amount of ground building work that was necessarily advanced in all haste, albeit not in an area of endeavour best suited to my talents.

I therefore resolved to take ownership of the idea on behalf of the project, but was happy to have Gaynor Coley, Eden's Finance Director, taking over the complex areas naturally within the remit of her Chartered Accountant's skill base whilst I prepared the presentation papers to the various landfill operators with whom we might expect good prospects of collaboration.

Then with eyes firmly fixed on matters global I put together a substantial draft paper, the prose polished by my friend Henry Boettinger from Crackington Haven a project proposal which I called *'The International Partners in Eden Programme'*. It was an idea and a project proposal of and for its time. After all, the Eden Project was now being developed as a response to the issues raised by the Rio Conference on bio-diversity (1992) and Agenda 21 which reflected an international recognition on the paramount importance of environmental conservation and bio-diversity protection. My paper started with connecting this to the turn of the Millennium.

"Global problems demand local solutions, the engine of change is the individual, the fuel is education.'"

The science, engineering, architecture and vision of Eden had already been endorsed by world class experts. As both an idea and a unique construction Eden is founded on the merging of environmental concerns, educational initiatives, advanced engineering and architectural technologies.

Eden appeals to the wider spectrum of humankind, its mission to interpret the reality of conflicting pressures of exploitation and conservation on land resources, and through education and public awareness create a climate of opinion that allows our Eden philosophy to work on projects throughout the world.

I said, 'Destination Eden' was to be an international showcase for the study of human dependence on plants – the home and mission control for a new Institute, focussing on the question of how, in our overcrowded planet, land can be apportioned between the needs of conservation and economic production. Given its purpose and awareness our desire was to have other nations become international partners who would support and participate in our exhibits and our programmes. It was indeed timely to seek to consolidate relationships now with overseas partners who would like to be part of the vision. My paper argued that this international programme could and should be part of Eden's funding strategy, thus cementing our ambition to become a global centre to act as a non-competitive resource facility to supplement and join with the endeavours of other existing international institutions. Publications would range from specialist papers to children's publications all orientated towards the vital inter-dependence between humankind and plants, and recognising that the most sustainable development projects in the world are husbanded by the very communities they are intended to benefit.

Eden should be offering its international partners the opportunity to show millions of people from all over the world features of their country, its plants, environments and culture; participation as a partner would aid their international efforts for projects requiring cooperation with other countries by becoming a member of a like-minded, on-going network of competent, concerned agents of progress.

I prepared documentation tailored to suit different nations, particularly those with the richest bio-diversity and facing the greatest threats. Eden was a platform for displaying these countries' unique contribution to, and stewardship of, diversity of their indigenous ecology. And, of course, Eden would evoke interest and enthusiasm which could lead to enhancement of their own visitor economies, truly a win-win proposition.

These ideas were certainly eye catching and I was invited to join a Department of Trade and Industry (DTI) Trade Mission to Australia via Malaysia and taking in New Zealand. Victoria and I grasped this as an opportunity to detach ourselves physically and metaphorically from our Watering Lane wars. What emerged through detailed planning was an affordable three week trip with no more than a couple of nights in a hotel and the remainder of our accommodation with friends and surf life saving colleagues of long standing, many of whom reciprocated my hospitality they had enjoyed in Cornwall, some 30 years previously during student days when Antipodean members of

Bude Surf Life Saving Club veterans at the 60th commemorations in 2013, re-enacting the Reel, Line and Belt march past with the author at the Reel, second right.
(Bob Willingham)

London Cornish RFC would decamp to Bude for summer weekends.

Throughout my lifetime there has been a close association between Bude and Australia born of our fabulous Atlantic surf and a shared love of the life of the beach. I had joined Bude Surf Life Saving Club in 1959. The Surf Life Saving movement in Britain started in 1953 in Coronation year when I was six years old. Bude was the first British Club to be formed and was based on the Australian Surf Life Saving movement. The Aussies had declared Bude to be Britain's Bondi and the club soon became the largest youth organisation in the area and the central focus of our young lives. Voluntary beach patrolling was a public duty we took very seriously and the ethos of our motto 'Vigilance and Service' underpinned a rigorous and disciplined training which kept us fit, fine tuned our competitive spirits in sporting contest against other Surf Life Saving clubs and has delivered so many of my happy memories of growing up in Bude.

This affinity with Australia and its people was to hold me in good stead with a feast of established contacts and massive good will awaiting us on arrival in Sydney. In 1994, the same year Tim and I became Eden co-founders, I had been President of the Cornwall Region of Surf Life Saving GB when Cornwall hosted the Life Saving World Championships and as one of the host organisers pledged to ensuring our important visitors had a good time I had got to know the world President Kevin Weldon. I needn't have worried when it came to Kevin, a personality well known nationally in Australia, and who seemed intent on proving to me that here in Britain drinking was still in its infancy.

When he had implored Victoria and I to be sure to look him up when we next visited Australia I hadn't quite anticipated the level of reciprocal hospitality that would come our way. Kevin ran his own helicopter fleet via one of his many businesses, Weldon International. Kevin arrived in his own

The author showing Challenger astronaut, Paul Scully-Power the delights of Cornwall, a sedate passage on the King Harry Ferry at a more gentle pace than his 133 earth orbits where at times the shuttle travelled at nearly 5,000 metres per second. *(JB archive)*

Oceanographer and Astronaut, Paul Scully-Power, was the first President of the United Nations International Commission on Space Oceanography, flew on the penultimate Challenger flight, the 13th Shuttle Mission which studied earth sciences. His book Oceans to Orbit tells the story of Australia's first man in space and his inscription in the copy gifted to us when leaving Brisbane says it all ...

"To Jonathan, A Book of Photos of The Real Eden. Here's to our joint team."

(JB archive)

helicopter to pick us up at Brisbane Airport to take us off to his global eco retreat of Gwynganna, high in the rain forest hinterland of Queensland's Gold Coast. Here he had assembled one of his regular long weekend house parties. I was invited to give presentations on the Eden Project and its international ambitions to my fellow weekend guests who included the recently retired Cabinet Secretary to the Queensland Government and renowned Australian astronaut Dr Paul Scully-Power. Paul was to become a good chum and Ambassador for Eden and subsequently we greatly enjoyed the opportunity to entertain him and his wife Fran in Bude.

At the time Paul was Chairman of the Science and Technology Council for the Queensland government and Chancellor of Bond University, Brisbane. This delivered massive support and offers of collaboration from the Government of the State of Queensland. We had enjoyed similar success with the Government of New South Wales having spent time in Sydney with an old London Cornish Rugby chum Jim Sloman and his wife Liz. Jim had been a regular summer visitor to Bude during his time in London but 1998 found him as Deputy Chief Executive of the Sydney 2000 Olympics. Before we left Sydney we had secured the draft of a letter from Bob Carr, Premier of the State of New South Wales with the fulsome support of the chairman of tourism of New South Wales offering financial linkages and ecology showcasing with Eden. And to crown all that Jim generously made available the Sydney 2000 Olympics sponsorship strategy document for Eden's use to optimise our capacity in securing the necessary match funding to our public funds.

Before Australia we had first touched down in Auckland New Zealand where chums from London Cornish RFC and Surf Life Saving accommodated us for a week and facilitated our Eden partnering ambitions.

Whilst at the AA in the late 1960s I played in the same London Cornish Rugby team as a 6ft 8in Kiwi, Maurice Purdy who, a few years later, was to return to New Zealand but only after marrying Karen Black from Bude. Maurice and Karen lived in Auckland in the next road to the famous Eden Park rugby stadium and had put together an impressive set of contacts that sat alongside strong support from the British Consul General in Auckland and the New Zealand High Commission in London.

Victoria and I had become good friends with George Gair and his wife Fay, George having been NZ High Commissioner in London and they had attended one of our luncheon parties in the Bude Belvedere.

Another retired NZ High Commissioner to London, John Collinge, had also been to Bude during his London term of office and through all these contacts I had given an interview to the New Zealand Herald, had developed a good relationship with the Horticultural and Food Institute NZ and had a working breakfast with Sir Roger Douglas, former Chancellor of the Exchequer in the NZ Government.

The Marketing Manager for New Zealand Post was keen to engage with our international stamp programme and by the time we departed for Australia discussions had advanced on how we might bring together Eden Team NZ.

New Straits Times, Malaysia. From left: Victoria Ball, Bob and Johnna Giles.

(JB archive)

Similar success was to be awaiting us in Malaysia. From the moment we touched down in Kuala Lumpur we engaged in a whirlwind tour that had been prepared for us by a British architect chum Bob Giles and his Danish wife, Johnna who was serving as Commercial Secretary at the Danish Embassy. They had been resident in Malaysia for several years, Bob had served on RIBA Council with me for many years and was currently Chairman of the Malaysia Chapter of the Royal Institute of British Architects.

Not only were we their house guests, but in anticipation of our visit Bob had prepared a detailed itinerary with assistance from the British High Commission whose advice and contacts gave us immediate access to those Government agencies that would control any Malaysian involvement in the Eden Project.

By the end of an exhausting five days meetings had taken place at Director level with the Forest Research Institute Malaysia (FRIM) the office of the Government's Science advisor in the Prime Minister's office, Tunku Imran, prominent businessman and younger son of the King of Malaysia, other senior Civil Servants within the Prime Minister's Department and the Ministry of Primary Industries and the University of Malaysia. The British High Commissioner, H.E David Moss, could not have been more helpful. One of Malaysia's most prominent architects, Dr Ken Yeang, internationally acclaimed for his high rise buildings in South East Asia and yet another alumnus of the Architectural Association, pledged all support to our securing Malaysia's involvement in Eden. As one of the world's most diverse and rich habitats this was surely of incalculable value to the project and everything my International Partners in Eden Programme sought to achieve.

A detailed report was prepared by Bob Giles concluding that the foundations had now been laid for a formal direct approach to Dr Mahatiar the Prime Minister of Malaysia.

We returned to Cornwall with Reports and letters of interest and commitment that fulfilled my every expectation, delivering evidence of warm and enthusiastic support and tangible proposals for international investment in Eden, financial from Australia and engagement from Malaysia that would greatly strengthen Eden's showcasing of habitats.

At Watering Lane this abundant progress was treated as a threat rather than an opportunity. For Tim it validated my co-founder status and the Eden Executive Group soon laagered up general opposition to the programme. It is not difficult to disable legitimate activity by a combination of resource starvation and control of flow of information. It starts with avoiding the answering of letters and faxes, telephone calls remain unreturned and all protests are met with a response that everyone is too busy doing more important things for the Project at this time. An unvirtuous circle can surround a good idea and halt its progress – and that is exactly what happened. My protests that my legitimate signed off programmes were being disabled went unheeded with the Trustees. They were already battle weary and were fighting enough fires on other fronts with Watering Lane.

Despite this and a range of other positive initiatives it was clear that I was being progressively marginalised and distanced from my co-founder role. I was disappointed then to be told by Evelyn, on advice from Druces & Attlee, that the Millennium Commission had confirmed their approval to the constructor, the operator and the bank all having equity in the project, on account of the requirement for them to have invested some 'hurt money'. However this consent for equity in the project did not extend to the co-founders whose own 'hurt money' had substantially carried most of the early project risks. Why? Because the co-founders are no longer fundamental to securing and achieving the business case. Meanwhile Druces & Attlee were advising the Trustees they had no obligation whatsoever either to Tim or myself.

I protested to Sir Alcon that if this was the case Druces & Attlee had been in default to us the moment we had signed off the Trust Deed. The sympathetic ear of the Trustees remained ever open and wanting to assist in coming to a generous solution, and Sir Alcon confirmed the Trustees would be happy to listen to any view Field Fisher Waterhouse had on the matter. Contrary to what Druces & Attlee were advising the Trustees, the Field Fisher Waterhouse view was that the Trustees needed to recognise the rights belonging to us; we were not asking the Trustees to grant rights to us, but for a negotiation that attached to the transfer of our rights to the Trustees and thence onward to the project.

There was no greater champion of my cause at this time than Tim Jones who, for a number of years, had led the private sector interests in Cornwall and Devon in their interface with regional and central government and, most importantly, the various European funding regimes supporting Cornwall's low economic base. He was to become a cherished friend of the Project, playing a pivotal role in Eden's negotiation for matched funding from European programmes. Our professional association stretched back to my early years in practice and we had collaborated on a number of project ideas over the years, aimed at increasing the prosperity of our region, and I had ensured his engagement on every step of Eden's journey. My ever growing problems were matched by his ever growing concerns and he effectively assumed a role as my Campaign Manager.

My historic costs memorandum submitted as requested to Evelyn for absolute return of all my disbursements, the recovery of all my time costs, and confirmation that founder shares and a remunerated Board appointment on a fixed term contract, all as advised by Field Fisher Waterhouse and against audited costs, took eight weeks to elicit a reply. Evelyn's offer, which had been drafted by Druces & Attlee, was derisory. Against proven costs she offered a sum of just over one third of the claim and stated the Millennium Commission would not accept that either Tim or I should receive any equity stake, also commenting that the European Regional development Fund (EDRF) had similarly said no. This was wrong and clearly dismissed by Tim Jones in his subsequent evidence when it came to interrogation of this point in the Royal Courts of Justice before Sir Robert Nelson. (RCJ.No.03/TLQ/0035 paras.203-209) Furthermore I would have to wait until after financial close for settlement and the only offer for the future was that I be appointed as a non Executive director of Eden on a consultancy agreement the terms of which added insult to injury and required me to take further risks before any reward. All this was wrapped up as only being available if I forthwith hand over all my rights and intellectual property for all time to the project.

The gloom of 1997's autumn was compounded for me by the news that A L Rowse had died. A handful of mourners were invited to his private funeral at Bodmin crematorium and we gathered on a dank and grey October day:

Cornwall's history in the moment, the passing of a chum united in friendship by our shared passion for Cornwall. My friendship with A L had first been formed at the Members' Table of the Athenaeum in I think 1985 with he and I making up probably a third of the Cornish membership. He loved my passion for Cornwall and I loved talking to a man who was widely accepted as one of the great historians and men of letters of the 20th Century and who was without doubt the most celebrated, if irascible, living Cornishman. On each occasion we got together it was Cornwall, past, present and future that captured the conversation and I was sad to be saying goodbye to such wisdom and authority.

The Trustees meeting for February 1998 followed soon after some phenomenal coverage in the Times weekend section on Saturday 24th January headed 'Welcome to Cornwall 2020'. It contained fabulous images and lengthy Tim Smit-centric coverage with Tim indicating my only involvement as being a local architect who had introduced him to Nicholas Grimshaw & Partners. **1998**

This prompted another raft of indignant inward phone calls, mostly reassuring me that there were a lot of people out there who would make sure the Cornish co-founder would not be shafted. Most worrying was the view from Tim Jones, Chairman of the private sector steering group. Tim Smit, in displaying his total absence of trustworthiness, was causing alarm and concern with those in the business community whose support would be necessary to see Eden through to financial close. If Tim was doing this to me, what would he in turn be doing to them and were they at risk individually? Deborah Clark rang in PR dismay. Tim had released too many good images too early and this was a PR disaster for Eden's various relationships, most particularly with the Western Morning News. She was appalled the management of information had been blown by Tim to serve his own purpose. Sir Alan Donald rang, furious that Tim was so cavalier and arrogantly disrespectful of all the hard work of so many people, not least the Trustees, that had got Eden firmly on political agendas. Henceforth, he would be calling Tim Smit by a different name, changing the second letter of his surname from the fourteenth letter of the alphabet to the eighth. My erstwhile business partner was no longer palindromic.

At the February meeting of the Trustees I again protested that battle lines were being created by the legal advice of Druces & Attlee who had been my lawyers and Tim's and they, the Trustees, were now in place because we had instructed them to create the Trust on Druces & Attlee's own advice. My grievances, as ever, were listened to and a few weeks later, although unbeknown to me at the time, in response to my protestations, Druces & Attlee had written to their clients, the Trustees, confirming they had,

> " … never acted for Jonathan Ball, in his personal capacity or at all either in connection with the Eden Project or any other matter."

Their being called to account for this letter by the High Court Judge in the Royal Courts of Justice in December 2003 brought forth one of the most charged moments of the trial. (RCJ.No.03/TLQ/0035 para.127)

Evelyn was as ever candid with me saying she was using cash flow to get everybody in line and acknowledged that remunerated offers had been issued to all members of the team, except me. I would be offered a 'paid on results only' basis. I was now being positively excluded from meetings and my complaint to Evelyn brought forth the riposte, 'I call the meetings, I decide who attends'. Without informing or consulting me she then instructed Ernst and Young to remove from the business plan the paragraph securing the co-founders' rights.

With Tim securing his own future by other means, including through his first person singular media campaign, I saw my own prospects best secured by hanging in there, continuing to add value at each regular meeting of the Eden Project Limited Board and in all the ways I had positively contributed to our successes since 1994. What mattered most was Eden's onward and upward progress and it would be a disaster for the project and for Cornwall if the true management culture prevailing was exposed to the media. Sticking close to Field Fisher Waterhouse I maintained a World War 1 trench warfare approach for my own interests which achieved similar, historic, inch by inch progress.

Evelyn formed what she called The Executive Group, Tim Smit, Peter Thoday, Philip Macmillan Browse, Gaynor Coley and Kary Lescure as her core team, leaving me in no doubt I was positively excluded from her inner circle in moving the project forward.

A large official looking envelope arrived in the post at the beginning of August on the morning of my departure to the Isles of Scilly for our family break. I stared at the contents in blank amazement; they were the registration certificates and trademarks for The Eden Project. The Intellectual Property Title Deeds to Britain's landmark Millennium Project had arrived safely in Bude, as the process had been completed unchallenged. An extraordinary event, but was it? We had dreamed up both the project and the project name and taken the entrepreneurial risks. The application to make the registration by the original creators of the intellectual property had been undertaken against the advice of Druces & Attlee. I had personally paid all the prescribed application fees and attendant legal costs, so how were Druces & Attlee going to advise either or both their clients Eden Project Limited and the Eden Trust to make a challenge and what would be the legal basis of any such challenge? Meanwhile the publicly funded millions flowing inwards to Eden and its realisation were on a strict condition precedent basis (a legal obligation) that the recipients of the Award, the Eden Trust, owned and controlled all the Intellectual property of the project. They did not.

There was, nonetheless, much to celebrate for all of us who had shared Eden's journey thus far. At the beginning of September, with the words, *'Eden is quite simply one of the most important projects in the world today'* we were able to announce that Sir Ghilean Prance, shortly to retire as Director of Kew Gardens, was joining the Eden Project as Director of Science. This recruitment of one of the world's leading experts was for me a defining moment in the evolution of our Project, which was due to start on site within weeks with our design team under Ronnie Murning's disciplined superintendence playing a blinder. World class reputations side by side, this was the endorsement of scientific gravitas. Eden, Cornwall and Britain had accepted the Millennial challenge of making the world recognise the critical importance of plants to mankind.

Autumn in Cornwall is often mellow and golden: but in contrast the darkening days close in and bring with them resignation rather than optimism, a season when, as the leaves gently fall, the days hang heavy. Shadows lengthen and the autumn of 1998 had the legal profession casting these shadows wider and longer.

At the October meeting of the Eden Project Limited Board Sir Alcon in his joint role as Chairman of the Eden Trust and Chairman of Eden Project Limited explained Druces & Attlee were proposing a course of action to strengthen legal entity and governance. It was a complete mess. I was being told by Field Fisher Waterhouse that there was clear indication in correspondence that not only had the co-founders been paying Druces & Attlee's fees, but they were still taking instructions from us after the Eden Trust had been formed at our behest. By Druces & Attlee's own admission the Eden Project was not a legal entity and yet they had written a letter to confirm that they, Druces & Attlee, were, and had been, legal advisers to the Eden Project since its inception by Tim and I in 1994. Quite simply Field Fisher Waterhouse's firm conclusion was that certainly up to the formation of the Trust, the Eden Project can only have meant Jonathan Ball and Tim Smit. The days to Christmas darkened further with conflicting legal advice dominating an unhappy working environment for all. It must be said this was in part arising from nothing more than the Eden Project's uniqueness. It was delivering so many varied challenges, both technical and human and Field Fisher Waterhouse commented to me how the legal solutions that have had to be found are consistent with Eden's pioneering characteristic. Anyone who has had lengthy dealings with lawyers will be all too aware that you should steer well clear of any issue that strays into novel law. Every step along that path should be undertaken with foreboding.

Early in 1999 the temperature rose at Eden Project Limited Board meetings with me refusing to approve the draft annual accounts wanting my protest recorded that the Finance Director was refusing me, as a director, access to the cash book records of the company. Evelyn wanted me off the Board. By chance I had a meeting on the platform at Paddington Station with my Member of Parliament, Paul Tyler, whose continuing interest and support for the project from the outset had greatly assisted Eden in charting

Westminster waters.

We had always enjoyed the most cordial personal relationship and Paul was widely regarded in North Cornwall and beyond as an excellent constituency MP. He would regularly come to Bude to see me, wanting to know about what he described as 'my latest brainwaves'. I had been particularly delighted when it was his turn in June 1993 to be written up in the House Magazine 'Hansard'. His Commons diary item highlighted his visits to me in Bude saying, *as usual Jonathan Ball is buzzing with positive ideas for the sensitive development of Cornwall'*. One of his visits had coincidentally been on the 5th October 1994 only five days after Tim and I had shaken hands as business partners. This had cemented his keen interest and engagement in the project.

He was close to disbelief, having pressed me for more details than I had first offered in respect of Eden's tangled governance issues. He wanted an early meeting and following this asked me for more information which I gave him by return. Not least he was appalled to learn that since first being told about the scheme in October 1994, my professional practice had plummeted from nine full time jobs in Bude down to three and a half. Worryingly enough for us both, but what incensed him was the apparent breaching of the agreement relating to the terms and conditions of grant between the Millennium Commission and Eden which had charged the project with entering into suitable terms with the project principals etc.

1999   The start of the New Year had me and my family in high octane financial crisis, not knowing which way to turn and morale at the Jonathan Ball Practice at a low ebb. It brought a new dimension to the words 'hurt money' and I suspected Tim and Heligan Gardens were likely to be in a parallel crisis. What I did not know was that they could and would deploy leverage to save their day. Here was Tim in 'everyone for themselves' mode and once again Orwellian equality prevailed. Tim was a member of the Eden Project Limited Executive Group, I was not.

Demands now made upon the Trustees for ratification brought from them united disapprobation. With Druces & Attlee advising Heligan, the Eden Trustees were presented with the demand to purchase forthwith from Heligan the Watering Lane Nurseries for a consideration double that of the original McAlpine's independent valuation two years before. This was notwithstanding that Heligan had been paid a monthly rental of £2,000 for this facility. The Trustees described this as a shotgun demand, being faced with the threat of the project falling if they did not give their immediate approval. Heligan insisted in linking this with Tim's historic costs and the deal was done. By this arrangement Tim, who was already drawing a £60,000 salary for a three day week, now additionally recovered six figure historic costs whilst Evelyn was able to continue her resistance to me receiving similar treatment. And so at this critical moment for me, on the stroke of a reluctant Trustee pen, for Tim and Heligan all their Eden risks were erased. Tim's eye watering salary was in stark contrast to the equally eye watering knife edge on which I sat - no income, the family home and the practice in peril.

Each and every subsequent meeting when Sir Alan Donald was present found him muttering his disaffection with the Heligan shotgun transaction and the inequity of my circumstances. The paperwork he was receiving in response to his requests as a Trustee for accountability from the Eden Project Limited Executive Group he described as jejune. It was these particular issues that led to his resignation soon after.

Affectionately forever stored in my memory is one of the last pieces of advice my father gave me shortly before he died in 1978. Early years in Practice saw long hours for short reward. I went to Dad for reassurance, for a pat on the head, for him to say everything would be OK. What I got was a forthright blast, *'Just remember, if it was that bloody easy, everybody would be doing it.'* We all remember the nuggets of parental advice most valuable in securing our future. Dad had also consistently reminded me it was not a fair world.

My gloom was lifted via a phone call from a good friend, Ralph French who had been peripherally engaged in helping move Eden forward. My London chums were worried about me, he said, not only our survival in terms of our finances and family home, but also my sanity. Not without justification, I replied, and briefly relayed the latest 'Tales from Shit Creek'.

Ralph was pleased to know that my eternal optimism had not quite deserted me. History was on my side, he said, in that relief eventually always comes to the besieged. I told him that what I needed was a Relief of Mafeking moment. 'It's funny you say that' said Ralph, 'because that's the main purpose of my call. What are you doing next week, and whatever it is, clear your diary because I need a bag carrier for a week long trip to South Africa and you are

The 120th commemorations of the Battle of Isandlwana, Kwa Zulu Natal, January 1999 with the Royal Regiment of Wales and British High Commissioner Maeve Fort with massed Zulu warriors. Photograph taken by author. *(JB archive)*

just my man. We are off to fight the Zulus', he said. *'The Anglo Zulu wars, you will recall only just predate the Boer War and in geographical terms Mafeking is only just up the road.'*

It was a wonderful opportunity and I jumped at it. Having had so many assegai spears thrown in my direction from the Eden Executive Group the thought of facing an impi of Zulu warriors mustered to commemorate the 120th anniversary of the battles of Rorke's Drift and Isandlwana was an entirely attractive diversion from my troubles. Anyone who has visited these breathtakingly beautiful battlefields so heavy with history and evocative of a heroism and valour equally shared between Zulu warrior and South Wales Borderer, will understand what a powerful experience it is. For me, here was a heaven sent well-spring for topping up my courage.

The author in Bude lifeboat t-shirt with a multitude of Zulu warriors mustered for the re-enactment of the Battle of Isandlwana.

(JB archive)

On the borders of Natal Province and Zululand infantry of the best equipped Imperial army of the day, at a time when the British Empire spanned continents, and numbering about 1,800 men armed with the British Martini Henry rifle, and who had chosen their own ground on the saddle of Isandlwana with the Royal Artillery in support, were overwhelmed and annihilated by some 20,000 Zulus armed with no more than assegais and raw courage. The following day B Company the South Wales Borderers, about 120 Welshmen, many of them ill and wounded, repelled a massive Zulu onslaught against the Mission Station at Rorke's Drift, a feat for which 11

David Rattray, photographed by the author, having just received the replica Queen's colours from Ralph French.

(JB archive)

The author courageously took this photograph amongst a Zulu Impi in full battle dress chanting their traditional war cry 'Usuthu' and about to charge in the re-enactment of the Battle of Isandlwana, in the presence of King Goodwill and Chief Buthelezi. (JB archive)

Victoria Crosses were earned, a record that holds to this day as the most for any single engagement.

Isandlwana was the only occasion throughout the reign of Her Imperial Majesty Queen Victoria when the Queen's colours were lost in battle. With Nelson Mandela's release and return to power South Africa rejoined the Commonwealth and it was only then that British serving officers could travel to South Africa. Accordingly the centenary of these battles had passed without appropriate remembrance. In consequence, the decision had been made and approved by Her Majesty the Queen that a replica set of colours to those lost would be commissioned and taken out to the 120th commemorations and this task had fallen to Ralph. Also in attendance was the Rorke's Drift Company of the Royal Regiment of Wales and the Welsh Divisional band of the British Army.

What a week. The replica colours were presented by Ralph to David Rattray at a dinner held at Fugitive's Drift Lodge close by where the Victorian colours had been lost, and placed in his care to be displayed at his wonderful museum which also serves as a dining room and shrine to the memory of the engagements; alas also now to the memory of David himself, brutally murdered there in 2007. David Rattray's gift for storytelling, for which he had become internationally famous, transported the listener through anecdote and Zulu fluent language back to the dawn of each engagement and tales were narrated that conveyed a shared nobility of purpose.

Wherever he went, David Rattray spoke to capacity audiences, at his

The Die-Hard Company, historical re-enactors, representing the British Infantry muster within the final redoubt at Rorke's Drift posed for photograph with the author and Ralph French the day following the presentation of the replica Queen's colours.

(JB archive)

regular lectures at the Royal Geographical Society in London and on one occasion even at St Mary's Methodist Church in Truro. But to be there 120 years to the day and to the hour, walking the hallowed landscape with David's hour by hour narration standing on the very ground left us all in awesome wonder and by the time we had attended the first ever Beating of the Retreat at Rorke's Drift with the Royal Regiment of Wales and the other commemorative events of the week, our spirits had soared to new heights and our emotions left in tatters.

Most people of my generation have seen the film Zulu and seen it more than once. It's a classic film and as I collected my thoughts and my memories at the end of an amazing and regenerative week my mind was already back to the Eden battle I was facing in Cornwall. Into my mind came the poignant moment in the film Zulu when Lieutenant John Rouse Merriott Chard, Royal Engineers, played by Stanley Baker and Lt Gonville Bromhead played by Michael Caine survey the slaughter near the end of the film with Chard saying to Bromhead, *'I only came here to build a bridge.'*

This line chimed with me in the circumstances in which I now found myself back home in Cornwall.

Chapter 8

Unveiling the Dream

The Millennium Commission was chaired by the Secretary of State at the Department Culture, Media and Sport (DCMS) Chris Smith MP who paid us a visit to turn the first sod on Tuesday 9th February 1999, in a gale of sleet and snow, with the Secretary of State vying for media attention with a couple of characters from a travelling theatre company who by Paul Travers's design had arrived by helicopter with extraordinary plant pot headgear sporting flourishing narcissi blooms.

Secretary of State, Chris Smith, turns the first sod at Eden   *(JB archive)*

We had invited 200 guests who all turned out in the freezing cold to hear Chris Smith hail us as truly one of the world's major environmental projects as he shovelled some quartz and mica around our inscribed Delabole slate foundation stone. Tim Smit captured the moment for our invited audience by endorsing Eden as a spectacle and an heroic piece of architecture, but this was simply the froth on top of something much more serious, he said. I was reported as describing Eden as being 'pregnant with possibility for every local person and will offer wonderful opportunities for your children and grandchildren.'

In truth Chris Smith would have little idea as to the gigantic technical and design hurdles we had overcome to reach this important milestone in Eden's journey. Work had actually started on site four months earlier in November 1998 but on a scheme radically different from that which had won Millennium funding.

We had used Waterloo Station as an exemplar to the funders and the first scheme echoed this structural form with large, curved trusses spanning from the base of the pit onto the cliff face. It was all looking good and our first model based on this structural principle captured many hearts and minds. But there was a huge problem. The Millennium Commission had only been prepared to advance sufficient funds for us to secure an exclusive option to purchase Bodelva Pit. Whilst these design proposals progressed so it was that the china clay company

3D model of the first Waterloo Station inspired design. (NGP)

continued the extractive processes winning china clay from the site. And so every time our design team travelled to Cornwall to review their design proposals, the site had changed shape!

A radical response was clearly needed and at this point the genius of Anthony Hunt Associates engineers, Nicholas Grimshaw Architects and the late Buckminster Fuller all came together to establish the basis of what is now before you. Quite simply the structural form of the linear geodesic domes could proceed and the biome envelopes resolved and advanced with the intersections between this superstructure and the ground determined once the final purchase of the pit had taken place. A design resolution that none of the previous schemes could accommodate.

As you stroll down to the Humid Tropics Biome think of them as giant childrens' soap bubbles. In your mind then take hold of these connected bubbles, locate them at the bottom of the pit against the cliff side. And there you have it. It doesn't matter where the edge of the cliff is; it doesn't matter where the base of the pit finishes up; the design will accommodate its geography. Pure genius.

All the detailed designs progressed and the cladding materials and

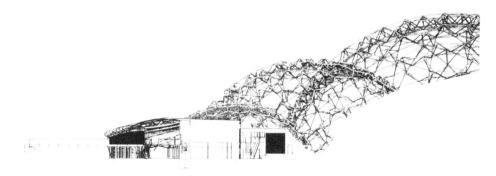

The radical response to the site constraints. (NGP)

structure could be resolved before the pit was finally purchased in order to meet our tight programmes. The Millennium clock was ticking and the political imperative was in place to deliver this wonder in time for Millennial celebrations.

This solution also had another significant advantage: glass is heavy and inflexible. It is difficult to install and even more difficult to replace, with the need for large crane capacities to reach over the buildings on a permanent basis. This solution proposed pneumatic pillows with each cushion fitting within each module of the structure. The panels are formed from several layers of ETFE foil, the material is called Ethyltetraflouroethylene, but to you and me it is glorified cling film.

The pillows were then fixed into aluminium frames which in turn bolted onto the steel structure giving the eye catching characterful appearance. The surface of the pillows is extremely smooth with a self cleaning surface so bird droppings are washed off by the rain. Each pillow is inflated with the pressure controlled by computers and back up pumps and power supplies provide that air can be diverted from one pump unit to the next should for any reason a pillow start to deflate. And another great advantage is that air does not weigh anything so the foundations to the building and the ground preparation necessary for the

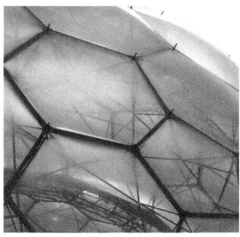

The ETFE pillows that add so much to the magic of the Eden experience.   *(NGP)*

downward thrust is less complex and costly. Indeed the foundations in part have to take into account an upward thrust should a gale of wind get inside the structures. We did not want our biomes to end up in Lostwithiel.

What needs to be understood is that here we were breaking new ground with the pillow design as the larger of them were greater in size than any ever previously attempted. A test rig was set up in Bremen in Germany and the mock ups were tested to establish the inflated pressure for normal operating conditions and what enhanced pressure needed to be established to cope with a loading of heavy snow. Environmentally the biomes were in the safe design hands of Alistair Guthrie of Arups and a simple-to-understand solution soon evolved.

Look at the base of the biomes and you will see louvred panels which are designed in full and part hexagons. The whole system works on a combination of natural ventilation and giant air blowers. And this explains the eye catching

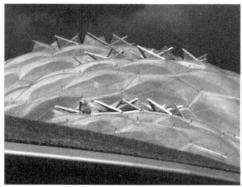

The eye catching triangles that form opening vents. *(NGP)*

triangles that stick up like jagged teeth at the apex where the hexagons are sub-divided into triangles to form opening vents. The temperature sensors set to the requirements of the plant exhibits then control what ambient or man managed air comes in and what goes out at the top, and of course dissipates the excess heat on a sunny Cornwall summer's day.

As Chris Smith took in the full scale of Bodelva Pit he must have secretly wondered however were we going to achieve such an audacious dream and how could the sides of the pit be made sufficiently stable into the future. One of the most fascinating aspects was how the embankments were consolidated after their re-profiling and stabilised to complement the final design appearance of the project. With the assistance of rock anchors to stabilise and secure the embankments the wizards from within what we called the Green Team came up with a special mix of seeds of grass, shrub together with fertiliser and an adhesive gel which was then sprayed onto the embankments. There was a really nice touch here. Into this spray mixture was applied a green dye so that it all looked great on day 1. As the seeds took and the vegetation grew away so the green dye faded from view with no-one the wiser but it had delivered the right atmosphere for our first visitors.

Chapter 9

A Culture of Mistrust

Sir Alcon Copisarow, the first Chairman of the Trustees, welcomes Secretary of State Chris Smith. (JB archive)

Concurrent with the Secretary of State's visit to the Project, Paul Tyler had written as my constituency MP to the Secretary of State, in respect of what Paul thought was likely to be some absurd anomaly or bureaucratic bungle now being quoted by Eden's Chief Executive Officer as an excuse for failure to meet obligations to his constituent, Jonathan Ball.

This sent Evelyn Thurlby into quite a tizzy ... and this made for quite an interesting board meeting. On 25th February 1999 Evelyn swooped off an Exocet memorandum to all Directors (including me), Trustees and lawyer Toby Stroh entitled 'Jonathan Ball - update on activities.' This memorandum read ...

"I have been informed this week by both the Millennium Commission and Government Office South West that approaches have been made to them on behalf of Jonathan Ball. The Millennium Commission have been sent a letter from Chris Smith, Secretary of State DCMS, Chairman of the Millennium Commission, enclosing a letter to him from Paul Tyler MP on behalf of Jonathan Ball. Various project documents were enclosed as attachments.

This item has been added onto the Board Agenda to give Jonathan a chance to account for his actions, clarify what he has done and inform the Board of which documents (some of which may be confidential) have been disclosed. "

Finally, it appeared, the solids had hit the air conditioning and it made for an interesting Eden Project Limited Board meeting held on 2nd March

1999 at Watering Lane. Scheduled for an 11am start we sat down at 11.10 and immediately the Chairman went to Agenda Item 4, Jonathan Ball, he didn't even take Apologies for Absence, Minutes of the last meeting, or Matters Arising.

Evelyn launched into an attack on me saying I had breached my fiduciary duty (*i.e.* one of trust) to the project by talking to my Member of Parliament. Evelyn and Gaynor Coley (Finance Director) had attended a Millennium Commission meeting the previous week on another matter and were told a letter had been received from the Secretary of State and Paul Tyler MP. The Commission would be writing to Evelyn but would be wanting to take the matter of my historic costs away from her jurisdiction. Evelyn immediately wanted my resignation from the Board for talking to my MP and failing this there would be a resolution for my dismissal. I replied this was not a matter for the EPL Board. It was a matter for the Trustees as recipient of the Award of Millennium Commission funding and the Company's shareholder. I had certainly not discussed any EPL Board papers nor had I made them available to my MP.

Gaynor Coley launched forth saying the EPL Board had not been given the opportunity by me to do something about all this and going to my MP was a breach of fiduciary duty. My robust retort was there had been so many breaches of obligations to me as a Board Director, absence of decency and natural justice and for goodness sake how could she say that the EPL Board had not been given the opportunity to address these matters when I was still awaiting a reply to my letter of last July?

Hostilities rumbled on until 11.50 when I was asked to leave the meeting until invited back in some 50 minutes later to receive the Board's ultimatum from Company Secretary, Gaynor. I must forthwith supply the Company with all the documents that went to Paul Tyler MP. The Board wished to offer me the opportunity to stand down from the Board but meanwhile required my non-attendance at all meetings and no papers, formal or informal would come to me without the express consent of CEO Evelyn Thurlby. If I did not accept this immediately then the EPL Board would endorse the vote of no confidence.

I replied I would not submit to what I described as this kangaroo court where the Board's legal adviser, Toby Stroh, had been brought down to Cornwall and I had not been informed of this, nor given similar opportunity to have my own lawyer present. I would take my own legal advice but must be given this opportunity to have my own lawyer present.

I telephoned Hayley Stallard of Field Fisher Waterhouse who first said either I was a member of the Eden Board or I was not. Evelyn had refused to enter into any parallel corporate arrangements with me she had already entered into with Tim. Evelyn's recent requirement and direction for me not to attend Board meetings whilst still calling me a Director of Corporate

Affairs, was unacceptable and my removal was either by negotiated resolution or dismissal by the shareholder, the Eden Trust. All information given to Paul Tyler was given by me as Eden's co-founder.

My removal from the Board was either by negotiated resolution or dismissal on resolution of the shareholders, the Eden Trustees. What is on the table probably can't be achieved under Company law, you cannot accept the responsibility of being a Director without having access to the information which the EPL Executive team continue to withhold from you. Jonathan, you have historic rights and this is still not a matter for the EPL Board. We had been negotiating this for 18 months. If there is a Board Minute now to say there is a Vote of no Confidence against you, so what? The Millennium Commission will want to know why the Co-founder has been voted off the EPL Board and will be asking its own searching questions and seeking explanations. This whole situation is totally bizarre because you have already indicated your willingness to resign when the Trustees have agreed and signed off your historic costs and future arrangements. What an omnishambles.

By this time Sir Alan Donald had also resigned, indicating he felt he could no longer discharge his absolute obligations as Trustee and shareholder of Eden Project Limited being concerned about channels of communication and accountability both cultural and financial by Eden Project Limited towards the Trust. In particular he was deeply concerned about the circumstances of the Eden Trust's acquisition of Watering Lane, particularly the arithmetic and the issues surrounding undisclosed related party transactions. By request I attended a further meeting with Paul Tyler MP who was hopping mad over what he saw as breach of parliamentary privilege in the demands Evelyn was making of me. Her requirement for me to resign for talking to my MP, when Eden was a publicly funded project, was outrageous. I had to send him extensive papers in relation to the history of the project from inception, validated information concerning my time and expense for the whole historic cost period and a review of the current balance of benefit between Tim and myself as the two equal co-founders.

April saw the departure of Sir Alcon as non Executive Chairman of Eden Project Limited and at the May Eden Project Limited Board meeting Evelyn and Tim presented as a fait accompli Philip Macmillan Browse as Acting Chairman of the Eden Project Limited Board. Peter Thoday had retained his complete independence throughout Eden's evolution, but Philip Macmillan Browse had clearly taken a different line. I sat there a little dismayed on receiving this news: our new Chairman was first and foremost Tim's emissary.

Matters came to a head on 21st May 1999 with a meeting called at the offices of Druces & Attlee in London. I had written to the remaining Trustees Sir Alcon Copisarow, Sir Richard Carew Pole and Sir Ralph Riley in protest that things could not go on as they were and explaining how strongly I felt that my financial, emotional and intellectual contributions of the last four and a half years as co-founder of the project had now been expropriated. I made the point that I had given too much of myself to ensure the Eden Project's success for any wish to have it harmed. However, several eminent persons who had been aware of my treatment had agreed it as being both unfair and shabby and the continuing refusal of the Finance Director and Chief Executive to allow me access to the cash books of the company and their refusal to give me answers to important matters I raised with them was both unlawful and must surely be of great concern to the Trustees. My personal and professional assets were now so drained by the obduracy of these executive officers that the consequence of my not reaching an urgent settlement to restore and redress these circumstances which would not have arisen had fair treatment been given, may be of lasting damage to the project and the reputations of those charged with its proper management.

The meeting was strained with Sir Alcon opening our discussions by explaining that (unbeknown to me) Tim, Evelyn and Gaynor Coley had travelled up from Cornwall and were sitting in the next door room having just concluded a meeting with Sir Alcon and the Millennium Commission Officer, Steve Porter. Here was another extraordinary moment for the Project. From my viewpoint the sense of a stitch up was inescapable.

With Eden Project Limited still in default in the preparation and delivery of annual accounts and with Ian Hay Davison and Sir Alan Donald having resigned as Trustees, both with reservations concerning the management culture and competence, I said there was an overwhelming need for cultural and management change if the Project was to survive.

Steve Porter was then invited to join with the Trustees for the remainder of my meeting with them and a general resumé followed of all the issues that had delivered this crisis point. I then asked Steve whether financial close on the project had been agreed, that is, that the conditional Millennium Award was now unconditional. The answer was either yes, or about to be so and in his answer it was also confirmed the project must have control of all its intellectual property rights as a pre condition to the award going unconditional. Steve then went on to me saying that the Trustees simply could not dispose of or grant rights without the lead funder's agreement. My reply to him was 'but you don't own the rights in the first place, so how can you talk of disposing of them?' There was a stunned silence.

In this brief silence thoughts scampered through my head. Millions of pounds of public money were being poured into a huge hole in the ground in Cornwall on the condition precedent that the recipient of the public funds owned all the intellectual property rights. But they didn't. The Trustees knew this, Eden Project Limited knew this, the Millennium Commission knew this, the Secretary of State DCMS who chaired the Millennium Commission knew this but New Labour's Cool Britannia political imperative had clicked in. The Millennium Commission had already been witness to a number of failures or doomed projects, some heroic, but many naïve to the point of being comical. Eden was clearly going to be a winner. If there were to be a few casualties along the way, such as Eden's co-founder Jonathan Ball, so be it. That was the clear sense I was getting. Somewhere further up the political food chain decisions had been made.

Sir Ralph Riley had had enough. Throughout our friendship, I had only once seen him depart from his softly spoken, erudite demeanour and this was at a meeting some months earlier at Watering Lane when both he and Sir Alan Donald had been incandescent in their condemnation of Tim's behaviour and disrespect. But no such emotion was expressed today. We exchanged a warm and sympathetic glance, whereupon he left the meeting saying he had to catch his train, but the look on his face said it all. He resigned shortly afterwards as a Trustee. Three months later news came that he had died.

Steve Porter then went head to head with me, *'are you saying'* Jonathan, *'off the record, that without these matters being sorted you will hold the project to ransom on its intellectual property?'* I replied that reimbursement and then the rebalance of injustice and the necessary redressing is not ransom. These were issues that urgently needed resolving in order for a solution to be finalised. It was my bank that was calling the shots, not me. 'OK' said Steve,

> *"... this is what we will do. You have expressed your serious concerns about conduct and irregularities within Eden Project Limited. As lead public funder I now require you to prepare a report in respect of your concerns. We will then institute an independent forensic audit. If this audit finds truth and validity in your assertions, then as lead funders the Millennium Commission will step in and make the necessary changes.'*

I was left in no doubt by Steve that if they found no validity or truth in my assertions, then Jonathan Ball would be history. I rose to my feet and maintaining eye contact leant across the table and held out my hand. *'I'll shake on that, Steve,'* I said. Shortly afterwards KPMG were appointed by the Millennium Commission to institute this forensic audit.

Back in Cornwall a culture of mistrust had firmly taken root at Watering Lane. The shifting sands of the Eden Project Limited landscape were puckered and holed with inconsistencies and half truths, a rabbit warren of intrigue. With the prospect of the Millennium Commission interrogator heading westward, those in the know scampered, rabbit like, down the nearest bolthole, away from prying eyes. Command and control had slipped through Evelyn's fingers. It was unquestionably true that Evelyn had worked long and hard and to the best of her ability and just when she needed it most the support she had given to her closest colleagues was not available to her. She suddenly now found herself isolated. Evelyn had done what had been required of her and those of her immediate circle who had enjoyed the most generous of her arrangements and from whom she could have expected loyalty at this time deserted her. Her usefulness to Tim had come to an end. Her hour glass had run out.

The Trustees were effectively disabled, feeling manipulated and concerned that information was being withheld from them. In short order the Trust became inquorate. In legal terms the recipient of the Millennium Award and all other public funds no longer existed. Equally, in legal terms, the Directors of Eden Project Limited no longer had a shareholder to answer to. Evelyn secured generous departure terms, drafted by Druces & Attlee and signed off by Tim, was legally gagged and was gone. Tim installed himself at Evelyn's desk in the Wendy Hut as Obergruppenführer. With Evelyn's departure and with Sir Alcon no longer Chairman of Eden Project Limited there was no Accounting Officer.

One of Philip Macmillan Browse's early actions as Acting Eden Project Limited Chairman was to write requiring me to absent myself from Board meetings, firmly blaming me for the KPMG forensic audit into the Project's administration. I replied that I was sad his letter was silent on matters of Eden's leadership and management style, with Evelyn already departed as CEO and with the continued prevarication in addressing important Project issues which had prompted the Millennium Commission's intervention. I made the point that the KPMG audit should be viewed as a reaffirmation of good stewardship and as such this was not a good reason for him to require my continued exclusion as a Director from meetings of the Board. Philip made no secret of the fact that he sat firmly in the camp of those who wished to see my exclusion from any further involvement with the Project. I, in turn, had replied a little waspishly about his own confliction, being Tim's horticultural right hand man and fellow Executive Director at Heligan, which did not leave him independent. Philip and I understood each other. It was Tim's firm hand on the knife that spread the butter generously on Philip's bread.

The 6th July 1999 Eden Project Limited Board's meeting with Philip Macmillan Browse enforcing my absence, received a report from Gaynor Coley, the Finance Director, confirming the Millennium Commission would shortly be instituting their forensic audit. Sir Richard Carew Pole, who had recently been appointed as Eden Trustee representative to the Eden Project Limited Board, expressed his firm view that the Eden Project was now weakened with only two Trustees (the Trust being legally inquorate), no CEO and accounting officer of Eden Project Limited, and only a temporary Chairman of the Board. Candidate Trustees were reluctant to put themselves forward until the KPMG forensic audit had been completed, he advised. At the end of July Tim's Project Director's Report confirmed the KPMG forensic auditors had been at Watering Lane for a week, ' *... senior staff interviewed and meeting notes issued and confirmed by individuals as being an accurate reflection of their views... ' * was his minuted report to the Board.

I had come to know Sir Richard Carew Pole well during his ten year tenure as President, Surf Life Saving Great Britain, through the 1980s, an appointment I was to succeed to in the Millennium year. We had a shared and equal passion for Cornwall and I spared a thought for the personal conflict he must have experienced in charting his pathway of duty through this governance imbroglio.

As was pointed out to me by a concerned observer, Eden Project Limited was not an independent commercial enterprise. It was publicly funded and as such all contracts should be open to as much public and funder scrutiny as is requested or required. If the Eden Project Limited Executive Group was refusing a Director of the company financial accountability, their position was fast becoming untenable. Tim, meanwhile opened further one-to-one discussions with me concerning our Intellectual Property Rights. To my complete astonishment he confirmed he was now receiving further advice from Druces & Attlee on a personal client basis in this regard.

Toby Stroh of Druces & Attlee was now advising Tim to donate his 50% claim to Intellectual Property to the Trust, a gesture that would also strengthen the relationship between Eden Project Limited and the Trust, they said. However, Druces & Attlee had also reported that they, our legal advisers in such matters, were unclear themselves as to where the IP rights lay and in turn had employed specialist consultants to comment upon and clarify this. The specialist report came through that I had established rights which could be difficult for the Trust to contest and only Tim was in a position to contest in any way as he had the best (and only) parallel and equal claim, this view being entirely consistent with Field Fisher Waterhouse's advice. Tim meanwhile, had opened his own negotiations with the Trustees indicating his intention to donate his IP to the Trust and forego any future interest providing the Trust settled its relationship with Eden Project Limited and modified its Constitution to prevent any divesting to any third parties without Tim's exclusive personal permission.

At the beginning of September I received a note from Steve Porter confirming that I would not be allowed sight of the forensic audit and nor indeed would the Millennium Commission confirm to me the terms of reference they had given to KPMG. Paul Tyler MP wrote on my behalf to the Secretary of State Chris Smith MP requesting sight of the terms of reference and the final report saying,

> *"I know that you share the general anxiety that transparency and accountability must be paramount when such large sums of public money are involved.'*

Within the prescribed time required for a Minister to reply to an MP writing on behalf of his constituent, The Secretary of State wrote as Chairman of the Millennium Commission to my MP denying him his request.

Paul replied protesting and saying that notwithstanding any difficulties caused by commercially confidential issues, he at least required to know the terms of reference given to the auditors. In reply Chris Smith once again declined to provide the information save a bureaucratic paragraph saying he was requesting a review and comment on the effectiveness of the Eden organisation.

Comfort zones for me and my family were distant memories long departed. Paul, soon to be the Liberal Democrat Leader in the House of Commons, confided to his constituent that here was a Ministerial absence of accountability which went beyond his long parliamentary experience. What was going on? This was not a matter that related to, or threatened, the defence of the realm. Why was it that I was in such hot water? And it was just about to get hotter.

In mid September I again wrote to Steve Porter at the Millennium Commission enclosing a copy of a communication I had received from the Prosecuting Solicitor at Companies House, Cardiff serving notice on me of intended criminal prosecution as an Eden Project Limited Director for breach of company law.

> 'Steve, I hope the absurdity of my dilemma will be apparent. On the one hand here is Her Majesty's Government threatening me with prosecution and on the other hand Her Majesty's Government as represented by the Secretary of State DCMS is telling me I am not allowed to see either the terms of reference or the findings of your forensic audit into, inter alia, the alleged issues of breach of company law'.

I ended my note by saying this law abiding, tax paying, proud to be British citizen had done no more than respond to the Secretary of State, Peter Brook's exhortation five years ago this very week to lift my eyes from the familiar and look to the glory of my nation. I sought Steve's early advice.

Eden had spent hundreds of thousands of pounds on lawyers fees and financial advisors fees and had a highly paid Chartered Accountant as Finance Director and Company Secretary: how has it come to this that I have been served notice of intended prosecution as a Director of Eden and why wouldn't the Millennium Commission disclose to me, or even my MP, the findings of the forensic report that the Millennium Commission have commissioned in respect of these alleged irregularities?

By this time the Chief Executive of the Millennium Commission was Mike O'Connor who was robustly holding his ground, saying there was no case to answer, but refusing me and even my Member of Parliament sight of the forensic report or even the terms of reference. This report had been commissioned by the Secretary of State, and paid for by public funds to examine forensically matters concerning the allocation of public funds. I went into Christmas and the New Year deeply upset with the lack of transparency and questioning how the Millennium Commission could deny such accountability. The political imperative of New Labour was violating my citizen rights with the complicity of the British Civil Service. Shit creek was not only wide, it was deep and very murky.

I took a step back, sat down, thought long and hard and took counsel from a swelling number of voices rising in a chorus of concern. With conflictions to the right of me and conflictions to the left of me I was cautious in the headlong charge of my indignation. It was abundantly clear that if my deeply held concerns about irregularities could be answered, they would have been. The cannons were on the hills to either side, but there was not yet either the political will or legal ammunition to blast me into oblivion. One shrewd supporter observed that I had now secured the position where no one could put me in check, but equally I was not yet ready to put others in checkmate. But what a waste. So much negative energy and fire-power that would otherwise have pushed Eden ever onwards was devouring our dreams.

I never lost sight of the fact that the best interests of the Project were paramount. With the Millennium Commission due to give us a significant funding tranche I could at least acknowledge their dilemma. Either the forensic audit had to result in a clean bill of health and on that basis a further £3m of public funds would be swiftly released to the Project, or the funding had to be withheld and the Project would collapse. Likewise, as Sir Richard Carew Pole had pointed out to the Board, no prospective Trustee in their right mind would entertain an invitation from the Secretary of State or what was left of the Eden management to make the Eden Trust legally quorate until they had been assured of a clean bill of health. Notwithstanding my own parlous circumstances, it was certainly in Cornwall's best interest that the Secretary of State moved to protect the Project's future. Besides, the British Civil Service probably wrote the Bible on how to obfuscate and withhold information at critical times.

One thing was certain: the circumstances of the moment were peeling away Tim's body armour. This money was to be advanced from the Millennium Commission subject to the proper settlement of my historic costs and resolution of what they termed the 'dispute with Jonathan Ball' and additionally agreement on a new Non Executive Chairman of the Eden Project Limited Board and a new CEO to be appointed as soon as possible. With the Eden Trustees inquorate and thus the recipient of the Millennium Award effectively defunct, and with Eden Project Limited now without an accounting officer, the matter of who this £3m of public money was actually being given to didn't seem to be an issue in the politics of the moment.

Having received a partial recovery of my historic costs following the Historic Costs Agreement Document of July 1999, family and Practice pressures had marginally reduced in intensity and the conditions attached to the latest Millennium Commission funding tranche accelerated matters to what was now an earnest desire to put the past to bed as comfortably and swiftly as possible. In order to satisfy the requirements of the Millennium Commission two significant appointments followed. Ken Hill Finance Director of the Pennon Group, South West Water's parent company, came in as Chairman of Eden Project Limited on 8th September 1999 and discussions advanced with Sir Ronnie Hampel for him to take up an appointment as Trustee and Chairman of the Eden Trust with his appointment effective from 1st January 2000.

Ken Hill delivered immediate gravitas and confidence to the business community of Cornwall and Devon. His reputation for fairness and decency in all his dealings was soon evidenced when, as his first task, he rang me to say he would travel to Bude to receive a full briefing and explanations as to the history of my involvement since co-founding the project with Tim in 1994 and to get a better understanding of why the project was in such current difficulty. He was authoritative in his demeanour and generous in his observations and preliminary conclusions and would be drafting a note to the Eden Project Limited Board that would also be reviewed by Sir Ronnie to, at the least, sort out the historic costs as a prelude to negotiations concerning our intellectual property. If the matter could not now be agreed Eden Project Limited would be suing me to hand over my intellectual property and the trademarks. I made the point that it was both Tim and I who had the rights which would pass to the Trustees and that the Board only had those rights invested in them by the Trustees when our birthright issues had been resolved.

2000   As Chairman of ICI Sir Ronnie Hampel had produced the Hampel Report on Corporate Governance in Britain and was arguably the single most qualified person in the land to bring order to our chaos. Eden's introduction to Sir Ronnie Hampel had come via his son Peter whom we had first met as the Eden Account manager within the Imagination organisation charged with developing the Eden Destination brand and experience. Peter had accepted Tim's invitation to leave Imagination and come and work full time for Eden in the post of Creative Development Director. It had been agreed that Sir Alcon would be retiring at the January 2000 meeting of the Eden Trustees and in turn Sir Ronnie and Secretary of State Chris Smith MP would consult with the Eden Project Limited Board on new Trustee appointments under Ronnie's Chairmanship that would establish good governance and create stakeholder confidence for the future of the project.

The Historic Costs Agreement document covered past disbursements and time spent but not birthright or intellectual property rights. Within a few weeks Ken had gone a long way to resolving the impasse created by the intransigence of the Eden Project Limited Executive Group. He also accelerated the bringing forward of overdue draft Eden Project Limited statutory accounts. These were met with many raised eyebrows and reinforced my explanations to Ken of how the dispute had first gone legal for the refusal to return to me modest sums of £3,300 a month against my huge historic costs in order to keep my practice afloat, denied on the grounds of scarcity of resources at Eden Project Limited. The accounts confirmed this was at the exact time as unauthorised overpayments were being made to other Eden Project Limited Executive Group Directors over and above their already fulsome rewards which had been capped by the Eden Company and by the Trustees No wonder, as a Director, I had been unlawfully denied sight of the Eden Project Limited cash books. Ken had been clear in his view that there were lots of unresolved issues, but I should not be penalised for identifying these Corporate Governance shortcomings. I had presented a review paper of where things stood at this time which highlighted inequity and which was to find itself closely scrutinised years later in the Royal Courts of Justice. In his written Judgment Mr Justice Nelson was to refer to the helpfulness of this document describing it as '*a somewhat wistful review of the dispute by Mr Ball ending with a quotation from Kipling.*'

A 'keep your spirits up through the difficult times' postcard from one of the author's many well-wishers

(JB archive)

If you asked me to choose my favourite poem I would be in great difficulty. But certainly up there in the short list would be Thomas Hardy's Darkling Thrush. And I well recall a quiet evening within this Millennial festive season hunting out this poem knowing it to have been published on New Year's Eve 1900. It was so apposite in so many ways. Here we were in the centenary week of its publication and here was I, like the poem's eponymous frail subject, so inadequately equipped for facing the forces so formidably marshalled against me, and yet with such joyous prospects of entering the new Millennium as co-creator of a project with so much capacity to express the spirit of our age and blessèd hope for Cornwall's future.

My own family Christmas carolling proceeded with characteristic gusto undiminished by all this mischief I had endured and which continued to cascade in my direction. Our Eden vision had now transported everyone's imagination with the first glimpse of the awesome scale of the humid tropics biome enclosure that would allow Nelson on top of his column enough room to raise the Union flag of the nation and wave it vigorously above his head with his one remaining good arm and still have plenty of headroom to spare. The purpose of our project was to send a signal to the world about purposeful Britain in the new Millennium. The world, if not quite holding its breath, was mesmerised by the audacious scale of the lusty, generous proportions of our emerging bosomy biomes.

The Guinness Book of Records was being petitioned to include what we all believed was the largest free standing assemblage of scaffolding ever erected to facilitate the lift off of our fantastical homage to Buckminster Fuller. Our fair maiden Eden was no longer a figment of our imagination.

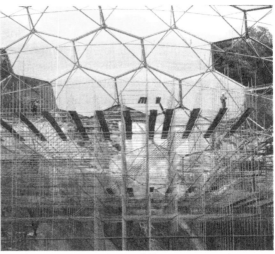

At the time it was the world's most extensive 'birdcage' scaffolding. Another first for Eden. (NGP)

Ken was then to have a meeting with Sir Ronnie Hampel but meanwhile left me in no doubt that whilst he might privately be entirely sympathetic to my circumstances this would be irrelevant when the matters came to formal offer. This kind disposition sat alongside an abrasive and somewhat uncompromising manner from Sir Ronnie, a well publicised and deserved characteristic of his formidable reputation. The prospects of resolution were receding. Sir Ronnie had a job to do and would do it his way.

And so continued the culture of exclusion with second generation trustees aligning with the core Eden Executive Group, delivering for me wave after wave of dark clouds across what should have been the matchless blue sky of the general excitement that surrounded our emerging Eden spectacle.

Through all this my multitude of well wishers were there for me and I took every opportunity to convey to them the sense that my personal troubles should not diminish, in any way, their enthusiasm for the project. The Rotary Club of Bude, representing the local business community, was particularly supportive. For some two decades the Bude Club had been twinned with the Rotary Club of Bandon, West Cork, in the Irish Republic whence had come the twinning of lifeboats and much raising of right elbows. And Eden saw several visits from the citizens of West Cork which added an extra dimension to my International Programme.

Meanwhile with Ken Hill's steadying hand being brought to bear a change in the culture of Eden Project Limited was becoming apparent. Richard

The Rotary clubs of Bude and Bandon, West Cork, have a jolly day out to view Eden's progress. At such times as these first and foremost it is friendships that keep you safe, quicken the pace of feeling secure and make you unfearful of the future. (JB archive)

Sandbrook's appointment as an Eden Project Limited Director had brought a welcomed improvement to management and accountability. In attempts to unblock the impasse it was agreed that I would travel to London for a meeting with Richard in order for him, in his new capacity as Chairman of the Eden Project Limited Audit Committee, to be able to arrive at a balanced view. I did not hold out great hopes for our meeting; after all, he had been appointed by Tim. But what soon emerged was a vastly experienced man of integrity and fairness and I got the early impression he had an insight into my predicament. Richard, a Chartered Accountant, had co-founded Friends of the Earth together with Jonathon Porritt and he commented fraternally, 'everybody remembers Jonathon Porritt, and nobody remembers Richard Sandbrook'. I was competently interrogated and asked to write to him with evidence as to Trustees Birthright agreements and additionally why the finger should not be pointed at me alleging breach of duty to Eden. He received my confidential memorandum the following day which included the full resumé from Field Fisher Waterhouse establishing evidentially why the accusatory finger should be wagged not at me, but at Druces & Attlee. Most importantly I had received a fair hearing, thanks I am sure mainly due to Ken Hill's compassion and even handedness. Richard and I parted on terms that were both cordial and, to say the least, unexpected. As we said our goodbyes he commented that interestingly enough he had only once been really shafted in his commercial life, and that was by a Dutchman.

Chapter   10

An Unforgiving Government

Delivering a giant pasty to 10 Downing Street with Bill Kneebone and Lords Tyler, Teverson and Taylor as part of the Jobs for Cornwall campaign.
(JB archive)

I had in Paul Tyler MP a staunch ally who in his further letter to the Secretary of State on 31st January 2000 stated, 'I had hoped I would not have to come back to you again about the extraordinary, irresponsible and unacceptable treatment of my constituent Jonathan Ball'. He reminded the Secretary of State of the increased risk of a public and messy legal challenge which, apart from being a tragedy as it was so avoidable, would be embarrassing for all concerned. Paul had recently visited the Eden site with me and told the Secretary of State how impressed he was with my continuing 'infectious enthusiasm' for the project.

This letter was copied to the Prime Minister, Tony Blair, who was due to visit the Project a few days later. The Eden Project Limited Executive Group having withheld this information from me, a Director of the company, this was the first knowledge I had of the Prime Ministerial visit to Eden. Paul rang me in Bude to tell me he had been summoned by Number 10 out of a meeting in Westminster. The letter on my behalf which he had copied to the Prime Minister had arrived in Downing Street on Tuesday afternoon and, in Paul's words 'had gone off like an IRA car bomb"! The Prime Minister's office was demanding a commitment that he and his constituent Jonathan Ball would not spoil it for the Prime Minister's visit. In Cornwall's interest our solemn pledge was given. Contrary to assurances, I was positively excluded from meeting the Prime Minister and from his attendant photo calls with Tim in front of 60 national media who had been bussed in for the occasion.

The Eden dream takes shape. Photograph by the author. *(JB archive)*

This high profile visit captured a good deal more column inches and Tim and Tony Blair smiling out from the national papers set the phone lines ringing once again, some predictable, some unexpected and reassuring – Steve Porter from the Millennium Commission, nice as pie, saying he had read most of the audit report. He then rang off having told me nothing of consequence. Deborah Clark rang to tell me that Alistair Campbell's iron fist had choreographed Eden's day which is why I had been excluded from meeting the Prime Minister. The New Labour authoritarian culture was no respecter of fair play. Spin was King. Here, shoulder to shoulder, Tim and Tony, two masters of media manipulation, dauntless in conduct and in self-serving unison.

The visit prompted a long conversation with Rod Hackney and from my experience all those years ago of working closely alongside him as RIBA Honorary Secretary when he was RIBA President I was in admiration of his political astuteness and knew you had to be up very early in the morning indeed to be ahead of him. We reviewed my circumstances. '*Remember we have a very unforgiving Government*' cautioned Rod, evidenced, he said, by the treatment of Jennie Page who took the blame for the muddle that was the Millennium Dome,

> *"Remember David will always beat Goliath with the right approach and tactics. Remember Eden Project Limited and the Eden Trust know full well that you cannot sustain a legal challenge against them if they ride roughshod over you regarding the trademarks, but equally they know that given Eden's profile and with all the great and the good involved they have much more reputational risk than you in the world at large finding out about this moral injustice and those who have attached their names to it. Tim can only trample on the seeds of justice for so long. Also remember the world of IP is strewn with exploitation and those who come up with good ideas and have intellectual inspiration more often than not get shafted. Continue to be honourable in the way you conduct yourself and as Eden's genius flowers over the coming years your primary*

motivation of achieving this for Cornwall will eventually be recognised."

Inexorably the matter was heading towards more fees for the legal profession and I was informed High Noon was set for Wednesday 8th March 2000 when I would face Sir Ronnie. No courtesies here of a visit to Bude. No courteous stroll over Nanny Moore's Bridge; this time London's Blackfriars Bridge over which I walked summoned for our 11 am encounter which I anticipated, with justification, would be bruising. Sir Ronnie was also at that time Chairman of United Media whose offices overlooked the Thames on the south side of Blackfriars and I was shown up to the Chairman's Room which I was sure had been witness to much power play.

There was equanimity that the past needed to be put to bed and it had to be either peace or war. If it was war any formal steps to enforce perceived rights legally by either side would de facto cast my Eden future adrift. The first part of the meeting was very formal, but friendly. Sir Ronnie said he recognised the need to be fair, but I needed to understand what fair is. That sounded ominous. He went on to say it was Tim and I who, on advice, had set up the Trust and the Trustees had an obligation to protect the project as the charity we had created for all time into the future under the legal arrangements that had been put in place by Druces & Attlee. 'The Resolutions enshrined in the Trust Minutes you rely upon are not formal agreements to your birthright. That was your mistake Jonathan.' I counselled myself to keep silent.

Sir Ronnie said he had carefully considered the invitation to become a Trustee and then its Chairman and wanted me to know he had attended a meeting with the Secretary of State Chris Smith MP to discuss his appointment and had required from the Secretary of State an undertaking that everything was 'clean' before he joined. He had been told the forensic audit confirmed this, commenting the Millennium Commission would not even allow him to have a copy but that he accepted the assurances from the Secretary of State.

I handed Sir Ronnie a copy of the report I had prepared on the instructions of Steve Porter at the Millennium Commission saying I believed as the new Chairman of the Trustees he had an absolute obligation to be aware of my concerns and misgivings. He took the document, looked at me and slid it back across the polished surface of the table unopened saying it was not his obligation to read the papers and he certainly did not intend to do so. He was answerable to the Secretary of State, not to me.

He went on to say both he and Ken Hill, EPL Chairman, were keen to listen to my point of view and were certainly resolute in their will to impose discipline to ensure the future conduct of Tim Smit, but they were not able to give me any comfort either for what I needed by way of full reinstatement or for what I might wish for in the future. Sir Ronnie was content with the Secretary of State's view that 'in macro terms the integrity of the project is intact'. They would give me my money back and an ex gratia payment of

£100,000 for the immediate transfer of all my pre-existing and accrued intellectual property rights for all time and the trade marks, together with my resignation from Eden Project Limited plus an undertaking not to speak to any third party about my concerns. I made the point that the ex gratia payment on offer to me for more than five years of my career and creative endeavours, above my direct costs and disbursements was what the Finance Director of Eden Project Limited, Gaynor Coley, had drawn for just seven and a half months work at Eden in her first year, excluding expenses and without having taken any financial risks whatsoever. Where was the concept of fair reward? I was required to resign forthwith from Eden Project Limited – so much for Ken Hill's view I should not be penalised for identifying the project's problems – and either Sir Ronnie received my resignation shortly or I would be removed.

I wasn't going to be bullied. Five and a half years of history was being ignored. Surely I could not let the Millennium Commission and others get away with this disregard of history and what I considered to be absence of good faith and a breach of trust, but into stark focus came the reality that I had no legal fighting capacity. I couldn't accept what was on offer without it having a terminal effect on my Practice and livelihood with life changing consequences for my family. I couldn't fight on without first establishing a resource base or whatever legal advice arrangement I could construct in this David and Goliath situation, with Goliath funded by the public purse. What I needed was a contentious lawyer prepared to accept me as a client on a contingent fee basis.

Field, Fisher Waterhouse had provided me with a life raft even if it was soon to prove legally unseaworthy in the view of Mr Justice Laddie, the High Court Judge who was to sit for our first Hearing in the Royal Courts of Justice. Their taxi meter had extinguished my fighting fund and in the absence of me putting new money on the table we would be parting company. In thinking long and hard on how I could stay in the game I decided as a last resort to take my lead from Tim's Machiavellian tactics. My story thus far had all the ingredients of a blockbuster and surely out there was a contentious lawyer hungry for personal reputation advancement who would instinctively grasp the legal strengths of my position, thus offering him the prospects of a high profile case; John Citizen from a small town in Cornwall having his livelihood and future expropriated, aided and abetted by Her Majesty's Government was quite a story.

The chorus of concern as to my well being was growing ever more audible. I received an unexpected call from the Chairman of Cornwall County Council, David Roberts to comfort me saying that my positive exclusion at the time of the Prime Minister's visit had been noted with concern. The Borough of Restormel whose risk taking at the outset of our journey had been defining, continued to offer political support at both Project and a personal level.

Two great public servants to the China Clay area of Cornwall were

Councillors Edgar and Jean Rowe, a husband and wife team who had committed their lives to the well-being of their community. On many occasions during my years in practice I had visited their modest bungalow at St.Stephens and had helped move to one side the mountain of Council agendas and civic paperwork sufficient for us to eat one of Jean's pasties at her dining table and talk of positive ideas for Restormel's future. It was Edgar who, in friendship, had been the very first to tell me not to trust Tim back in the autumn of 1994, a note of caution that went unheeded. There are none so deaf as those who do not wish to hear. We have all been there.

Jean, with terminal illness, had been afforded the respect and honour of being elected Mayor of Restormel for the Millennium year. She in turn had extended me a special kindness by inviting me to be her guest of honour at the Restormel Millennium Ball where I sat between her and the Lord Lieutenant of Cornwall, Lady Mary Holborow. My dinner companions on either side expressed similar sentiments to those articulated by David Roberts from Cornwall County Council.

This well-spring of support in Cornwall and London found me a few days later on my way to London to meet with Larry Cohen from the law firm Hammond Suddards. Larry had read all the papers and, yes, he would help me. He certainly applied Day One imagination to my predicament. I was entitled to my historic payments now and how about requesting payment within seven days or we would petition to close down Eden Project Limited? That would get the Secretary of State jumping. We would again reconfirm the trade marks were immediately available to the Eden Trust which in fact and in interpretation maintained the moral high ground that I had now commanded for some time, but that I was entitled to fair quantum meruit (a Latin legal term meaning 'as much as is deserved.') Larry's tactical advice was to press Eden to agree a position of accepting quantum meruit and he would immediately recommend what he termed leading experts for establishing the proper value for my rights.

He further advised I should be surprised that Sir Ronnie Hampel was seeking to renege on Trustee agreements in his capacity as the new Chairman of the Trust but I should offer forthwith to give up all my rights subject only to being paid fully and fairly for them. Eden have consistently acted in bad faith over a long period and they either agree to a quick and clean resolution on quantum meruit basis or face the consequence of Parliamentary questions in the House and embroiling the Secretary of State in this whole nasty business. Larry could see fair prospects for his personal professional media profile and there were good opportunities to his firm for media coverage; after all, Tim had warmed up and exploited the media magnificently as a battering ram to his own purpose.

I received a letter from Mike O'Connor at the Millennium Commission on 21st March 2000 confirming they had now received the final KPMG forensic audit report, *'which finds nothing of substance in respect of the grievances examined'*. He went on to confirm that the terms of reference given to the auditors excluded all essentially legal issues. Here it was. The terms of reference given to the forensic auditors excluded 19 of the 28 areas of concern I had raised, including all the issues that had any legal implication or consequence. It appeared areas where I had complained or alleged Eden Project Limited had acted unlawfully in the conduct of any matter had been specifically excluded.

This was shortly followed by a communication from Druces & Attlee enclosing a cheque to me personally for £136,000 as being in full and final settlement of all my Eden interests, a figure which didn't even cover my costs since January 1998. *'Which planet are they operating from?'* commented Larry and replied on my behalf returning the cheque and enclosing a Draft Assignment of all my trademark interests against fair quantum meruit to be determined independently by judicial process. Implicit in this was a requirement for a copy of the KPMG forensic audit to be made available by the Secretary of State as being necessary in establishing quantum meruit.

With them still running for cover I received a further letter from the Millennium Commission informing me,

> *"I am now satisfied the Report did not support the allegation which you made. The Report was not commissioned or prepared with a view to it being distributed."*

The prospect of the KPMG Report surfacing via judicial decree must have been viewed with discomfort by the Secretary of State.

Chapter 11

Friends Rally to the Cause

The Eden Visitor Centre opened on Monday 15th May 2000 and the Eden Trustees met in Cornwall on that day resolving formally that I either resign as a Director of Eden Project Limited or be sacked. I attended the opening wearing my black and gold striped Cornish blazer and with my head held high. The new Trustees legally fortified by the appointment of both the current senior partner and a retired senior partner of a leading City of London law firm had clearly been briefed to my disadvantage, but Ken Hill led the general sense of

Eden's visitors' centre. (NGP)

sadness at the prospect of legal proceedings. The Director of the Millennium Commission Mike O'Connor spent the day with his press officer studiously ignoring me until I went up and said *'Hello Mike, welcome to Eden'* whereupon he took the stance of a startled rabbit and shot off. Within the month the Queen's Birthday Honours announced that, amongst the Civil Servants being honoured, Mike O'Connor was appointed a CBE.

I received a letter from Sir Ronnie Hampel on 25th May to say that as the forensic audit *'had found nothing of substance in respect of the grievances they examined'*, they were proceeding with my removal from the Board. I replied that his letter presented me with the ultimatum of resign or be sacked for highlighting inadequacies, the majority of which had been excluded from review and which in my opinion involved matters of serious impropriety. Sir Ronnie had accepted he had scant knowledge and understanding of the complexities of the project history, so my question to him was this: what would he have done as a Director of the project in these circumstances given he was arguably the most qualified person in the United Kingdom in matters of Corporate Governance? As Chairman of our Trustees what did he suggest I now do in respect of the 19 alleged improprieties the Millennium Commission had purposely excluded from the forensic audit? My removal from the Board followed shortly after.

The Eden Project, whilst being the most consuming in every sense of the word, was one of three public projects I had thrown myself into for marking the Millennium in Cornwall. The Bude Light emerged as a tribute to Sir Goldsworthy Gurney, Bude's 19th century hero of scientific invention and was sited on the eastern boundary of his Castle grounds, less than 100 yards from where I had received my primary education at Bude Church of England Voluntary school.

As a statement of cultural value there surely could not be a more fitting way to celebrate the new Millennium in Bude than the innovative 30 ft high beacon of light designed by Boscastle artist Carole Vincent, a concrete cone with colours of the sand, sea and sky it comes alive at night using the latest fibre optic techniques designed to reflect the constellations at the time of the Millennium. As an architect what appeals to me most is that the Bude light, funded by Arts Council Lottery Board, is leading edge technology in the application of coloured pigments in concrete looking towards the future and celebrating the past but speaking of our times. It is set in an amphitheatre designed for casual meeting, yet also a performance area fit for civic and ceremonial occasions.

The Bude Light. The Jonathan Ball Practice.
(Ross Hoddinott)

The Millennium Book launched in Truro by the HRH Prince Charles, Duke of Cornwall. 29th June 2000. *(JB archive)*

Of the three my most enjoyable project as a Cornishman was being appointed to the editorial board for The Millennium Book for Cornwall. Our inaugural meeting took place in May 1998 at the Falmouth College of Arts under the Chairmanship of Michael Galsworthy. The rationale was that we would publish a book celebrating the Millennium, recording some chosen achievements and a selection of key events in the milestones of Cornwall's history and finally to invite a glimpse of its future as seen through the eyes of young people. The content would be wide ranging covering the economic, social and cultural life of the County with an overall emphasis being given to Cornwall and events as witnessed by local people. We would involve local schoolchildren and the aspiration was for a high quality book that, subject to funding, would be presented to every school child in education in Cornwall as a Millennium gift.

We enthusiastically set about our business commissioning and reviewing chapters and other submissions and our regular meetings were a joyful and positive relief from the Eden disharmony. Each member of the editorial board was asked for a quote and my reply was, '*this book is a celebration of ageless splendour conveying to the school children of Cornwall a strong sense of belonging, delivering hope for and belief in Cornwall's future ... which belongs to them*'. It was such a lovely project and ensured a whole generation would be better equipped for 'telling the tale' about Cornwall and the Cornish. It is a handsome volume, gloriously illustrated and 84,000 volumes were distributed with the Prince of Wales, Duke of Cornwall coming to Truro for our book launch day with hordes of school children bussed in for the happy occasion.

Also in June 2000 came Eden – the First Book put together by Tim and the Eden Project Limited Executive Group and published without my involvement or input and, in legal breach of my Eden Project Limited agreement of July 1999, failed to recognise properly that Tim and I were the co-founders and, blow me, Ronnie Murning and Tim Carter who headed Davis Langdon's project management delivery on site didn't even get a mention. The project's genesis was heavy with Tim's reconstructive spin. It was classic Tim Smit. Setting aside the fact it was a combination of the truth, half the truth and nothing like the truth, it was a jolly good read, well illustrated and it sold well. Tim was ensuring history would be kind to him, he intended to write it as he wanted it portrayed.

Talk of Eden at this time was inescapable, which was working as much in my favour as it was draining to my spirits. Paul Tyler had suggested I have a word with Lord Rodgers of Quarrybank and off I went to the House of Lords to meet Bill who by now was Liberal Democrat Leader of the House. Bill was pleased to see me and after a brief reminisce about our times together at the RIBA we watched old Father Thames rolling by as I gave him an update on the Eden story. Bill had been one of my guests at the early London dinners at my Club and had been following Eden's progress with interest since that time. He immediately pledged his help in any way; I could rely upon him as one of my Battalions, he said, and he would work closely with Paul Tyler in seeing where he could best assist. Our friendship had a professional rather than a social base. Nevertheless, Bill and I knew each other well and he is one of the few wholly decent politicians I have come across. '*Always be true to yourself, despite ambition*' was his consistent counsel.

In September Peter Thoday, one of the original Green Team members, resigned as a Director from the Project. Paperwork destined for Peter had come through from the Eden Project Limited Executive Group to me in Bude by mistake, so I rang him to say I would forward it on. Peter was very pleased to

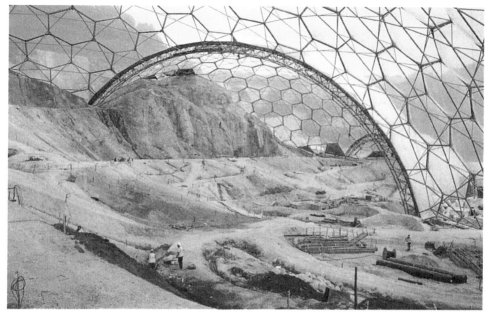

Landscaping of the cavernous Humid Tropics Biome. (NGP)

hear from me because he hadn't wanted to ring, however he had had enough and resigned, utterly frustrated by no line management authority and irritated by so much of what was going on. He and Tim had parted on cordial terms but he was particularly disappointed that Ian Cunningham, the talented and relatively recently employed Operations Director, had also just resigned. Peter had thought Ian was such a vital ingredient to the way forward, but Tim had come to view Ian as a threat. *'The plants are the handmaidens of the message but the big problem is Eden is a wonderful ego trip for Tim'* said Peter. *'Tim believes in his own PR and there is a Tony Blair Presidential style which isn't what we all signed up to'.* We shared a general sadness in the out-turn of such wonderful hopes and beliefs for us all at the beginning. Eden was unstoppable as a world Millennium project for Cornwall and for Britain, but it was irritation and sadness rather than bitterness that summed up our emotions.

Peter is a man of great personal integrity, an integrity that was never tradable or compromised for personal comfort or benefit. He had always been clear in saying to me that contrary to the way Tim had presented the birth of Eden in his book, until Tim and I had got together there had simply been 'a few unstructured chats' between himself, Tim and Philip Macmillian Browse.

I commenced legal proceedings to secure my quantum meruit against Eden Project Limited and the Eden Trust on 4th October 2000 in the High Court Chancery Division Royal Courts of Justice with Druces & Attlee acting for the Defendants. The previous day I had attended a lengthy meeting with Larry Cohen who was clear there were two audiences to this action, firstly the Judge and secondly the Secretary of State. Back in Bude I had a telephone conversation with Henry Boettinger who was amazed that Eden would not come to the table for immediate quantum meruit settlement discussions, noting I had shouldered huge risks including my family home where most others had enjoyed their generous rewards without having to take any risks. A lawyer chum expressed the view that Eden were being badly advised and any competent City of London law firm would have advised their client to settle the claim before it got this far. Presumably due to their hopeless confliction, this advice had not been forthcoming from Druces & Attlee. They could not so advise without being exposed for the inadequacy of their earlier advice.

But there was no solace in my moment. At such times in your life you suddenly find yourself in an emotional maelstrom. It creeps up on you. There is so much that can, and is, going wrong in your life. There cannot be many people who have co-conceived and set up a £100m charity only to find themselves issuing legal proceedings against that charity in the High Court. I couldn't not sue and survive, but for survival I was amputating my dream and casting adrift my own Eden future. The breakdown of trust was irremediable, made so by the absence or wild manipulation of the truth. There were no prospects for peace whilst the brutal politics of exclusion prevailed and the unwarranted retention of what effectively was my lifetime's accumulation of working capital.

The author on the steps of the Royal Courts of Justice, for the first time!
(Western Morning News 13/11/2000)

The media coverage of my issuing against Eden brought forth another raft of phone calls and correspondence from complete strangers, all of whom shared an injustice – the common denominator of having been put to the sword by Tim. One wrote a long, unhappy letter chronicling her and others' misfortune at Tim's hand at Heligan, how Tim had perfected a *'Stalinesque management style of quiet, quick and efficient removal'*, thanking me for the stand I was taking and inviting me to take heart that there were many such casualties who would be following my legal case with great interest.

Larry, meanwhile, had been headhunted by McDermott Will & Emery solicitors and US attorneys who were part of the new breed of international lawyers many viewed as nuzzling in on the comfortable club that had

Eden 19th December 2000, four months from opening.　　　　*(Western Morning News)*

previously constituted the City of London legal community. He had written to the Millennium Commission requesting the information within the KPMG forensic audit as being necessary to our preparations for the Royal Courts of Justice and received a reply from Mike O'Connor denying the information he sought. We were told KPMG did interview people so as to compile their report but it was a condition of the interviews that the information contributed was supplied for KPMG and the Commission's internal use only. Why? Given this forensic audit interrogated conduct in relation to public funding, this response raised far more questions than it answered. The letter finished by saying,

"... you are correct in your comments that I have previously refused to release the KPMG report and for the reason given above, and I am afraid I must continue to do so."

This was taken up by my MP Paul Tyler who wrote to Chris Smith MP pointing out that the Millennium Commission was accountable to Parliament through him, as Secretary of State, for the huge sums of money invested and he could not understand how and why the information contained in the forensic audit could be considered secret and inappropriate for public examination, adding it would be doubly unfortunate if disclosure had to be obtained by judicial direction. Larry sagely reminded me that I was a man of modest means from a small town in Cornwall. The Al Fayeds of this world can take on the Government through the courts, but not you, Jonathan.

My prospects still remained gloomy, but I was fortified by expressions of support suddenly popping up in the most unlikely places. 15 years earlier I had had a libel run-in with the Architects' Journal when I was RIBA Vice President they had got their wires completely twisted and ran a story in the weekly Journal under the banner Balls up in Bude. At the time it had put a minor

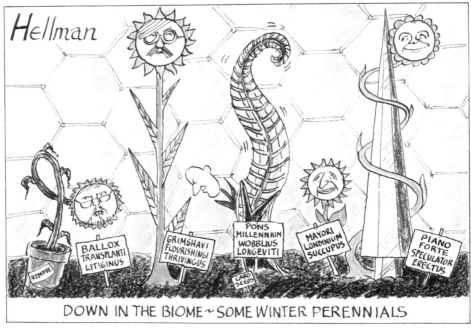

Louis Hellman's cartoon, The Architect's Journal, 14th November 2000.   *(JB archive)*

Cornish architect in major professional difficulty by implying I had condoned the demolition of a listed building, an allegation that was totally false and soon recognised by the AJ as such. We quickly made our peace and I was happy when, years later, the Editor presented me with an inscribed gift on my 50th birthday. On 16th November I opened my copy of the Architects' Journal to see the profession's weekly cartoon by Louis Hellman dedicated to my support and the inequity of the circumstances in which I found myself.

Larry had meanwhile drafted a formal complaint to the Office for the Supervision of Solicitors about Druces & Attlee continuing to represent the Trust in litigation. Druces & Attlee were now acting against me seeking to remove the very same pre-existing and accrued rights they ought to have properly secured for me three years ago. How could they now advise the other side impartially? Druces & Attlee themselves had a significant personal interest in the outcome of the case.

Correspondence was flying between Druces & Attlee and McDermott Will & Emery with Larry highlighting the further confliction of Toby Stroh, Partner of Druces & Attlee having been concurrently a Trustee of Heligan Charitable Trust including at the time in January 1999 when Watering Lane was profitably sold by Heligan to Eden with Druces & Attlee also acting in that transaction. Into my Statement of Claim to the Court, Larry had set out in detail how the arrangements surrounding the sale of Watering Lane Nurseries to Eden were such that there was an over payment to Heligan of more than

£100,000 on the transaction which was subsequently characterised as part of an historic cost payment for which I alleged there were no adequate records. It was presented to the Eden Project Limited Board as a property transaction. When I complained about the propriety of this transaction I had been overruled.

The planting inside the Humid Tropical Biome takes shape. (NGP)

Soon after Druces & Attlee served notice applying for Summary Judgment on Counter Claim to have all my trademark rights pass to Eden, notwithstanding they were already in receipt of a Draft Assignment against fair quantum meruit. Both sides agreed that a sum of money was due to me and all I wanted was fair quantum meruit, judicially determined. As Larry commented, why would Druces & Attlee send me a cheque in the post for £136,000 out of Trustee funds if they did not acknowledge that they owed me at least that. My supporters commented that the wheels were falling off at Eden and it was pointed out to me that we had now seen the resignation of as many Eden Directors as we had seen Eden Trustees depart.

In mid November the Sunday Times ran a small piece breaking the news of my legal action and in consequence it became a significant news item in the national press the following week. More unsolicited phone calls followed and resulting from one conversation I found myself on the way to have lunch with John Nelson who had been Tim's original business partner in the development and realisation of the Lost Gardens of Heligan project. Others had alluded to John's own unhappy Heligan termination. John and I had become chums from the early weeks of Eden in October and November 1994 with my regular visits to Heligan and we often enjoyed sundowners at the end of the working day. Tim was the first to acknowledge that John worked all daylight hours and vivid in my memory is John coming into the Heligan office at the end of the day wet through, raindrops departing the end of his nose, and with a broad Cornish smile recounting the achievements of his day's hard labour. Here was Orwell's loyal and trustful workhorse 'Boxer' from Animal Farm out in all weathers between the shafts putting in working days beyond his age and delivering Heligan's remarkable re-awakening for his business partner's glory. By Tim's media manipulation John was in time to become no more than a workhorse's hoofnote in Heligan's history.

Both John and his wife Lyn, who also worked at Heligan, carried deep upset about destiny's unfair hand. But I found it interesting that, like myself, I sensed his strength of ill feeling towards Tim fell short of the measure his unworthy treatment justified. Like me John had mortgaged his family home in pursuit of Heligan's success and had never received a penny for taking such astronomical risk. John's heavy smoking had caught up with him, but despite emphysema he was in good form. Given that legal proceedings had been issued I checked any potential conflicts of interest, John replying how happy he was to help in any way he could providing it didn't compromise his own capacity to have a legal pop at Tim at some time in the future.

Back in Bude, Tony, my former neighbour and legal friend of long standing had wanted a word. He had been a friend for over 25 years and had always been there for me as a legal advisor and as a chum. He had one question for me and asked that I consider my reply very carefully. At this hour of my life would I look him in the eye and confirm that I could fully discharge my professional and financial obligations to my clients and to my staff in the Practice. With heavy heart I had to reply in the negative.

2001   And so it was on 18th January 2001 I made the public announcement that I was no longer associated with the architectural practice in Bude, Cornwall that for 27 years had carried my name. I assigned all my equity and ownership rights to my colleague Neil Tibbitts who had been with me in the Practice since 1986 and I entrusted its destiny to his safe keeping. He went on to further award winning achievements with my professional name disappearing from view for all time two years later when he merged with a larger firm whose Cornish pedigree stretched back more than 100 years. There was generous local press coverage highlighting the national and regional design awards for our buildings and our ideas noting that this was necessary in order for me to concentrate on my legal battles in asserting my rights as co-founder of the Eden Project.

The full impact of my loss of the Practice came as a sledge hammer blow. Certainly there were no hard feelings from within my Practice colleagues, just the strongest sense of betrayal of us all. There was no choice but to hand over the business in its entirety to Neil and remaining colleagues in order to protect and preserve our clients and the remaining jobs in Bude. But for the so many friendly eyes and well wishers here was cruel proof of the real impact of what had been going on, the near wipe out of a well regarded Practice by dint of Eden taking all the working capital of that firm and then refusing to give it back. The Practice overdraft transferred to me as a personal debt.

In particular Paul Tyler MP was incensed that as his constituent I had been hung out to dry. The Practice had been operating successfully since 1974, the very same year that Paul Tyler had first been elected to Parliament to serve for the now defunct Bodmin constituency. The second generation Eden Trustees and the Millennium Commission were enjoying the glory of a £100m internationally acclaimed Project with fabulous prospects for the nation, but had not complied with the condition precedent to the public funding and their obligations to me. Here was my Member of Parliament being continually refused answers to legitimate questions central to the Secretary of State's

Putting out the flags out at Eden for the visit of HRH Prince Charles, Duke Of Cornwall, Prince of Wales. *(NGP)*

accountability to Parliament. And to cap it all, the Secretary of State Chris Smith MP had used a stunning image of Eden for his annual Christmas card.

We were now on the approach to the Grand Opening of Eden set for Saturday 17th March 2001 and it was clear I was going to be positively excluded from the opening celebrations.

At least this made it easier for me to respond to calls from several key Eden supporters who, also denied invitations, shared this sadness. The prodigious national press build up to the opening day, with its focus on Tim, brought forth other phone calls and letters from complete strangers sympathetically sharing their own Tim experiences with me. They were to a core theme: Tim is a fabulous wordsmith, but is all tip and no iceberg; Tim wants to be seen as a leftie with his views and woolly jumpers, but actually he's pretty far right; Tim's a very creative person who creates so much havoc through his unscrupulous processes, humiliating and abandoning so called friends and colleagues at every turn. Another call came from Neil, a chum from my RIBA days, ' ... *remember, Jonathan*,' he said, ' ... *if you deep freeze bullshit you can polish it, but eventually the temperature rises and then Tim will be in all sorts of trouble.*'

Two days before the opening the phone didn't stop ringing in Bude with well wishers and various journalists preparing for tomorrow's press day at Eden. They all received the same response: I'm celebrating for Cornwall...and when pressed I acknowledged my co-founder issues as no more than a little local difficulty.

Two calls defined what my project journal would record for the Press Day. Knowing me to be excluded from the Press Day, and with commendable even-handedness, I was invited to lunch with the Editor of the Western Morning News in Plymouth. I also agreed to an interview with the Arts correspondent of Channel 4 News, Nicholas Glass, who was travelling down from London for Press Day and their investigations had shown me to be an integral part of the Eden story.

Friday dawned rain swept and wind blown, not a good day for Cornwall to take a bow to the world's media. My lunch with Barrie Williams, WMN Editor, was scheduled to last an hour and a half and I left plenty of time for my drive from Bude.

The old Western Morning News building is Nicholas Grimshaw's flagship architecture in the South West with strong nautical metaphors linking to Plymouth's proud maritime history. When we had visited the building with the Cornwall RIBA soon after its completion in 1992 we marvelled at the way the ship's company of some 250 staff went about their business; the huge printing presses for all the world the engine room of an ocean liner, and reporters' work stations on decks with glass walls suspended externally from great ship's masts. Most of all it projects a friendly visitor atmosphere to reinforce that the newspaper is of and for its community, informing, debating, challenging and crusading on behalf of the people of Cornwall and Devon.

Lunch was in the Board Room, the bridge of the good ship Western Morning News, a single room structure towering over the building giving a distinctive day and night profile and affording spectacular views over Plymouth and the sea to one side and the moors on the other.

Barrie and I were sitting in isolated splendour and he opened our lunchtime discussion by retelling our first encounter, '*Oh, and two blokes from Cornwall want to talk to you about a giant greenhouse ... such marvellous understatement as my secretary ran through my orders for the day back in 1994*', is how Barrie explained his first introduction to the Eden Project and to Tim and me.

Barrie had been there for the project throughout, celebrating our triumphs and sharing our moments of adversity. '*OK Jonathan, we're off the record, tell me what the f***'s been going on*'. I had nothing to lose. I was safe in the knowledge that we shared a love of the project and regardless of what had gone on no harm would be done journalistically to Eden. When I finished three hours later, and after cancelling his afternoon schedules, Barrie exclaimed that this had been the most riveting story he had listened to in all his professional career. The shenanigans I had suffered as the Cornishman co-founder struck at the very heart of government and it was a strong public interest story. He gave me an undertaking the Western Morning News would run it with the backing of their libel lawyers, not yet, but at some time in the future when no damage would flow to the project itself. As I was saying my thanks and departing he said he had one final question for me - 'did I check under my car every morning?'

It was a dash from Plymouth to Bodelva Pit to meet the Channel 4 news team and their wagon was already waiting in the pouring rain at our agreed meeting spot outside the North Entrance to the site. I met Jessica plus her cameraman who had already been down in the pit interviewing Tim along with 20 TV companies from around the world, including Russia, Canada, Australia, New Zealand and the USA, all sharing equipment as there had been technical failures due to the immense heat in the humid tropics biome. Clearly it had been a phenomenally successful media day.

Royal Visit to Eden.
(Western Morning News 14.05.2001)

We agreed to conduct the Nicholas Glass interview on the top road with the biomes in the background below us and my piece was positive and celebratory. We parted company and I went to seek shelter in the Davis Langdon site huts on the eastern lip of the pit and have a yarn with Tim Carter. Ten minutes later the site hut door burst open and there was Jessica from Channel 4 delighted to have tracked me down as this was, for her, now a legal imperative,

Her story left Tim Carter and me with our jaws touching the floor in amazement. Just after I had left, Jessica and her team had been hit by what she described as a Rambo style raid, the Eden Discovery Land Rover having roared up and parked across the bows of the Channel 4 wagon to block its departure. Two Eden staff demanded she hand over the tape of her interview with me. Her long experienced cameraman had quickly removed the tape cartridge and had hidden it from view by sitting on it, then refused their demands to hand it over. According to Jessica's description Deborah Clark then arrived, saying Channel 4 cannot use that interview; how Deborah is a friend of mine, that I had been trespassing on the site which is private property, and that her demands were no more than to protect me legally. The Channel 4 team delivered a robust response pointing out Eden could not invite them down from London to cover the Project's opening and then treat them like this. An immediate call was put through to Channel 4's London lawyers who confirmed the item could be broadcast so long as I agreed. Consent was immediately given, subject only to the tenor being my enthusiastic support for the project. Tim's PR police, paid for by the public purse, had given the Channel 4 news team a whole new experience in their professional lives and unequivocal victory to me as to who held the moral and ethical high ground. Tim's respect and adulation had not been won, it had been commanded and engineered.

At least amongst the wall to wall media coverage I could point my 88 year old Mum in the direction of Channel 4 news for her to see a fleeting glimpse of her son saying a few words about the project that had consumed our family life for so long.

Despite the foot and mouth epidemic, and despite my having been written out of all the press briefings and despite my having been the subject of confidential negative briefings to the Trustees (something that only came to light in later legal proceedings), I felt a sense of immense satisfaction that six and a half years since our first six and a half hour meeting at Heligan when Tim and I shook hands to pursue a dream of unimaginable scale, here Eden was

The Spectator 24th March 2001

David Austin captures the goings-on at Eden for the Spectator and The Guardian.
2001 (JB archive)

opening its doors to huge public acclaim. The public meeting at Poltair School just prior to our planning consent had been my moment of awakening. As I had shaken so many hands that evening I knew we had taken ownership of a lot of Cornish dreams. Today those dreams were finally being realised.

I was delighted when a cracking cartoon, so full of symbolism, by David Austin appeared in the next week's Spectator and following a nice telephone conversation with its renowned creator, for a small consideration the original was given to me as a keepsake. David Austin was pocket cartoonist to The Guardian with a daily production for 16 years until his death in 2005. That my small difficulty entered his radar was a delight and his gentle incisiveness chronicled the moment.

Chapter   12

The Plug Hole Theory

The day of the Summary Judgment Hearing in the Royal Courts of Justice before Mr Justice Laddie in April 2001 was soon upon us. My legal team was adamant that of the multitude of issues and imponderables surrounding this dispute, there was no way a Judge could take one issue, the Counterclaim for me to hand over my trademark rights, and determine it without full investigation of the evidential base to all the interconnected issues. But that is exactly what Mr Justice Laddie did.

There were legal skirmishes about the construction of value, good will and the conduct of lawyers and how everything at Eden was in Corporate Governance disarray at crucial times. *'It could be said Eden operated the plug hole theory,'* said the Judge. *'You simply opened the plug hole and sucked everything into Eden's ownership'*. But the day went to the concept of fiduciary duty, that is, the obligation for a Director, at all times, to act in good faith. Mr Justice Laddie found that in making the application to register the trademarks I breached my fiduciary duty to Eden Project Limited. How could I at the relevant time owe a fiduciary duty to a company that was not yet trading, was refusing to enter into any corporate arrangements with me, whilst desperate to take ownership of something that belonged to me (and Tim) as co-founders. Eden Project Limited was a company which in any event had no rights to the trademark name other than through the Eden Trust who would own the trademarks when they had settled the birthright issues with us, something they had previously resolved to do. In many subsequent conversations the view has been expressed to me that Field Fisher Waterhouse gave me legal advice that was correct in law and proportionate to my circumstances of the moment and that Mr Justice Laddie, in determining the matter on the basis of fiduciary duty, was wrong.

Leading Silk for Eden, David Oliver QC, had run fiduciary duty as his flagship point. The Millennium Commission had withheld the KPMG forensic audit from evidence to the Court. Had Her Majesty's Government not positively refused to disclose this key evidence, the first mention of fiduciary duty would had set hares running that would have been quite a challenge to Eden and to David Oliver QC.

But it was not to be. Our journey back to Cornwall was dispiriting and two days later I returned to the Royal Courts of Justice without Victoria, to be present when the Judgment was handed down. The matter had been judicially determined; we had lost. I was to hand over the trademarks and it was for another High Court Judge later in the year to determine my quantum meruit, how much I would be paid. Mr Justice Laddie encouraged me to pursue Eden to trial for reinstatement.

I surveyed the Judgment, as did my legal team and those closest to me. Views expressed were incredulous. Eden had used a legal device to extend their bad faith which had been shown to me since 1997; they had not come to the High Court with clean hands. The Judgment was narrowly constructed and specious, it being an issue Her Majesty's Government could not afford to lose either in the current climate with a General Election looming, or in answer to being challenged as to why so much public money had already been spent in disregard for the key condition precedent, that Eden owned its intellectual property when the Secretary of State clearly knew this not to be the case.

Here was another despairing moment for me to survive, both financially and emotionally. I had been badly let down by my first City lawyers Druces & Attlee, and now here was a High Court Judge telling me my application to register that which belonged to me and Tim on the strong legal advice of Field, Fisher Waterhouse, my second City law firm of repute was, in his judgment, illegal. And my third lawyers had assured me that what had just happened to me was almost inconceivable. In the run up to the Hearing the McDermott Will & Emery advice, supported by Counsel Pushpinder Saini, was clear: it cannot be argued that fiduciary duty was breached as these rights belonged to me (and Tim) in the first place and never to the Company. It was not the Company's property to register in the first place, therefore how could they argue that I had misappropriated that which was mine. My ownership as originator of the IP well predated the incorporation of Eden Project Limited.

The nadir of the moment was, however, a voice mail on my mobile from Victoria. In the madness of the day a BBC TV news report got to her before I did and to listen to a recorded message from my wife in full distress presuming we had now lost our family home had me likewise emotionally shot to pieces.

An unspoken understanding had evolved for the quieter moments Victoria and I shared. Eden's overpowering invasiveness was set aside by neither of us referring to it, or its consequences for us, in any conversation. Then occasionally the moment would chose itself. To Victoria it was all such a shame, that so much emotional energy was going into the defence of my position rather than my advancing the project. She knew, and I guess I did too, that she could have ended our torment by insisting on severing all further involvement. Equally she knew she had to let me go on as far as I felt I needed to go in order for me to live comfortably with myself. We both have few, if any, regrets in life. She knew there would come a point that I would have to reach that sufficiently repaired the injustice I faced in order for regret not to take a hold in our lives.

With friends rallying round and my bank manager, Mike Jane, restructuring our mortgage, I was able to discharge the other side's substantial costs of nearly £30,000 within the time prescribed by the Court and our close chums Clive and Jane immediately insisted they pay for a QC's second opinion.

I have always enjoyed a close and loving sibling relationship with my older sister Jenny. She has always been there for me and championed my successes and put her arm around me to console me when picking up the pieces in consequence of my enthusiastic yet fruitless pursuit of an idea too far.

Her support along my Eden journey was unswerving, from banging off letters to the press when the project needed added impetus, to moments such as this with me facing utter despair. I will never forget her phone call of reassurance that followed this unwelcomed moment. She made the offer that I could have all her personal savings there and then if it helped, an offer I declined but a sentiment that, to me, was all the world.

My legal position in respect of my protests about the conduct of Druces & Attlee was certainly strengthened by this Judgment. There had been nine months for Eden to challenge my application for registration of the trademarks, but they had not done so, because quite simply there was no legal basis that Druces & Attlee could construct for such a challenge.

Our second opinion from a leading Silk, Geoffrey Vos, QC was not to deliver the comfort we so desperately needed. I was told I had been shafted and the use of this word even surprised Larry Cohen. I had been shafted by progressive conduct in bad faith from Eden and there had been no way of stopping this process other than by my deploying sanctions that would have destroyed the project for Cornwall. *'And therein is your problem, Jonathan. You have, throughout the process, declared what I understand to be your true position, that you put Cornwall's interests ahead your interests of personal reward. You have properly signed truth statements in the High Court to that effect and by so doing, in legal terms, you have acquiesced.'*

Larry was as equally upset and dismayed as was his client. *'The law has become a thief's Charter'* he cried, *'London Mandarins stealing from the Cornishman ... these are the guys that gave you the Greenwich Dome and have failed to disclose the publicly paid for KPMG forensic audit to the Court,'* he ranted in an explosion of fury provoked by Mr Justice Laddie.

Louis Hellman's cartoon, The architect's Journal, 17th April 2001 (JB archive)

Ronnie Murning sent in his letter of resignation from the Project to Eden Project Limited, a hugely destabilising occurrence for the company, the Trustees, the professional team, the constructors and investors. The press coverage of our day in the Royal Courts of Justice was generally supportive of me in tones sotto voce, with the Architects' Journal in their 17th April 2001 publication devoting a second Louis Hellman cartoon to highlighting the injustice.

But for me there was a silver lining in the dark clouds Mr Justice Laddie had drawn across my sky. Druces & Attlee's position had worsened considerably; the Court had ordered them to deliver up to my legal team original documents from their files that evidentially would have life and death implications for them and for me. By now Duncan Curley, Larry's right hand man, was in day to day charge of my case and we established an exemplary working relationship which, for Victoria and me, quickly moved to a position of true friendship. Duncan was appalled by what he had seen, not just on his client's behalf, but also the professional conduct of Druces & Attlee which he considered shameful to his profession, and the conduct of the Millennium Commission, in withholding information from the Court that he considered to be a disgrace.

Where Larry was legally inspired but a little impetuous, Duncan was measured and methodical. Whilst Larry blasted off warship 16 pounder guns with battle ensign flying high, Duncan followed astern and below the radar stealthily torpedoing each defensive encounter until the other side were left hopelessly exposed to face the consequence of their own impropriety.

Were we finally to prevail it would be Duncan's total and absolute commitment to seeing fair play and justice for his client that would see us to final victory.

Armed with Mr Justice Laddie's direction Duncan and I marched to the offices of Druces & Attlee, my first visit since the encounter when Steve Porter from the Millennium Commission had laid down the forensic audit proposal, to inspect documents and so began months of legal contention, with Druces & Attlee seeking to deny me access to attendance notes (their written records of my meetings with them as client), and redacting key originals. As a lay person I was astonished by this procedure just as the electorate of Britain were outraged several years later when redaction was widely employed to suppress proper public examination at the time of the MPs expenses scandal.

My legal taxi meter was running furiously and what soon became apparent was my inability to pay the fare on this legal journey. The difficulty both Larry and I faced flowed from the unequivocal yet unfulfilled expectation that Mr Justice Laddie would despatch the Summary Judgment application and Druces & Attlee to our joint relief would have picked up all the legal costs.

Clive and Jane had now committed to covering all non McDermott Will & Emery legal costs for the next period, and Larry reaffirmed my circumstances were overpowering in their moral and ethical worthiness and would, beyond his any doubt, translate into appropriate legal remedy. The big question was when. Getting to this goal was now our joint endeavour and our joint salvation. Confusion to Mr Justice Laddie, we both choroused. I reminded Larry that throughout our professional relationship, I had followed his advice virtually without question and had not sought to challenge him when faced with legal setbacks, minor or major. Things that might have been said, I had left unsaid, which had strengthened our joint purpose. What was clear, a view reinforced by Herbert Smith, heavyweight London lawyers now consulted by Clive and Jane to help my cause, was that the one question on everyone's lips was whether political motivation had smudged the line between justice and politics in our last Judgment.

I concluded the moment with Larry by noting any loss of progress, legal or political, would put in peril our getting to goal within a time scale satisfactory to the partners of McDermott Will & Emery, and to put to an end the misery visited upon me, my family and my architectural practice of 27 years standing which, by this painful process was no longer mine. In the September I sold paintings off the wall of our family home, forwarding the cash to Larry as a gesture.

Larry wrote to my MP Paul Tyler on my behalf, grateful for his support in ensuring all relevant facts are out in the open. The KPMG forensic audit would surely contain a number of the same issues now coming before the Court, and the interests of justice could only be served by both parties being able to see it. The Millennium Commission should not be seen to discharge huge sums of public funds with no apparent accountability. Withholding disclosure where such public documents could materially assist the interests of justice was a serious matter.

This prompted a humdinger from Paul to the Secretary of State, Tessa Jowell MP as yet another new Chairman of the Millennium Commission. Paul again emphasised how he remained an enthusiastic advocate for the Eden Project. 'However, we who represent Cornwall and remain answerable for the use of public funds cannot ignore past problems ... and indeed its present triumphant success (Eden had welcomed its one millionth visitor in only six months) removes any excuse for further delay'. He copied his letter to Prime Minister Tony Blair.

In reply Tessa Jowell MP repeated that the forensic evidence was confidential to the Millennium Commission. She recognised the dispute between his constituent and Eden was coming before the Court but these were matters to which she was not party and she had no wish to intervene. We would soon have cause to question whether the Commission really was so committed to a hands-off approach.

Paul was not to be fobbed off. He had recently been appointed Liberal Democrat Leader of the House and came to visit me in Bude, bringing with him Nick Harvey MP who was the Liberal Democrat Shadow Minister for Culture Media and Sport. After a half day briefing and update they left pledging full support up to and including, if necessary, laying down a question in the House in late October.

There are moments in your life when it is hard not to get a little despondent. There were a lot of things I could have done with the last eight years of my life, arguably at the height of my earning capacity, and most of which would not have involved putting my family and those close to me in peril. There was unwelcomed symbolism in selling family possessions to pay for just a few hours of a lawyer's time. The unspoken hurt of not being required on and indeed positively excluded from the Eden voyage ran deep, but survival is all about refusing to make room for melancholy.

Political and legal progress prospered side by side. I had written to Eden Project Limited Chairman Ken Hill enclosing a non-contentious factual chronology of Druces & Attlee's early involvement in the project, and making the point they, Druces & Attlee, were using Eden Project Limited and the Eden Trust, and their publicly secured funds, as a vehicle to fight me in the existing litigation in order to bury the history of their own involvement. How could they possibly continue to act for Eden and give impartial advice? I copied the letter and enclosure to the two new Trustees who were both respected City lawyers in the hopes they of all people would act decisively in pursuit of Trustee obligations. The enclosures to them included a letter that had been unearthed during our Mr Justice Laddie directed inspection of Druces & Attlee documents. It was from Toby Stroh to Tim Smit at Heligan STRICTLY PRIVATE AND CONFIDENTIAL and was dated 12th October 1994, two weeks after Tim and I had shaken hands on our 50/50 agreement. In this letter Toby Stroh confirmed,

> *"and will let you have my further thoughts on the structure which will facilitate your control of the scheme."*

Where for heaven's sake did that leave me and where did that leave the Trustees in respect of relying on Druces & Attlee's continuing advice? An early and somewhat terse reply indicated there was nothing new to them in what I had sent and Trustees and Company were proceeding on the basis that the action would continue.

Notwithstanding this reply, what was soon to become clear was that the legal tide had already turned in my favour. There were serious concerns that some of the evidence before Mr Justice Laddie had been misleading. Had we raised our concerns at Court over certain statements that ran false to the incontrovertible paper trail, Mr Justice Laddie could probably not have proceeded with his Judgment.

The circumstances of the times dictated that Tim and I only saw each other very occasionally and one disagreeable consequence of his every attempt to erase me from Eden's Hansard was the difficulty in which this placed all the professional team. They had looked to me gratefully for their individual appointments to this prestigious project, yet their professional obligation and loyalty was now to their client which was no longer me. Nick Grimshaw had written me a kind note saying he hadn't forgotten that I was the co-founder of Eden, or that I had originally appointed his firm, free of competitive process, as architects for the Project, 'a wonderfully generous gesture' he said.

An exclusion zone operated against me for many award events, but Grimshaw's was faced with an inescapable dilemma when the Eden Project was shortlisted for the Stirling Prize, a huge international architectural accolade. The announcement of the winner, presentation, dinner and party was to be held in the Great Court at the British Museum on 20th October 2001 and protocol dictates that on such occasions the architects host their clients and those who have most contributed to the securing of international acclaim. The solution lay in Grimshaw's taking not one, but two tables with Nick Grimshaw and his wife Lavinia hosting, with others, Tim and Gaynor on one table, and the Project Architect Andrew Whalley hosting Ronnie Murning and me, with others, on a separate table.

... "But I wanted that award as well!!" ... Colin Weekes, Cornwall Today, December 2001. Inscribed: To Jonathan Ball from Colin Weekes 6th December 2001 *(JB archive)*

I arrived at the British Museum in good time anxious about the out-turn of the evening and with everything crossed for Eden's success. The heads of all the professional firms were ever courteous and each found an appropriate form of words in expressing their concerns for me and disappointments at what had come to pass. For myself, I was just pleased to join in the celebration of the moment, regardless. Eden's architect Nick Grimshaw had, like me, trained at the AA and, funny old world that it is, one of the three Stirling Prize judges for this year was none other than Janet Street-Porter who had been a brief contemporary of mine at the AA before she left to pursue a high profile career in journalism and this forever connected her celebrity status to the profession.

As we moved to the awards announcement, my having spoken to RIBA Presidents past and present and Paul Finch from the Architect's Journal all of whom were supportive and sad for me, Tim and I came shoulder to shoulder for polite, strained conversation until the moment the Stirling Prize was announced.... and it was not to be Eden's night. Tim, visibly upset, and I exchanged glances, '*Please remember, Tim*,' I said, '*there is as much that unites us as divides us*'. His gaze once again contrasted with the same warm smile that had accompanied all our early days together, that warm smile that never migrated north to melt the glacial coldness in his eyes. He clenched his right hand and gently, (was it fondly?), punched my shoulder and without a word turned his back and was gone.

Tim's personal star continued in its vertical ascendancy. In addition to appearing on Desert Island Discs, he was the subject of This is Your Life on prime time TV with Michael Aspel. With the world watching Tim nervously pre-empted John Nelson's entry on set by acknowledging it was John who had done all the work at Heligan. John walked on to his moment of glory by confining his words to agreement with what the star of the show had just said. What I might have said as Tim's parallel Eden business partner was clearly a risk

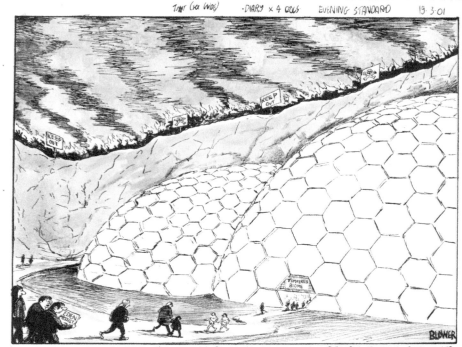

"APPARENTLY IT SHOWS WHAT THE ENGLISH COUNTRYSIDE WAS LIKE BEFORE FOOT-&-MOUTH"

Patrick Blower Evening Standard, Inscribed: For Jonathan Ball by Patrick Blower on the opening of Eden March 2001.   (*JB archive*)

too far for the programme's production team to even pick up the telephone to me. Reports trickled back to Bude that the party after the show was not without its moments.

Concurrently wide national media coverage coincided with the publication of Eden, by Tim Smit. The Western Morning News carried a series of five extracts. In his inimitably engaging way Tim had committed in Chapter 1 to explaining frankly and openly that he was and had always been a compulsive liar throughout his life. The Mail on Saturday colour supplement of 3rd November 2001 had Tim in full flood extolling the benefits of dishonesty,

> *"I made it (Eden) happen by telling lies ... what would you have done? ... told the truth? ... that would be the cynical defeatist English way..."*

Given that we were mid way through a High Court legal action where he had been responsible for drafting, with Druces & Attlee, Eden's Defence and Counterclaim, this had to be arrogance beyond hubris. Equally the KPMG forensic audit must surely have clearly and substantially relied, inter alia, (it cost me a huge amount of money to learn those words) upon Tim's word for the 'no case to answer' stand the Millennium Commission and Her Majesty's Government continued to maintain.

Live 8 Africa Calling Show 2nd July 2005, one of the hugely successful Eden Session concerts. *(Western Morning News)*

On 7th November 2001 I issued a High Court Writ against Druces & Attlee for negligence and seeking to have them disqualified from acting for the Eden Trust and Eden Project Limited in the continuing action. By this time we had an impressive Queen's Counsel assisting our preparations; John Slater, QC had been a Deputy High Court Judge since 1994 and enjoyed a substantial reputation in matters of professional negligence. John had a portly presence that gave weight to his views and his golf swing. The Western Morning News ran the story noting success for Mr Ball could cast doubt over the earlier Mr Justice Laddie High Court Hearing, but failure would land me with sizeable additional costs. This was entirely accurate reporting. With my failure would come the prospects of our family future home being a tent on Bude beach.

Legally, all hell was breaking loose. The Laddie Judgment showed that my rights had been overtaken and assisted in my restitutory claim against the Eden Trust and Company. Druces & Attlee, by their failure to give proper advice, had placed me in an untenable position and my turning to Field, Fisher Waterhouse for help and acting on their advice only compounded my misery when Mr Justice Laddie found I had breached my fiduciary duty in making application for registration of the trademarks which belonged to me and Tim. Druces & Attlee had put me in my appalling position and we now had to ensure and prove that legally they were fatally compromised.

A significant development in my favour soon followed. I received notification that the Solicitors' Indemnity Fund had instructed City of London lawyers Reynolds Porter Chamberlain to take the matter over formally. Druces

& Attlee were removed from the record and the case was now in the hands of the insurers.

Ronnie Murning, ever perceptive, rang to say Tim repositioning himself by promoting dishonesty as a virtue is a signal that I was winning and *'where for Heaven's sake does this leave the Eden Trustees?'* Tim's parading of this entirely unreliable and untrustworthy characteristic had surely exposed everyone – Mr Justice Laddie, Druces & Attlee, the Millennium Commission, but most of all the Eden Trustees - to sky high risks and Eden was faced with the prospect of having secured legal title to the trademarks by deception and deceit in the High Court.

It was not for me to question the Laddie Judgment. By common consent the trademarks were where they should finally reside and but for the failure of Druces & Attlee to advise properly and their subsequent hopeless confliction, none of us would have been in this mess. And what is more, why should the public purse be paying for the defence of this action?

Duncan counselled turning off the heat in our pursuit of the KPMG forensic audit; the progress through the Court was already sparking a huge legal conflagration and now was not the time to have Her Majesty's Government even more interested in the outcome than it already was. After all, the Millennium Commission chaired by the Secretary of State was up to its armpits by complicity, and pursuing the forensic audit at this moment only muddied the waters.

The prospects were promising of a win on all counts, best of all with minimum damage to the project itself. Both the Architects' Journal and Building Design ran supportive reports on my High Court Writ and this was soon followed by a letter from the RIBA President, Paul Hyatt asking me what he might do in exerting Presidential influence to assist my extraordinary circumstances.

Even with the generous support of Clive and Jane I was still in some difficulty with Larry's fee demands as Duncan was now working daily on the case, repelling Druces & Attlee's various protestations and their extreme legal manoeuvres in attempts to mitigate their increasingly beleaguered position. After a face to face with Larry I undertook to go back to my Bank Manager Mike Jane for yet another negotiation. Meanwhile some personal family items were put up for sale and the proceeds were forwarded to McDermott Will & Emery.

In November Mike Jane agreed to yet another mortgage extension against our family home. We had evolved a pattern of monthly meetings, usually in Bude and with Mike's senior position in the bank and in his last two or three years in post, mercifully he was left to his own judgment when dealing with customers of long standing. He had witnessed every twist and turn of the whole Eden saga. The foundations of my financial survival, subject to his continuing risk assessment, had been shored up in our detailed discussions in February. He was passionate in his condemnation of dishonest practices and was fearful for Cornwall that Tim's media excesses and the disgraceful conduct of Druces & Attlee would cast Eden's future adrift. It was surely ironic that his supportive resolve on my behalf flowed proportionately to the shabby treatment that had come my way calculated to bring me to my financial knees. Mike Jane, a Devon based Cornishman, had married a Bude girl and our mutual respect was long established. *'I've known many customers with a steel outer casing and soft inners ... but you Jonathan have a soft outer with a granite core. They've hit the Cornish granite. You are not going away - I understand that and I'm here to see you through'.* Tim's qualmless conduct was facing growing resistance from those who truly believed in Cornwall and in Eden's future in it.

The full Christmas Card for 2001 with the family portrait and all the cartoons from the national and professional press for the year.   *(JB archive)*

Since my first days in Practice in 1974 it had been my custom to design a Christmas card that would promote the Practice in an imaginative and amusing way and topical to the times. On the occasions when we had been overtaken either by workload or other intervening variables we had fallen back on supporting the RNLI, buying our cards via Bude Lifeboat Station. Despite the huge pressures that were upon us I felt it important that I customise our card for Christmas 2001, not least to let our many true and loyal friends and supporters know that we were still in the land of the living. Attached to our message that it had been an eventful year, but we were still smiling was the David Austin cartoon from the Spectator and the two Louis Hellman cartoons from the Architects' Journal that amusingly characterised the previous 12 months.

Chapter 13

Gone for a Burton

In the run up to our return to the Royal Courts of Justice desperation hung in every Druces & Attlee manoeuvre. The evidential base against them was indisputable, leaving them in pretrial disturbed days of constructing cynical legal argument. With growing confidence in the quality of our robust witness statements, thoughts turned to the repercussions of Eden having Druces & Attlee disqualified. All Eden's own advice had been tainted, Druces & Attlee couldn't throw in the towel without probably voiding their professional indemnity insurance, but meanwhile where did Eden go for pretrial advice? How much of Druces & Attlee's advice to Eden from the start had been defective by conflict to secure Druces & Attlee's own interest?

In Court room 76 in front of Mr Justice Burton we were to find ourselves in happier circumstances on Wednesday 12th December 2001. From the outset positive signals were ringing out loud and clear with Mr Justice Burton opening the proceedings noting that Tim and I were originators of what had become a very successful project,

> " ... which illuminated the Millennium by its originality ... that Mr Ball has been dropped from the project and all that has been paid to him is a certain relatively small sum of money by way of alleged remuneration on an hourly basis, while Mr Smit, his partner in the original project, remains with that successful project."

It was to get better. Mr Justice Burton noted,

> " ...that Laddie J found that the trademark was registered so late that he (Ball) was, by the time he did so, in breach of his fiduciary duty as a Director of the now existing company. That did not involve, as I see it, any substantial or material consideration of the facts."

he commented gravely, incorporating these words into his Judgment (RCJ 12.12.2001. No.S/01/0232 page 18 lines 20-22.)

My case opened with John Slater, QC, and David Oliver, QC again appearing for the defendants. With John Slater QC in full flood on my behalf mid morning in the first session Mr Justice Burton interrupted and turning to David Oliver QC said ...'the evidence is overwhelming, Mr Oliver, should you not be considering your position?'

We stopped early for lunch 'to give time for David Oliver QC to take instructions' with Mr Justice Burton further commenting 'you need time to address me Mr Oliver – you have quite a mountain to climb.'

After the break, I had to endure further arcane legal argument including what, to a layman, would be felt a cynical ploy that I had no funds to give a cross guarantee to the Defendants costs if the injunction was found to be wrongly granted by Mr Justice Burton. To my rescue came my brother Christopher who, from the public gallery, immediately stood surety to defeat this last contemptuous legal sneer, that justice only comes to those with deeper pockets than those possessed by the ordinary man. Mr Justice Burton immediately despatched this Defendants' manoeuvre noting that my brother,

" ... is willing to back up both of those cross-undertakings by a guarantee in the sum of £100,000 in the case of the undertaking to the solicitor Defendants, and £25,000 in the case of the Chancery Defendants ... ."

The day was ours. Down came the shutters. The injunction was granted with immediate effect, the right of Druces & Attlee to appeal the decision was denied and my costs of this action were to be paid to me 'immediately'.

And so, for a moment at least it was with unqualified pleasure that I vacated my lengthy tenancy of shit creek in favour of the second generation Eden Trustees who with immediate effect were faced with an injunction prohibiting them from communicating with their own legal advisors in the discharge of their Trust duties attendant to the managing with probity and propriety of multi millions of public funds that had passed to Eden. It's no wonder the majority of the founding Trustees had already resigned.

We had scored a significant victory and had conducted an honourable campaign throughout. It was of enormous personal importance to me that Mr Justice Burton had gone out of his way to clarify my proper conduct in respect of the trademarks and this firmly and effectively extinguished Eden's unmerited innuendo that I had, in any way, acted improperly.

Back in Bude in time for Christmas and at 6pm on 21st December, Victoria's birthday, I turned the key in the door below the signage of the Jonathan Ball Practice for the very last time. We had a good family Christmas and New Year. A good festive season was also assured for Nicholas Grimshaw, knighted in the New Year's honours for services to architecture with Eden images attached to the wide media coverage of his knighthood. In the same honours list Tim Smit, as a Dutch national, was appointed Honorary CBE.

In what was to be a short but happy respite, we were able to survey some heart warming headlines including major coverage from the Western Morning News under 'Judge Bars Lawyers from Eden Case' and also good coverage from the professional journals including Legal Week who gave main news page coverage to the story that Druces & Attlee was 'facing a multi million pound negligence claim and had been barred from acting for a leading corporate client after ignoring a confliction situation in the High Court'. Henry Boettinger decreed it to be 'your first best day' and we enjoyed other letters from well wishers including Peter Steege, my Rotary chum from Boscastle, who had travelled to the Royal Courts of Justice in my support and wrote observing that 'Druces & Attlee had gone for a Burton'.

My MP Paul Tyler was delighted and called for sight of the Burton Judgment as soon as possible and also a copy of the Eden Witness Statement that had gone to the Courts in the name of the Eden Trust as represented by Sir Ronnie Hampel, as Paul was concerned that this was contrary to the assurances that Sir Ronnie, who in turn presumably had acted on assurances, had given to him as my MP. Paul also wrote again to Secretary of State Tessa Jowell reaffirming that both he and his constituent Jonathan Ball remained wholly enthusiastic supporters, noting Eden had proved to be such a major success in all respects not least in giving Cornwall and the Millennium itself a much more positive image particularly compared with the Millennium Dome.

He went on to point out my success before Mr Justice Burton and that the comments of the Judge would leave little doubt that all defendants to my further claims in the Chancery Action were going to have a very difficult time when that case came to Court and he urged the Secretary of State to redouble efforts to settle the matter. In reply she again made it clear the Millennium Commission was not party to the action and would not be getting involved. Sir Ronnie Hampel was copied in on both letters.

Chapter 14

Truth Trust Peace

One thing was crystal clear – my substantial victory before Mr Justice Burton would stimulate Eden's appetite for conversations and helpful communication channels were soon open with Ken Hill. Many of the assurances given to the Trustees by Druces & Attlee and by Tim Smit were now being filed under 'F' for Fiction. Where there had been a sense that those Trustees who had not already resigned in protest had been sleepwalking into this legal minefield, they were now wide awake, especially to the Eden atmosphere of distrust. In all this repositioning and running for cover Ken Hill stood pragmatic, courteous and anxious to negotiate a settlement at the earliest moment. This was now clearly a possibility as the Project was moving into a new phase. The question was, how culpable were Druces & Attlee, how culpable were those at Eden directly responsible for instructing Druces & Attlee and, were indeed Druces & Attlee about to become Eden's Get-out-of-Jail card?

I formed the impression that Ken Hill felt the solution lay at this time in keeping Tim Smit well away from the levers of decision making. By his own conduct he had surely forfeited any further right of influence in my Eden future. Where Tim and I had been united in co-creating and delivering a once in a lifetime dream, we had now become divided by values, by Tim's studied duplicity and by a culture of mistrust which a number of people told me had become a contagion that prevailed at Eden and permeated everything. Who was saying what to whom, and when, had apparently become a potent force disrupting harmonious working relationships at Watering Lane and making everyone nervous. Well wishers reported back to me that these harboured discontentments surfaced at team social gatherings and the many glittering awards ceremonies as Eden claimed one prestigious accolade after another. The heady oxygen of public adulation coupled with a liberal lashing of celebratory bubbles brought to the surface and overflowing these simmering distrusts with some occasional unseemly conduct in public, giving forceful credence to the West Country wisdom that alcohol is a preserver of all things except one's dignity.

Tim could no longer carry the line of trumpeting dishonesty as a virtue and as an acceptable means of delivering Eden's end. Tim's amazing talents were alluring for all the world to see and to admire but his buccaneering bravado had a romance and an attraction that was firmly superficial; losing perhaps one distinguished Trustee to his unmanageable and cavalier conduct was arguably acceptable, but now four of the five original Trustees, exasperated by Tim's behaviour, had departed, which sent unwelcomed signals of a different nature.

Ken Hill and I both clearly understood that the disqualification of Druces & Attlee by the High Court had huge significance for me and for Eden. The nearest parallel was, perhaps, a love triangle. The High Court had forcibly removed the protagonist in this extraordinary saga, delivering a shared optimism that the remaining issues between Eden and myself, with Druces & Attlee no longer there as an impediment to settlement, could now fall into happy resolution.

From the very outset I had accepted the legal advice that I could not sue Tim Smit without bringing down the whole Eden project. My legal team now assembled to determine our strategy in the light of the latest judicial decree. Any legal case regardless of complexity can only go two ways from the starting point: some get better and some get worse. This was a very Larry Cohen pronouncement but in truth the combined Judgments by Mr. Justice Laddie and Mr Justice Burton had delivered legal clarity as to my way forward. Happily, I need seek no more from my own Project, Eden, than reimbursement, having my money back please, and my claim for full reward for all my endeavours since the inception of the Project would be framed as a claim against Druces & Attlee, whose conduct had been firmly censured by the highest civil court in the land.

Getting me back to zero was morally and legally incontestable by Eden and events quickly moved towards early agreement. All parties at last now understood where the finishing line to this tortured legal marathon would be. The Mr. Justice Laddie Judgment in transferring my trademark rights to Eden purely dealt with ownership and not with quantum. The subsequent Mr Justice Burton Judgment enshrined the clear and solemn view that the trademark award to Eden was found by Mr. Justice Laddie on a narrow legal point, ' ... *which did not involve any substantial or material consideration of the facts.*' This left Eden's legal advice throughout as discredited. For Eden, the Laddie J Judgment had been a double edged sword. He concluded that I was to have no ongoing legal rights in the Project but when vesting my rights in the Trust he made it clear that the Trust had yet to pay me for those rights. There was already a strong evidential base to my audited costs and it was no more than getting representatives from each side together to negotiate and sign off the reinstatement quantum.

The position of Druces & Attlee, of course, was in complete contrast to this. By their alleged negligence and confliction they had lost me, my co-founder position in its entirety and also my opportunities to secure legitimate rewards from my innovation, creativity and gigantic risk taking. It therefore followed that my claim for reward should be against Druces & Attlee.

I was on the train returning from London to the West Country, close by where Tim and I had been when we heard from the BBC that our first Eden submission had been unsuccessful, when my mobile signalled an incoming call from Larry Cohen. Eden had settled. Although the formal agreement signed off by Sir Ronnie Hampel on behalf of the Eden Trust and Ken Hill as Chairman of the Eden Company was to be confidential as regards both financial and other terms, Eden unequivocally and publicly recognised my *'significant contribution to the vision of the Eden Project from its inception'* and enshrined my status as *'equal co-founder'* for all time. This status was to be acknowledged in all media coverage and I was to continue to be invited to all important events concerning the Project such as Openings, Gala and public events and the like. Satisfactory as they sounded, I suspected in my heart of hearts that these provisions, though legally binding, would never be generously applied as long as Tim and Gaynor remained in post at Eden; and so it has proved.

The Eden financial settlement brought further welcome relief, but only by degrees. I had lost my professional practice, I was reinstated, but I had no livelihood and nothing to show by way of reward for the past seven and a half years of my labour and enterprise. Additionally, the 'pick yourself up, dust yourself off and start all over again' maxim was not open to me as I now faced what was to turn out to be the commencement of legal proceedings against Druces & Attlee that were to consume my energies and emotions for a further 22 months to the final incontrovertible show down in the Royal Courts of Justice before Sir Robert Nelson in December 2003.

Despite all my accrued wisdom and experience I had not fully grasped the cynical disregard John Citizen from a small town in Cornwall faces when he has the audacity to

"Cut!!! ... Mr Smit could you come out of the bushes and stand this side of the camera please??!!" Cornwall Today March 2002. Inscribed: To Jonathan Ball, very kind regards, Colin R. Weekes, 24th March 2002. (JB archive)

commence legal action against a significant City of London law firm whose provenance stretched back to the 18th century. What opened up was a legal ping pong with spurious manoeuvres and callous manipulations deliberately calculated to a single aim, that I would fall off the end of the world before I could prove my case. Druces & Attlee had behaved with a contempt towards me that left me with the sense I was regarded by them as something they would not wish to bring indoors on the bottom of their shoes.

The ever perceptive and ever wise observation from my caring lawyer chum Tony was that any delight for me in the Chancery action before Mr Justice Burton could not have had a better outcome, was set against dismay as he knew better than I that more turbulent times now lay ahead. Additionally, I now had to deal with Reynolds Porter Chamberlain who had taken over the case on behalf of the Solicitors' Indemnity Fund and their reputation for intransigence in the forthright protection of their insurer client's best interests preceded them. Of course, there was now no commercial incentive in Druces & Attlee seeking early settlement. My path would be long, winding and fraught with danger.

Ever since my Eden troubles first loomed large and seeped into the public consciousness I enjoyed not only the deep concern and support from close chums legally qualified and otherwise, but also an unending dialogue within Cornwall as to how Victoria and I coped with it all. How did we not sink under the emotional maelstrom and legal and financial onslaught that left us facing such profound uncertainty? My constant reply embraced my dictum of truth, trust and peace. Quite simply, without truth there is no trust and without trust there will be no peace. This holds good in every facet of our lives. Importantly, it needs even stricter adherence in times of trouble. The whole Eden legal imbroglio and corporate governance disarray which we faced were proof positive of this dictum's validity and in turn was to prove a vital component of our continuing survival.

When it was finally all over in 2004, we sat down with my legal team and closest London supporters for a celebratory dinner at my Club around the very same table where 10 years previous we had first captured key support for our dream. It was on this occasion a cherished compliment was paid to me by my legal team which was simply this: that, from day one of our professional relationship there had not been one single occasion when my lawyers had cause to query or challenge my version of events.

Whilst absolute truth has to be maintained, the proving of this sometimes requires more than just memory. During my professional training and as the head of my own professional practice it has always been my custom to keep meticulous notes of meetings and conversations. This ingrained habit was to become our lifeline. In the heady atmosphere of the Royal Courts of Justice I was to find contemporaneous notes defeat strongly held recollections every single time. Larry Cohen had wryly observed that beyond any possible doubt he considered me to be the best squirrel he had ever represented. Many times both Eden and Druces & Attlee were obliged to concede that what was stated was indeed the case, as supported by contemporaneous written evidence, and they had somewhat begrudgingly coined the term 'The Bude Files', to refer to my prodigious paper trail amassed in Bude. These files contained our salvation.

Meanwhile Victoria developed her own defence mechanisms. Her way of coping was never to get too excited when I returned home with good news, nor too depressed when we slid down yet another legal snake. She quite simply refused to climb onto the roller coaster that I had unwittingly created for my family. Speculation was banned. Each progress report she interrogated and distilled back to its bare established fact which was then considered on a 'we are where we are' basis. Her own emotional intelligence shielded our daughters Jemima and Morwenna from the worst of the news whilst making sure they were aware of our continuing plight.

Duncan, dear Duncan, Larry's no.2, was in daily contact with measured reassurance and his style throughout the legal switchbacks was unfailingly affable and companionable. I looked forward to his communications, rather than dreading them. Alongside this Larry was forever inventive and creative in keeping our battle ensign colourfully fluttering in the breeze and on several occasions had even Duncan and I exchanging glances of disbelief at a suggested audacious move. For example when Sir Ronnie Hampel and I had our showdown meeting the appointment of two top London lawyers as Trustees to Eden had fortified him to be able to present me with a take it or leave it offer that was anything but quantum meruit. This produced from Larry the suggestion that we go for judicial disclosure of these three Trustees' annual incomes to display to the world the inequity and poverty of the consideration offered to me by them. How could you not like the cut of Larry's jib?

The Burton Judgment reverberated on both sides of the River Tamar with equal force and what soon became apparent was that the legal profession had taken its seat next to Her Majesty's Government and the Secretary of State for Culture, Media and Sport in the front row of the gallery of the court of public opinion. Keen interest in the case became ever more widespread. Witness to this was the invitation from the Legal Editor of The Times for Duncan to write an article, following the Burton Judgment posing the question whether confidential information can truly be protected when solicitors act against a former client. On 16 April 2002 The Times ran nearly a whole page under the headline 'How Solid are Chinese Walls?' with an excellent treatise by Duncan alongside a magnificent photograph of the Eden biomes. The sub heading 'Lessons from Eden: the Law Society is [now] preparing rules on how and when Chinese walls can operate within solicitors' practices' was a portent of things to come within the legal profession and reassurance that the stand I had taken, partly on behalf of John Citizen, had not been in vain.

Foliage within the Humid Tropical Biome grows away.   *(NGP)*

The public gaze and interest continued in a somewhat bemused way, given the esoteric legal complexities, which were difficult enough for me to follow even with quality advice coming from every quarter. The Cornish have a well founded reputation for rugged individuality. The wise men came from the East but the clever buggers come from the West, so they say. Rural Cornwall has many similarities in its character and quintessence with rural Ireland, not least a parallel and proportionate Diaspora. It is perhaps rural Ireland without the Catholic Church and it is certainly tribal in its instincts, as indeed are all the Celtic nations.

But these Celtic nations all sing to a rhythm of innate well being that will forever elude the stranger. The concept of fair play and looking after each other goes back to the time of the ancient Celt when these concepts were a prerequisite to survival. I continued to be left in no doubt that Cornwall would not see me abandoned. For all his Tim Smiteries, the Machiavellian, the compelling and erudite and indeed the utterly charming facets of his character, he was the outsider, the stranger, he was David Penhaligon's definition of an expert - the Prophet from a distant land. Had Tim properly understood the Cornish he would have moderated his unscrupulous conduct by his own calculation in order to serve his own objective.

And then, for a moment, matters legal were set aside by quite extraordinary pronouncements that gushed forth from every media orifice. This was launched with Eden having a four minute slot networked on BBC breakfast television on 1 October 2002 ... the amazing success story of the Eden project, Gaynor Coley, now promoted to Managing Director, confirming the visitor figures for this year will again be 2 million and the next £100m worth of investment in the Project was being unveiled. The mouth-watering headline figure which spun the story into the stratosphere was that 'the Eden factor' was delivering £460,000 per day of additional revenue in the far South West. The Western Morning News issued a free supplement within the newspaper on The Wonder of Eden describing it as a true phenomenon and a world beating attraction. The Times ran a photograph of Tim *'The former record producer whose brainchild The Eden Project was'*, claiming the new proposed biome would *'make Eden as famous a landmark as the Sydney Opera House and help it to become one of the world's must-see destinations'*. The Guardian ran a small piece and The Independent ran a good news piece and also ran the story as its Leader under the headline 'Clotted Cream'.

The astronomical revenues Eden was generating daily in the far South West could not have been in greater contrast to my own financial circumstances of the moment. With two High Court Judgments behind me and with a paper trail that delivered beyond any reasonable doubt the validity of my argument and my claim, I was initially buoyant and upbeat about the immediate future, but soon what in my mind had been legal ping pong, changed more to a game of snakes and ladders where each throw of the legal dice found me slithering down two snakes for every ladder I climbed.

This said my sagging spirits had just received what Chairman Mao, in referring to his Little Red Book, had memorably described as a giant leap forward for mankind, by my Installation in September 2002 as a Bard of the Cornish Gorsedh, a world college of some 400 Bards committed, on a non exclusive basis, to maintaining and championing Cornwall's cultural heritage and traditions as a Celtic nation. All Bards are initiated at the annual Gorsedh Kernow held each September and in consultation with Bardh Meur, the Grand Bard of the day, you assume and are invested with your Bardic name which becomes unique to you for all time. A meeting with the Grand Bard ensued and a providential suggestion emerged. I was being Barded for my services to the Royal National Lifeboat Institution and Surf Life Saving in Cornwall. But Bardh Meur had one eye towards those in the future looking back and proposed I assume the Bardic name Tregarthen which, in the Cornish language, means 'of the Garden'. The thoughtfulness of Grand Bard Jowan an Cleth was to characterise his three year term of office where, by strength of personality he steered a greater re-awakening of interest in Cornish culture.

Meanwhile regular autumn conferences with my leading Silk, John Slater QC, set the agendas for Larry and Duncan, at the same time delivering to me more detailed insights into the legal complexities that place any high court action beyond the realms of layman's understanding. That we had a paper trail so comprehensive and compelling was not enough. I was being schooled to the mantra of retainer causation quantum, the three pillars upon which Druces & Attlee would need to construct their defence and any escape from severe censure, financial penalty and attendant professional opprobrium. In simple terms retainer is the professional relationship between a law firm and its client. Legal codes of professional conduct prescribe that the onus is firmly on the lawyer to have in place and in writing the terms upon which he is retained, the services he will provide, the duties and obligations he assumes on behalf of his client and the rewards he expects on discharge of those duties and obligations. Causation is the linking of any deficiencies in the conduct of the lawyer's retainer that results directly in loss to the client and Quantum is the battle at the end, putting a value to the loss when a client has been able to prove successfully that a lawyer has fundamentally breached his retainer and there is, beyond any peradventure, a causational link between that breach and direct loss suffered by the client.

The Burton Judgment condemned Druces & Attlee to hopelessness on any arguments they attempted to advance that they did not owe me any retainer obligations. In John Slater's words 'their case on retainer is a dead duck' and setting aside my own surprise that even Queen's Counsels mix their metaphors, John Slater added that he would be delighted to have Druces & Attlee fight retainer as it would be a public 'crucifixion job' in the Royal Courts of Justice.

As to Causation and quantum, our paper trail was strong but this linkage, and how much, was where the defence would set their sights on establishing wriggle-room. Legal argument would focus on what legal advice I should have been given and what should have been put in place to protect my interests. Yet more expensive experts delivering yet more costly witness statements as to how much loss had been incurred and how the legal advice deficiencies I had suffered were glaringly obvious and sat firmly at the Janet and John end of professional performance.

I was quickly disabused from harbouring any thoughts that Druces & Attlee's removal by the Courts from this action would ensure that the right thing would now be done and that such action was vital for the citizens of the land to have faith and confidence in our legal systems and in the High Court delivering justice. Reynolds Porter Chamberlain, now acting for the Insurers, were in place to protect narrowly constructed interests. The concept of whether conduct was right or wrong or downright outrageous, whether denials from Druces & Attlee in the Royal Courts of Justice were specious when, as a law firm they had the status of officers of the court, was not their concern. The reputation of the legal profession being further besmirched in the eyes of the public did not appear to be of any consequence whatsoever.

On advice we agreed to mediation and to appoint a Mediator in the hope of establishing terms upon which all issues could be settled without recourse to trial. Our Quantum experts, Valuation Consulting, who had produced expensive reports establishing eye watering losses way beyond my own sense of proportion and expectation, were confident that an appropriate settlement could be secured. Our evidential base to date on retainer and causation were inescapable. It was now Druces & Attlee's turn to be firmly up shit creek, an environment I knew all too well, but my tenure there had at least been with one paddle: Druces & Attlee, they said, had none.

The issue of quantum constantly has the client outside their comfort zone. The construction of value arguments remains timelessly unscientific. Any mediation has to be undertaken and entered into with an agreed bottom line figure acceptable to the client for him to settle the claim, but the legal team have their own fine line upon which to tiptoe in establishing what this is in the light of their own latest best estimate of quantifiable damage. In reality, it didn't matter.

We travelled to London heady with the prospect of putting the tormented years behind us and moving our lives forward to less stressful, more equitable and positive times with our family home finally and firmly free from risk. I was buoyant in my hopes that the anguish I had visited upon Victoria and all those near and dear to me was close to becoming history. Our immediate pre mediation briefings and the first part of the mediation process were all upbeat and my instructed bottom line of a settlement figure that was acceptable to me was aimed at putting our family lives back together rather than any life-style changing financial ambitions; a settlement that was light years away from the astronomical figures signalled by our valuation experts as being acceptable and achievable. Victoria had accompanied me to London but on advice was not in attendance for the mediation. My legal team had instilled in me a cautious confidence that settlement could and would be achieved and Victoria set off for the West End shops looking for a cashmere jumper that would have been our first symbolic settlement purchase.

But our mediation day the 11th October 2002 had started at 08.45 in the morning and ended at 18.50 the same day after tense and unsatisfactory procedures with the courteous and patient mediator entering our room for the last time to confirm he was unable to come back with any meaningful offer. I met a few days later with Larry and Duncan for our post mortem. Larry was desperately disappointed expressing his view that the other side had not entered the mediation in good faith. They had wanted to see the colour of our eyes and to know where we were coming from and would now wait to see the further construction of our evidential base. I came away with the sense Reynolds Porter Chamberlain had decided they would be recommending to their clients, the Solicitors Indemnity Fund, to have a go at knocking me for six in the Royal Courts of Justice before coming into settlement terms. The rights and wrongs of my claims, the moral and ethical justification, seemed to me as a layperson, to be completely immaterial to them. We had arrived in London hoping and thinking mediation was our last throw of the dice that would land us on the ladder to the finishing square on the board. All we had done was to slither down yet another snake.

More unwelcome news was soon to follow. My leading Silk the avuncular John Slater QC informed Duncan he had no availability for proceeding to trial until October 2003, 12 months distant. Both Duncan and Larry urged me to resign myself to this further disappointment. We must go with John Slater's best time; his sterling performance in front of Mr Justice Burton had left Victoria and me with the firm conclusion that here we had a best of breed with an advocacy style so admirably suited to our needs and the specialist legal complexities of our case. The best are always in high demand. But what a bittersweet moment. We could not demur, nor did we.

Legal processes distract from everyday life. Being consumed by anxiety is the trap set for the unwary. Quite simply it's the last thing you think about before you go to sleep at night and the first thing to come into your mind in the morning. The hours, the days, the weeks and the months stretch out. Lightening this darkness has to be a positive, proactive act of will and determination. How we were to survive this further year of uncertainty - emotionally, physically, psychologically and financially - without prospects of income or livelihood is a fundamentally good question to ask. In truth my state of mind was buoyant. How, in our troubled times, had I established a force for good and constructed harmony and personal well being out of the chaos our lives appeared to be in? I have always taken the view that good luck is the crossroads where opportunity meets preparation.

Chapter 15

...I Can Always Borree a Quid...

As RIBA Honorary Secretary I had come into contact with the Brahma Kumaris World Spiritual University, an international organisation working at all levels of society for positive change. It is a teaching organisation that fosters positive values and ethical living with 5,000 centres in 85 countries offering courses in meditation and spiritual knowledge embracing people of all religions and cultures working together to reach their highest spiritual potential. Between 1988 and 1995 I was to serve three RIBA Presidents as the Honorary Secretary, each a two year appointment. This providential encounter resulted from the Presidency of Rod Hackney, the first of the three, who for some time had worked closely with Brahma Kumaris in his social entrepreneurship that had captured so much media attention under the banner of Community Architecture.

On retreat with the Brahma Kumaris World Spiritual University, Global Retreat, Oxford. Photograph BKWSU.   *(JB archive)*

It was a moment for reflection on the hard work I had put into the RIBA, always beating the drum for those furthest away from the London decision makers, but also for what my service on RIBA Council had, in turn, given to me. The first day of my appointment as Honorary Secretary had introduced me to Shit Creek, its perils and how congested it is. Here I was in my last period as Honorary Secretary conversing with an organisation so admirably equipped to assist anyone and everyone in such predicament. Since my first encounter, Brahma Kumaris has been a constant in the background of my life and their teachings have given me a spiritual vocabulary for every moment particularly in times of stress.

I remain grateful to the RIBA and to Rod Hackney. My interface with this organisation over the years arose from my first extraordinary experience of going on retreat at Nuneham Courtenay, their global retreat centre just outside Oxford with handsome grounds stretching down to the banks of the River Thames. As RIBA Honorary Secretary I was one of five Trustees of the British Architectural Library, custodians of probably the most important collection of drawings, architectural books and associated cultural assets in the world. At this time the collection had an estimated value of £300m enshrining all the scholarship, cultural heritage and Charter Objectives promoting the art of architecture. It secured international admiration way beyond the world RIBA membership. The RIBA faced an enormous problem. How could we construct a sustainable future for this world resource when, with so many other calls on the membership subscription, we could only deliver a ridiculously small budget for so important a task? The Victoria and Albert Museum in South Kensington was minded to strengthen its architectural collection, but to facilitate this potential marriage-made-in-heaven would be quite a challenge. Each organisation had its own culture, traditions, history and sacred cows, together with various curators, department heads and staffing levels.

Rod had an idea. Selected Trustees, Curators, staff and other appropriate representatives from each organisation would go on retreat together to brainstorm the prospects. We all assembled for our first evening together at Nuneham Courtenay, cautiously optimistic. I was acutely mindful that what for us Trustees was an opportunity would be perceived as a threat by all in attendance whose livelihoods would be changed if this proposal was adopted.

That first evening was a revelation for me. We had as our facilitator and rapporteur John McConnel, who had recently retired from a distinguished career within the Prison Service and was dedicating his life to the World Spiritual University and assisting individuals in coming together to rediscover and develop the spiritual dimension of their lives. Softly spoken, articulate and caring, he gently touched upon the history and importance to the nation of our two respective organisations and how he would use his best endeavours to help us reach common accord in how future generations would benefit from a positive outcome to our deliberations. Over the next two days he cautioned we would each be experiencing the conflict between emotion and reason. The message I was receiving was clear. Our hearts should not remain firmly defending the status quo and the continuing integrity of our respective organisations at the expense of our heads signposting a lasting solution.

He introduced us to the wonders of traffic control, the name given to an important part of daily life within the global retreat. Every two hours you are suddenly aware of background music and at that moment you are encouraged to stop your conversations, sit upright, place your hands on your knees and adopt a meditative posture for two minutes of silence. During this powerful silence you are invited to review the last two hours of your conversations and deliberations. You have had four kinds of thoughts; positive, negative, useful and unnecessary and why not, in your own mind, ditch those that were negative and unnecessary and proceed with the positive and the useful. At the end of the two minutes the music fades and you resume your dialogue as if this intervention has not taken place.

That the RIBA and the Victoria and Albert Museum did come into accord and within a surprisingly short time line was, I am sure, because here was an idea whose time had come. Equally, I believe our deliberations during that retreat environment created an enabling trust and harmony that set aside barriers erected to protect perceived self interests. A culture of cooperation had emerged.

Throughout the world the Brahma Kumaris is partnering with community and private organisations and since 1981 has worked closely with the United Nations having consultative status with its Economic and Social Council and the United Nations International Children's Emergency Fund (UNICEF). The University is administered by elder Sisters, or Dadis, acknowledged throughout the world as spiritual leaders. The Co Administrative Head is Dadi Janki whom I was to meet the following year, my audience with her having been organised by the kindly John McConnel.

This set in train my continuing occasional involvement with an organisation that profoundly assisted me in the way I came to terms with my relationship with Eden. Notwithstanding the regular uncongenial assaults that were causing so much upset at a personal level I was receiving a guiding hand encouraging me to dismiss the negatives and accentuate Eden's multitude of positive messages it was sending to the world. And therein lay the foundation stones of my own salvation. Through this guidance I was able to develop my own mechanisms for continuing my positive contributions to Eden at every opportunity. As its Co Founder I took heartfelt pleasure at every opportunity to promote Eden, a pleasure now free from negativity which I compartmentalised away from the public gaze, marginalised and arrested in its personal invasive nature, a cancer confirmed benign and treatable.

And so I developed, side by side with legal conflict, a life of searching out felicity which came easily to me the moment I thought exclusively of all the good things about Eden and the opportunities it held for the young people of Cornwall regardless of those at Eden who would deny my full involvement. This emerging spiritual well being was fed by serendipity. The very week I had to walk across Blackfriars Bridge for my High Noon meeting with Sir Ronnie Hampel, I accepted a cherished invitation to be one of the guest speakers at an international residential seminar entitled 'Humanity, Quality and Ability' co-facilitated by the International Union of Architects (UIA) the world organisation for the architectural profession and the Brahma Kumaris. This was to be held at the Global Retreat Centre, Oxford in October 2000.

There are about 1.5 million qualified architects in the world with another 1 million under training, most are humanitarian in their principles and values, working for the common good of society and striving to create a better world. The idea was that 60 architects selected world wide for their humanity would come together in common purpose to brainstorm the 21st century. Of course my contribution was focused on the Eden Project, already internationally acclaimed in the architectural community, but this was a gathering in humility rather than mutual self regard. It was to be a very humbling occasion as I met many heroes who had lived their values in unimaginably more difficult circumstances than my own and I received a valuable object lesson in the connection between spiritual and cultural, aesthetic, ecological and humanitarian well being in the world.

A few months later together with Rod Hackney who had gone on to become World President UIA and had co created our architects' brainstorming event, I received an invitation to dinner in London with Dadi Janki. At the end of a memorable evening she gave Rod and me a challenge; to put our minds as to how we might harness architecture for advancing the themes and values we had discussed with such power and international resonance the previous October. Herein was one of the catalysts for my next project idea, The Great Atlantic Way.

The Brahma Kumaris helped clarify and connect together various strands of my life to date into a more coherent and more powerful sense of purpose and a focus for my energies. Dadi Janki had gifted me a book called 'Living Values'. Your personal values are never more needed than in time of crisis and this book affirmed how values are the treasures of life, values are friends, they bring happiness to your life: values expand your capacity to be self sufficient and liberate yourself from unwanted external influences; values offer protection, bring empowerment. On one retreat occasion we explored these matters in greater depth and took the enduring example of Mahatma Gandhi whose world changing power in the 20th century came from nothing more than the exercising of his values.

Of equal benefit was the clarity given to my understanding that feelings follow thoughts. Where your thoughts go, your energies flow. There is a distinct difference between worrying about the future and planning for the

Eden's pillows inflated to the higher pressure to cope with snow loading 25th November 2005. (Western Morning News)

future. Filling your thoughts with goodwill and kindly words and actions are repayed with kind regard on most occasions and control of your thoughts starts with learning the principles of meditation, the core curriculum of the Brahma Kumaris World Spiritual University. Meditation is taught as a method of raising self awareness leading to self realisation. Meditation stills the mind and empowers the intellect to achieve insight and understanding of the spiritual laws and principles which sustain harmony and bring natural renewal to all levels of life on earth.

At this hour of my life I thus began a new journey from contemplating to meditating. Contemplation is an activity that can be undertaken without too much effort. It is reflective in nature, undemanding of intellectual endeavour and whilst it results in often delightful observation is not, by itself, spiritually nourishing. Contemplation observes the present, that which one sees, the physical world. Meditation, by contrast has to be practised and observed diligently. It is an exercise that examines the inner reaches of belief and desire and has a deeper, more fundamental effect on the decision reached. It is the practice of examining the core of your being. It is not undertaken in an idle fashion, for no purpose other than to pass the time, but to help resolve inner conflict or turmoil and reach some sort of understanding and inner calm. It teaches acceptance of a certain condition, but does not advocate a surrender of values. It exclusively deals with positivity.

For me, neither sufficiently experienced in such worthy practices nor sufficiently disciplined enough by nature to commit wholeheartedly, dipping in and out emerged as my own preferred way. My traffic control experiences reinforced for me the power of quiet times which in turn connect to inner peace. As with everything, the more you practise the more you benefit and greater self awareness follows, better equipping you to face the day.

In this, my long season of distress, a technique was developing to deal with vexation, a calmness for smoothing the journey of my mind hand in hand with my troubled Eden journey. Even the most conscientious students in a normal learning environment suffer frustration and are upset by their own shortcomings. John McConnel, in long telephone conversations, knowing my Eden beleaguered state of mind, urged me to remove all battle words. 'If you fight, Eden fights back'. Of course he was right, but of course adopting this laudable approach was, in truth, not an option fully open to me, not least as the legal processes in Britain are promulgated and established on adversarial lines and confrontation. The future was adopting a path of personal progress rooted in pragmatism, steered by legal advice all counterbalanced by the solace of the way of truth and peace.

Certainly the harbouring of a strong sense of injustice promotes feelings of anger and my Brahma Kumaris experiences set aside swathes of anger and frustration at the circumstances in which I found myself. Others do not make you angry, you chose to be angry. It is a negative emotion, it cannot be given to you. Anger is not viral, you cannot ingest it and you certainly derive no benefit whatsoever from promoting such feelings within yourself. If you chose to be angry, and the choice is yours and yours alone, the friendly faces in the room avert their gaze and you risk lessening their kind regard. You make the world a hostile place; it is not inherently so. I was not able to put all such theory into practice, but at least any dark moments of self pity and despair diminished dramatically and there was now the ladder by my side in the pit I had dug for myself inviting me with nominal effort to climb free from any gloomy entrapment.

Despite the mediation disappointment and the harsh reality of having to wait a further 12 months for John Slater QC, we came to the end of the year and into Christmas 2002 with renewed purpose and the sense of having a transfusion of positives overtaking the negatives and delighting in every positive Eden news story without reservation. In late November the Western Morning News trumpeted that Eden was now employing 650 people, most of whom had been recruited from within Cornwall and the vast majority of all consumables at Destination Eden were being sourced within the County. 'The Eden Factor' was an economic lion that roared.

The festive season break gave time to give thanks for our many blessings, for family get togethers in celebration and time for reflection and review 30 years on from my graduation at the AA. How the mores of the times had changed. The lifestyle balance of living and bringing up your children in Cornwall far outweighed the professional disappointment of being passed over for the more exciting architectural commissions and professional opportunities that went the way of those of my generation who remained in London. The imperative of the New Year was to ensure that in mind, body and spirit I was fit for purpose to face the rigours of preparing for the final show-down in the Royal Courts of Justice at the end of the coming year. A few years previously on New Year's Day morning I had walked along the road outside our house in Stratton for fresh air to dispel the excesses of my New Year celebrations. The first person I met was a local farmer chum, George Heard.. *'Happy New Year to you George, with lots of good health and prosperity'*, I said. *''Appy New Year, to you too'*, he said. *'but what I wants is the good 'ealth – I can always borree a quid!'*. I heard nothing more profound throughout the year, nor have I since. You cannot borrow good health.

Festive indulgences are always dispelled with walks along the coastal footpath and my favourite is that amazing stretch of coastline from Marsland Mouth where Cornwall meets England about seven miles above Bude, down past Hennacliff rising some 450 feet above sea level, through Morwenstow and then past Sandymouth down the long, sweeping sandy beaches to Bude this coastline is remote, majestic, elemental. Here Cornwall wears her impress of well being; there are no finer ways to fill your days. This said, when the capricious sea conspires a lee shore with a wave fetch from a wild Atlantic Ocean, this coastline takes on a character more malignant than majestic.

The Royal National Lifeboat Institution (RNLI) has well tried and trusted procedures that attach to the launching of lifeboats in times of stormy distress. In my time on the crew of Bude Lifeboat it was the Station Honorary Secretary, usually affectionately addressed as Hon Sec, or SHS, who was in superintendent control of the Station. It is a common misconception that a Lifeboat Coxswain is in charge of all decision making, but the 'do we go or not' decision rests not with him, but with the Hon Sec as Launching Authority. This final decision and final responsibility is with the Hon Sec, nowadays called the Lifeboat Operations Manager, a term devoid of romance, but better suited for communication in times of crisis.

It is when the lifeboat puts to sea that the coxswain of all-weather lifeboats or senior helmsman in respect of inshore lifeboats takes command. At the end of a lifeboat service with the lifeboat safely recovered and ready for its next launch the Hon Sec is charged with sending a Return of Service to the Institution covering all aspects including the extremes of tide and weather, the performance of the lifeboat and God willing the safe recovery of any casualties. Bude Lifeboat Station was established in 1837 and its long and proud history can be charted by reference to these Returns of Service. There is one that always captures my imagination. It is from September 1863 where at the end of the Return of Service in elegant copper plate hand the Hon Sec of the day conveyed his comment back to HQ... 'Those of the Committee [of Bude Lifeboat] who witnessed this service observing the great exertions required on the part of the crew to make head on this occasion against the wind and tide have expressed their opinion that the Coast is at times subject to a sea and wind which no human power would be able to guide the Lifeboat through'. What must have been witnessed that night?

'Cawk, Cawk, then said the raven, I am fourscore years and ten, yet never in Bude Haven, did I croak for rescued men' is from Robert Stephen Hawker's poem A Croon from Hennacliff reminding us the sea is timeless in its commanding of respect.

I am especially drawn to this coastal landscape at the turn of a year. The hovering hawks, sharing the high thermals with your soaring spirits, swooping silently and deadly on their small mammal prey are the only predators I see. In being taught meditation you are encouraged to take yourself in your mind to a favourite spot, somewhere that is most precious to you; somewhere so inspiring, so full of energy and free from threat. Of all my large circle of Cornish friends and acquaintances whose company I so enjoy, it is my chum Les from Penzance who most shares this passion for Cornish landscape and the way it speaks to us. Les takes me for walks in his native West Penwith, and I, in turn, walk him along the remote cliffs of Morwenstow where our eccentric Victorian cleric, Parson Hawker, who initiated observance of the Harvest Festival, more than a century before, found so much inspiration. In one of our conversations that flowed effortlessly between landscape and grandchildren Les captured the fundamental nature of it all, *'It's not about the breaths that we take in this life it's all about those moments in this life which take our breath away'.*

Such shared passions are fed by observation, belonging, respect and appreciation together with a good slug of Pandora ... hope is the last thing left in the box. The starting point in any journey of creativity is inspiration. Had I been born and lived in ancient Greece or Rome it would have been to the Muses that I would have looked. First to the oldest, Calliope, the intellectual Muse and then perhaps to Erato the Muse of the emotions. Alongside medicine, architecture remains at seven years one of the longest periods of professional training and by the end you hopefully have acquired a keen sense of this inter dependency and how solutions to problems are best founded on a response that is both intellectual and emotional. Indeed, absent these thoughts and there would be no Eden Project.

But I was not born in ancient times and the land of my birth is Cornwall. My professional training reinforced in me my sense that Cornwall was the innate starting point for my inspiration, Cornwall was my muse. Just as you apply inspiration to the solving of a complex design brief, so it is with other problematic facets in your life you apply similar thought processes and creativity.

2003   My New Year resolutions heralding 2003 were to think only of the positives and to apply my accumulated problem solving skills and all my emotional energy into a set of project ideas that look to the future and reserving only that of my emotional energies that was absolutely crucial to defending my Eden past and my legitimate expectations within it that remained denied.

I had chosen the title The Great Atlantic Way for my new set of ideas and musings as, for me, it conveyed the sense of a journey that was both physical and spiritual. Its genesis had been my cliff walks around Morwenstow, sitting in Hawker's Hut and gazing westwards to the ocean's infinity. I took a notebook and started writing about it. I sought out those down through history whose eloquence I could never hope to match to read how they articulated similar feelings and responses.

Hawker's Hut, Morwenstow.
'Time tired rails on stablegate parting
Rust worn blacksmiths' nails betrayed
By the sea damp all invading
And wild whipped landfall wind decayed.'
(Bob Willingham)

Hawker's Hut is a well known, if not well visited, landmark hereabouts. They say it is the smallest National Trust property in Britain. It is constructed of ship wreck and was erected by Parson Hawker's own hand as a remote cliff side retreat where he went to write his sermons, poems and some say to smoke opium. It could not have a more dramatic setting, precariously clinging to the cliffs and certainly an enthralling sight from the seaward; I well recall pondering this on one occasion during my time as Senior Helmsman as I sized up taking Bude lifeboat in amongst the jagged rocks at the base of this cliff on a search, mercifully in fine weather, that was to turn out as a false alarm with good intent. It must have been a very evocative place for Hawker. Broken ships' timbers that had sent sailors to their mass graves dug by Hawker and his parishioners in Morwenstow churchyard close by Hennacliff and alongside the Church of St Morwenna and St John the Baptist where the Parish guide reminds us a church has stood facing the Atlantic for more than half as long as the entire history of the Christian faith to which it bears witness. To this day the figurehead of the Caledonia, the most famous of the wrecks driven ashore along this treacherous coastline, marks the spot together with Hawker's inscription 'They came in paths of storm: They found this quiet home in Christian ground'. A powerful testament indeed to my Great Atlantic Way thesis that every square metre of planet Earth has its own special stories to tell. Morwenstow has this spectacular, if solemn, peace and calm and it was here, in solitude, I could bring my turbulent Eden troubles.

On the first occasion I went on Retreat and my initiation into the discipline of meditation ... take your mind to a special place... Morwenstow and Hawker's Hut was the first place to come into my mind. It is a place where you can expect to bump into Calliope and Erato. It is somehow of, rather than imposed on the landscape. It is a place of shelter so small in a landscape so large, timeless yet for its time in our globalised world.

The day the Eden Visitor Centre opened in May 2000 and I was told by the Trustees either to resign from Eden or be sacked, the ever observant eye of the Western Morning News, unknowing of the detail, but sensing my uncertain future as Eden's Co Founder, supportively invited me to write their then weekly comment page under the banner of 'Viewpoint' covering this important Eden milestone.

I took my notebook and my thoughts to Hawker's Hut and wrote a piece which I entitled 'Dad, we are all global citizens now'. In my view there is no finer place to sit and think globally and it is here that I dreamt up someone whom I called ' Global John Citizen' later renamed by the Great Atlantic Way team as 'Global Jo', less of a mouthful and gender neutral for our times.

Our elder daughter Jemima's four year international business degree course had incorporated 12 months experience in India and so taken had she been with the enterprise and humanity of the sub continent that she had returned with a fellow student by riding two iconic Royal Enfield Bullet motorbikes 17,000 sponsored kilometres from Chennai, that most of us still call Madras, to Bude in order to raise funds to help the relief of female infanticide in rural Tamil Nadu. She raised several thousand pounds (an awful lot of rupees) and returned home truly a global citizen. It somehow captured for me the force of globalisation as the engine driving political and economic change and in recounting her Indian experiences it drove home such simple concepts as the need to achieve food and water security for populations around the world. I connected these thoughts with the hero of my own student days at the AA, Buckminster Fuller who not only gave the world the geodesic dome now so dramatically manifest in Bodelva Pit, but it was also Bucky who first articulated *we have to make the world work for everyone in order for it to work for ourselves*. My 'Viewpoint' introduced Global Jo and thanked Bucky for helping us focus on the issues that really matter and hoped he was looking down approvingly on the Eden Project.

Why was it that the Eden Project had so powerfully captured the spirit of the age? First of all it was a story, then it was dramatic landscape, then it was fabulous architecture and engineering, assembling amongst the finest creators of a generation to come together in such symbolic endeavour to mark mankind's Millennial moment. Originality, content and form in dramatic location with the plants as the dramatis personae and the total experience arising from your and my relationship with them.

Sitting in Hawker's Hut gazing seaward I started to ask myself, What if … rather than taking a single destination like the Eden Project, how about 500 square miles of planet earth – no one has ever done that before – some of the highest value landscape in Britain, combined with the lowest prosperity and comprising some one third of the inhabited landscape of Cornwall and establish a 21st century sustainability exemplar.

And what if … having stumbled across a closed completed landfill site only a few miles inland from Morwenstow in a wooded Cornish valley that has not had public access for 50 years we take that as a starting point for the journey. Recycling a closed landfill site by using it for an environmental building that touches the earth lightly and is an introduction for the story of weather and mankind sending signals of recycling… the final frontier, our conduct today not mortgaging our children's tomorrows. At Eden we had taken Bodelva Pit, landscape despoiled by the extractive processes of mankind, and symbolically turned it into an iconic Project. Of equal epic ambition, why not take a closed landfill site, landscape despoiled by man's detritus, and create a symbolic project out of the unsustainable conspicuous consumption of our times.

And what if … you think of linking weather, climate, landscape, mankind and a sustainable future – what a fabulous storyline, creating a set of ideas connecting the individual to the big issues of our time, delivering a proposal to reverse Cornwall's declining agricultural base and other enterprises, to distil the essential qualities of a whole landscape and an entire culture, both fragile, and present this as a product for the benefit of this landscape and culture.

The proposition was for Great Atlantic Way to tell the story of how climate and weather shapes and forms the landscape and the people who inhabit it. Following a visit I made to The Met Office in Bracknell before their move to Exeter I received fulsome support from Colin Flood, Director of Special Projects. In a letter from him dated May 2003 he declared '*We [The Met Office] are quite captivated by the whole idea, particularly the element relating to the story of man and the environment. There is no doubt that the climate has played a significant part in shaping man's destiny; … to enable individuals, society and enterprises everywhere to make the most of the weather and the natural environment …, Great Atlantic Way is very consistent with this.*' The Met Office declared their full support for the venture and confirmed sponsorship to developing my ideas.

History is full of glowing examples of good that has come out of adversity. Whether the Great Atlantic Way as a set of ideas would have come together at this time but for my embattled circumstances is a question I am unable to answer. But I had again assembled a hugely talented and creative team, all enthusiastic to join in my crusade and I entered 2003 upbeat and eager. As her father, Jemima's initiative and achievements made me so proud; like her sister Morwenna, she is someone who lives her admirable values. What parent could ask for more? After graduation Jemima joined the Great Atlantic Way team as Director in charge of Future Proofing, of having our eyes at all times firmly on the horizon. Whenever the Great Atlantic Way team came together for brainstorming sessions there was always a symbolic empty chair at the end of the table reserved for Global Jo as a powerful reminder of the need to bring benefit to the powerless and dispossessed citizens of the world who constitute the majority of the world's population. With Bucky's words ringing in our ears we constantly reminded ourselves that more than 800 million people will go to bed hungry tonight.

My own natural empathy for Cornwall and Bude's genius loci, its spirit of place, was, I always believed well tuned, but amongst those who contributed to these new ideas was my friend Richard England, eminent Maltese architect, sculptor, poet and author who presented me with a Masterclass in these insights. I had shared with him my thoughts which were that, just like you and me, landscape has DNA. Every square metre of planet Earth is unique. The thread of history is woven through our landscape and my Cornish Great Atlantic Way story would be told by the farmers, the fishermen, the quarrymen, engineers and inventors, artists, writers and many others whose connection to, working of and inspiration from this weather-hewn countryside had defined its past and its present ... our imagination would define its future.

What did Richard England think? He wrote me a seminal letter which I read, re-read and then read again. Along with Henry Boettinger's Springs of Inspiration, pivotal prose in Eden's evolution, here was undiluted wisdom and powerful intellect with its precise focus on the issue of the moment, an exhilarating treatise on our Atlantic armour, landscape beyond scenery.

"Jonathan, I must express my admiration for an idea which is above all about the particular 'spirit of place' of that wonderful area of the British Isles which is Cornwall ... always I have felt that it is necessary for us to learn about a place by listening to what I refer to as the voices of the site. The Great Atlantic Way is exactly about experiencing the energy of an extraordinary land, with all its present absences and absent presences: thus enabling the participating observer to absorb its unique magical spirit with eyes that feel and hands that see. This is the sort of dream project which can make man rediscover some of the 'inherent knowledge' which seemed to be so natural to the ancients but which the modern mechanized world has unfortunately lost, reminding us of T S Eliot's verses, 'where has all the wisdom gone – lost in knowledge?' The Great Atlantic Way project will enable us to be aware of and to care about the resonating spirit of all the magic of the landscape that is Cornwall. Here one will experience the alchemy of the land, the syntax

Low winter sun on Eden's biomes. (NGP)

of the sky and the great resonating song of the waters of the Atlantic. As one walks The Great Atlantic Way one will read the tale of time of the area in a mnemonic layering system not dissimilar to that of the geological stratification of the land itself. Here, land, sea and sky become shrines, sanctuaries, mandalas and temples ... oracles where man may once more find peace ... and learn to love again. This is a place where landscapes metamorphose into dreamscapes ... It was Axel Munthe who said 'the soul needs more space than the body' ...The Great Atlantic Way will surely provide such a space."

The Great Atlantic Way project was a multi-faceted set of ideas firmly within the public realm, aimed at improving the civic condition and creating a secure and meaningful future to those inhabiting the landscape of rural North Cornwall. The common theme running throughout the journeys creates stories of the interaction between weather and the landscape and how they have shaped the lives of the people hereabouts, not least my own life, landscape, sustaining, constant, always uplifting.

In ancient times the Muses were said to live on Mount Olympus with the other Gods. Having taken my steer from Sister Wendy Beckett in selecting Calliope for Intellect and Erato for Emotion and noting their whimsical interplay, I was sure, in my time they were alive and well and living here, on these remote and changeless cliffs, forever fortified by gazing out upon the Atlantic. All the muses love music and anyone walking the Great Atlantic Way and experiencing what Richard England describes as 'present absences and absent presences.... with eyes that feel and hands that see...' will surely have music in their soul.

If it be that Mozart is your passion then listening to your favourite piece is joyful and restorative. Greater joy comes if it is perhaps a live performance, perhaps your favourite orchestra; perhaps an internationally renowned conductor; perhaps the Royal Opera House Covent Garden: all these experiences from your fireside to an international concert hall, the pleasure is infinite but the core passion is still Mozart. Taking the muses as inspiration, now translate these thoughts across to majestic landscape. On the balmiest summer's day through the wildest winter storm when it is near impossible to remain in the perpendicular to a still moonlit night or perhaps that magical light that emerges following violent weather, just like Mozart, it is still the same landscape. The movements of music parallel the mnemonic layering of landscape made bare for all to see, where it meets the Atlantic Ocean. The landscape is there, you don't have to switch on the wireless, play a CD or buy a concert ticket: you just have to look at what you already know with fresh eyes. By looking differently, if only a fleeting glance, the Great Atlantic Way aspires to awaken in you, a new peace of mind.

These developing ideas and stories of landscape, so powerfully reinforced by Richard England, oozed inspiration. I couldn't wait to get out of bed in the morning. With this any Eden defensive encounter generated by legal process or Tim's continuing media excesses that would previously have put me in an indignant spin, were now demoted to the status of rude, but necessary, negative interruptions.

To mark the 50th anniversary of the United Nations the Brahma Kumaris published Visions of A Better World, with a moving Forward by Sir Peter Ustinov, and in which was set out a Global Vision Statement. In many ways the Great Atlantic Way vision offered a parallel journey to the Eden Project. It struck me that Bucky was the linking thread and the title of this seminal Brahma Kumaris publication could aptly be applied to both Eden and the Great Atlantic Way. The Great Atlantic Way story, however, is another idea for another time. For now it plays no further part in my Eden story

Chapter 16

Back to Stern Reality

The elegant prose of Richard England '... *Oracles where man may once more find peace ... and learn to love again ...*' haunted my thoughts at this time. In March 2003, a few short weeks before receiving his letter, the Mother of Parliaments had propelled our nation into a war with Iraq based on what the majority of the British people felt was a false prospectus. Gallant resignations such as that of Foreign Secretary Robin Cook followed, and cogent argument propounded by principled libertarians and a rally of more than one million protesting citizens marching down Whitehall could neither deflect, nor defeat, the zealous Blair fervour. Blair prosecuted for a war with Iraq on an interpretation of international law peculiar to himself. Personal Prime Ministerial ascendancy was arresting the will of the people.

Truth was in short commodity, trust evaporated and peace became the casualty. The lies and deceit of the Blair government were mirrored in my personal circumstances.

I was soon abruptly brought back to stern reality. For more than six months I had not been bogged down with legal comings and goings, but in June 2003 a phone call from an outraged Duncan informed me we were at the stage of pre trial exchanging of Witness Statements and lo and behold one of the middle ranking Civil Servants at the Millennium Commission was to be the lead Defence witness against me at Trial. I was utterly disbelieving: the Chairman of the Millennium Commission, Secretary of State Tessa Jowell, as her predecessor before her, had refused point blank any access to the Millennium Commission public records. They had ensured the forensic KPMG audit was not seen by Mr Justice Laddie in the Royal Courts of Justice, the consequence of which so nearly wiped me off the face of the earth. The Secretary of State had firmly stated to my protesting Member of Parliament that they were not a party in this issue and would not intervene in any way. And now I am told that Jerry Michell, who had conducted many of the meetings with Druces & Attlee, was now volunteering to be the chief witness in their defence. I viewed this as a staggering violation of my citizen's rights. Where was the level playing field? The Millennium Commission, through the Secretary of state, through its Chief Executive Officer, and through lower ranking officials, had refused to communicate with me, with my lawyers, or with my Member of Parliament on his constituent's behalf. Yet now they were quite happy to be talking to the Defendants Druces & Attlee and assisting them in the Courts.

Duncan and Larry had closely examined Jerry Michell's Witness Statement which referred to a number of documents and understood that the production of these documents was being blocked by the Treasury Solicitor. Be that the case, Jerry Michell was volunteering to appear and could then make allegations which could not be judicially challenged under cross examination. And to cap it all you and I were paying his wages, the public purse was shelling out for Jerry Michell's time in preparing for and in assisting the Defence of Druces & Attlee. I had long ago come to the inescapable conclusion that the Millennium Commission Executive were up to their armpits in complicity, but the only view I could now take was that here there was downright collusion. Why? Could it be that Mr Cock Up was firmly at home and Druces & Attlee and Jerry Michell needed the kind regard and protection of each other?

Larry drafted a stinging letter to the Secretary of State, as Chairman of the Millennium Commission wanting to know in what capacity one of her employees was giving evidence for the Defence. Could she please confirm to my lawyers the position of the Millennium Commission and its employee in relation to this litigation, and whether it intended to take a stand to enable justice to be done between the parties, and how it reconciled that duty with its present stance.

A letter was also sent to Tessa Jowell by Paul Tyler MP, again outlining delight that the continuing triumphant success of Eden ' ... *is a monument to the imaginative and enterprising skills of those involved in its inception.'* He brought to the Secretary of State's attention that in 2001 she had made it absolutely clear that the Commission could not be involved 'in any way' in the legal disputes and would have 'no wish to intervene'. She would surely share his amazement and dismay that her member of staff, Jerry Michell, had seen fit to volunteer evidence in support of Druces & Attlee having refused to provide any assistance to me.

> *"In view of your personal assurance to me, I find it all the more baffling that an Officer of the Commission should intervene in this way, and should give rise to clear 'inequality of arms' between the parties to this case. Since my constituent is acting as an individual and Messrs Druces & Attlee are funded by insurers, this is all the more deplorable. I am advised there may be a Human Rights issue as well."*

A reply was received by Larry on 19th August from an Ian Brack, Director of Policy at the Millennium Commission (we had never heard of him) emphatically refuting the charge the Commission had aligned with Druces & Attlee against me, repeating the Commission agrees the case was not its concern; however Mr Michell has provided a statement in his capacity as Director of Commercial at the Millennium Commission to ensure the Commission's policies and involvement are clear to all parties.

His evidence would serve to confirm how unclear the Commission's policies and involvement were to be, that Tessa Jowell was the fifth Secretary of State in quick succession to Chair the Millennium Commission, with each political appointment bringing with it policy tweaks and change of emphasis to accommodate the political whim of the moment.

The owner of the voice of caution from the past and his client were as one, '*the Al Fayeds of this world can take on Her Majesty's Government through the Royal Courts of Justice, but not you Jonathan, a man of modest means from a small town in Cornwall*'. It was becoming crystal clear that any further strenuous efforts on my behalf to bring a tin opener anywhere in the vicinity of the Secretary of State and this Millennium Commission can of worms would be perilous indeed.

Even the ever reassuring Duncan could not conceal his unhappiness on my behalf. Her Majesty's Government, the Secretary of State and the top brass at the Millennium Commission were closing ranks around Jerry Michell. It was becoming clear that Millennium Commission policy had not been properly put in place at that time and history was being rewritten discretely because no public body would admit such absence of defined policy.

I was firmly returned to my old habitat of murky Shit Creek, but with a new realisation, based on my Millennium Commission experiences, that Shit Creek was a tributary flowing into Banana Republic Britain.

In mid September Legal Week ran a front page regulation story confirming the Law Society was to bring forward its controversial conflicts rules review as 'Chancery Lane moves to head off criticism that the Law Society is failing to police City law firms'. The flow of the tide was now firmly with me and this added to the interest from the legal profession in the outcome of my action. From squirreled away papers we had contemporaneous evidence that ran entirely contrary to what was said at some points in the Witness Statements that had been served by Druces & Attlee.

The preparations of my own Witness Statement had filled the hours, days and weeks between the New Year and Easter 2003 side by side with the positive punctuations of my new Project. At this time of year Cornwall powerfully displays and parades her weather induced moods in this her most unhurried season. Days of bleak blasts from the Atlantic, cumulus nimbus moments suggesting imminent hell and damnation as if heralding Judgment Day on humanity; one day all windswept desolation, the next all calm, the sun so low in the sky, almost at eye level, penetrating and accentuating the shadows of solitary dog walkers leaving imprints in virgin sand to be erased by the next incoming tide. A good season indeed to be surrounded with endless volumes of files, news cuttings, project documentation and a feast of Eden memories – eight years and four months' worth of elation mixed with despair so consuming, holes in the hands scars - all in need of interrogation, substantiation and articulation.

The process starts by telling the story of how it was, free of embellishment and elaboration and supported by contemporaneous notes and key letters and other documentation. This is then reviewed and discussed with your lawyers. You go away and on advice you incorporate key points that you have unwittingly left unsaid and which are legally essential to the narrative. Periodically this all comes together for what the lawyers refer to as a 'Con', that is 'Conference with Counsel', a regular milestone which, for me, mirrored our early Eden days when Tim and I would report progress to the Eden Trustees for review and next steps agreement.

My substantive Witness Statement was signed off during Easter week and comprised 179 pages with 660 paragraphs all rigorously validated. It was actually my fourth Witness Statement, sitting alongside those prepared for the Mr Justice Laddie and Mr Justice Burton hearings, and was my penultimate. As you get close to the steps of the Court further work is often needed to elucidate previous Statements and challenge the veracity of contesting Witness Statements prepared in support of the Defendants. What was important to me and to my legal team was that my substantive Witness Statement was word perfect, painstaking in its compilation, robust in its integrity, as sound a body of endeavour as was within my competence. I was to find that standing in the Witness box under forceful cross examination by the leading Silk for the Defendants is one of the loneliest places in the world with your only and closest companion being your Witness Statement signed off before God as the truth, the whole truth and nothing but the truth, my Atlantic armour.

A month before there had been a confidence boosting Conference with Counsel with John Slater QC confirming we now had a secure position independent of all defences. It was now accepted by the Millennium Commission and both sides that in 1996 there had to have been an act of buying out the intellectual property and that Druces & Attlee had interfered in a way that had rendered this impossible. By this time we also enjoyed the benefit of a first class Witness Statement prepared in my support by Ian Hay Davison, the first of the Eden Trustees to have resigned and the Trustee who knew more than most people about the intricacies that were at the core of this legal battle. Both John Slater QC and his junior Counsel Jane Davies purred that Ian was a ten out of ten witness and not only would he be entirely believed but also command great authority with the Court. They were absolutely right.

It was all going well, too well. During the second week of October 2003, only a few weeks before trial with our interminable wait to secure John Slater's admirable advocacy nearly over, an unwelcomed event occurred, so contrary that it left Victoria and I wondering whether, after all this time, the Gods were finally conspiring against us. I sensed there had been discussions within my legal team as to who was going to tell me, who was going to take this hospital pass and convey it onwards to the poor client. There was no disguising this bad news: however upbeat and positive you remain, being at law stalks your thoughts each day, somewhere, somehow, and we had endured a further year of this miserable circumstance for one reason only, in order to secure the services of John Slater QC. It fell to poor Duncan to tell me. John Slater's current case was over-running and he would now not be available for us for the trial. Our disbelief and anguish, the embarrassment and feet shuffling attached to broken promises from the legal team were all played out. Here we go again, slithering down yet another snake, off balance, hurt, fearfully facing new uncertainty. Yet again it was a case of 'we are where we are'.

Duncan tried to be chirpy, *'It's not ideal, but our case is well prepared and it's in good order to be handed over'*. Both Duncan and Larry had met with Michael Kent QC whose style they ascertained was different, but helpful. Where John Slater relied on his junior Counsel Jane Davies to feed him, Michael Kent liked nothing better than to get his hands dirty with contemporaneous documents. It was this particular skill and ability which fostered greater confidence that we would prevail. But I could not disguise my dismay and nor did I. For me it was all to do with history and confidence and how could we replace two and a half years of confidence when John Slater had been so brilliant before Mr Justice Burton? It was the equivalent of an eminent surgeon informing you on the day before you are to undergo open heart surgery that actually, contrary to all your preparations and understandings, he is not in fact carrying out your surgery himself.

Certainly Larry was angry and upset at what had happened. Crown Office Chambers should have been able to manage this, but with only weeks to go it was now 'reading in time' and we had no option but to accept. My meeting with Larry and Duncan was foreshortened as the Chairman of their law firm McDermott Will & Emery was over from America and had called a meeting. Our own meeting concluded in sombre mood and Larry and Duncan departed knowing they had an unhappy client on their hands. A counsel 'Con' had been fixed for 15th October when I was to be introduced to Michael Kent QC who would be dropping everything to read in and take ownership of our survival.

Having slept on it my first job was to ring up Duncan to make our peace. I found that our meeting had left him with equal unease and upset. Duncan is no ordinary hardnosed City of London lawyer used to dealing with hard boiled commercial clients. He was acutely tuned to the fact that our lives

Eden's biomes shimmering in spring sunshine 2014.   (Bob Willingham)

completely depended on these moments and we knew in this we had all his professional skills, his personal friendship and his unswerving commitment. For Duncan, if for no other reason, I was determined to arrive at the Counsel Conference having conducted my own traffic control and without a negative or unnecessary thought in my head.

The Conference opened with John Slater QC who only stayed for a few minutes, profusely apologising that he had been caught by the over-run of his current case. Michael Kent QC, upright and urbane, exuded competence and secured my confidence from the first. From limited acquaintance with the papers he had already come to some over-view whilst reading in. Our biggest issue would be with the Witness Statement of Jerry Michell from the Millennium Commission whose evidence Duncan countered as believing it to be spun out of sight and all retrospective, the draft of which had been put together by Druces & Attlee themselves. But we had been promised new eyes to our case via Michael Kent QC as part of the John Slater QC departure deal and so I requested these new eyes review the whole Millennium Commission position. Why had the Millennium Commission refused my legal team any information and then aligned with Druces & Attlee? Why had the Millennium Commission forensic audit never yet seen the light of day? And how could Jerry Michell suddenly pop up volunteering a Witness Statement for the Defence? It simply didn't smell right, and if I understood Michael Kent QC correctly Jerry Michell, paid for by you and me, was now the final greatest threat to my family's future on evidence that could not be properly cross examined by direction of the Treasury Solicitor.

The day before our meeting the Royal Society of Arts (RSA), to which I had been elected to Fellowship in 1985, announced that Tim Smit was to be presented with the RSA's premier award, The Albert Medal, at a ceremony the following month to be held at Buckingham Palace when he would also be invested with his CBE. This honour was in recognising him as 'Creator' rather than Co Founder of the Eden Project and put him alongside previous recipients such as Michael Faraday and Marie Curie. In seeking more overview from our new pair of eyes we reviewed these headline-grabbing accolades, together looking at latest publications and information emerging from Destination Eden, the residency of Tim's voracious, unsleeping media machine.

With seven weeks to go to entering the Royal Courts of Justice, Eden issued its Friends publication with a lengthy review of a glossy new book, The Architecture of Eden which had been written by Hugh Pearman architecture critic and Andrew Whalley from Grimshaw's in which I had been demoted from co-founder to Tim's 'architect-advisor.' It was to Andrew Whalley that eight and a half years earlier I had sent my fax in April 1995, coining the phrase 'Eden the Eighth Wonder of the World', on the day of Grimshaw's appointment imploring him to keep the fax as a special memento for his grandchildren in time to come. The Eden website had now completely erased any mention of me and ran a large image of Tim Smit with attached text covering his spun version of the history of Eden.

I was greatly concerned that leading Silk against me could merely wave this publication before the Court and direct the Court to Eden's website in repudiation of my substantial Witness Statement. This was immediate and current evidence from Eden, however inaccurate and unfair, to influence the Court against me and ran entirely contrary to the facts and in fundamental breach of the legal agreement that attached to my settlement with Eden Project Limited and the Eden Trust.

What did Michael Kent QC think? After all, during our unsuccessful Mediation Reynolds Porter Chamberlain had referenced the latest Times press comment as part of their evidential base against me. First reaction from Michael was how Tim's receipt of the Albert Medal, the Architecture of Eden book and the official Eden website were excellent evidence demonstrating how I was being unfairly treated. Michael, upon reviewing my Eden settlement legal agreement with Jane Davies, advised me to write to Sir Ronnie Hampel as Chairman of the Eden Trust in protest. Michael and Jane Davies were in unison: these were good examples of the complete failure of the Eden Trustees and the Eden Company to honour their legal obligations enshrined in the document.

Fortuitously the settlement agreement had a dispute provision which provided that two wise men would review any alleged breaches and hopefully reach accord. For Eden this would be Ken Hill, Chairman of Eden Project Limited and for my side Tim Jones, Chairman of the Devon and Cornwall Business

Council. The two wise men provision was invoked and my protest that the progressive rewriting of Eden's history had been unfair, untrue and misleading was immediately upheld. A Public Statement was drafted in the names of Sir Ronnie Hampel as Chairman of the Eden Trust, and Ken Hill as Chairman by way of apology to me and at Eden's expense was published in The Times and The Western Morning News which prompted wider media attention and was there for all to see, not least the High Court if, in the event media coverage was to be dragged through the hallowed portals.

PUBLIC STATEMENT
THE EDEN PROJECT
JONATHAN BALL OF BUDE, CORNWALL

It has been brought to our attention that the role of Jonathan Ball as co-founder of The Eden Project has not been properly acknowledged in recent Eden Project publications and other media coverage. We would like to set the record straight.

In particular The Eden Project Trustees and Directors of Eden Project Ltd wish to endorse the fact that Jonathan Ball and Tim Smit are the joint co-founders of The Eden Project. It was their original exchange of ideas that forged the Eden vision.

Tim Smit's pioneering business venture with John Nelson at the Lost Gardens of Heligan in the early 1990s provided the background to Tim's subsequent idea to create a series of giant conservatories to tell the story of how the Great Plant Hunters changed the shape of the world.

Cornish architect Jonathan Ball's ambition was twofold: to deliver defining world class architecture which would make manifest Tim's idea of giant greenhouses and with which Cornwall would celebrate the Millennium, but also to extend the remit of the project to showcase the humanitarian issues of our age and the global challenges facing mankind in the 21st century.

The combination of Tim Smit's exceptional communication skills and Heligan experience, and Jonathan Ball's creativity, skills and professional contacts in the world of architecture, site assembly and politics was the catalyst that turned the dream into reality.

Between 1994-1997 the two co-founders shared equally the entrepreneurial risk in developing the concept, from the formation of The Eden Trust and Eden Project Ltd, to establishing the Business Plan that secured the Millennium Commission's landmark project funding, assembling the professional design and horticultural teams, securing the necessary public support and consents and masterminding all the collaborative arrangements necessary for the Eden vision to be realised.

Sir Ronnie Hampel, Chairman, The Eden Trust
Ken Hill, Chairman, Eden Project Ltd   (Nov 2003
                              Ref: LND99 285343-1.058840.0012)

Meanwhile, we kept our relationships with Paul Tyler in good repair and both Duncan and I attended a meeting with Paul at Portcullis House in his delightfully located office directly opposite and looking up at Big Ben. Paul's overview was, as ever, thoughtful and supportive. We should not expect formal support from the former Secretary of State. Chris Smith did not hold warm feelings about his removal from Office, he will have a hazy memory and in any event will want to duck: nonetheless Paul would arrange a meeting with him.

Jerry Michell's Witness Statement was volunteered in support of Druces & Attlee. The issue for Duncan and Larry was about Jerry Michell's evidence being subsequent to the time, being ex post facto, which made it imperative that we see the papers supporting his evidence, papers which were being denied by the Treasury Solicitor. Jerry Michell would be there defending his position of not being prepared to give us the papers. An issue for us would be to see their retention on an item upon which the Millennium Commission have responsibility, not whether or not this was fair or unfair to me. We would want to keep well clear of challenging the Secretary of State's veracity in the High Court.

Other points of legal detail were being swept up. Duncan had sent off a letter to Reynolds Porter Chamberlain requiring them to explain, on the record, why key notebook pages belonging to the relevant partner of Druces & Attlee had been removed. These pages covered attendance notes of early meetings with Tim and I at Druces & Attlee and Duncan required the denuded notebook to be delivered up for forensic examination.

Regular chats with my erstwhile neighbour and legal chum, Tony, delivered perceptive insights in response to my latest Shit Creek in the Banana Republic tales, observing that I was caught up in a spider's web of Tim's making. As he reflected, the problem I had was that the average attention span of an intelligent person is four and a half minutes. Tim Smit is a world class orator and is probably one of the world's leading authorities on how you fix the attention span of an average person to get them on your side for your own ends.

I was warned by Michael Kent QC that I had a talented and combative leading Silk against me in Bernard Livesey QC who would be out to provoke and exasperate me and had nothing to lose by forthright attack. Always listen carefully to the question, confine yourself to short answers (those near and dear to me would immediately be alerted to the fact that he was setting the bar very high on this point alone); be clear in your mind as to what you were doing from 1997 onwards as the Judge will probably ask you: and then, of course, particularly the time from 2001 after your removal by the Trustees as an Eden Director. I commented that I had been running two actions in the Royal Courts of Justice in London – quite a full time occupation really for an

Eden 2014   *(Bob Willingham)*

ordinary citizen from Bude in Cornwall.

Given that Cornwall is believed to be the lowest prosperity county within the United Kingdom, I received one or two observations of caution from chums concerning my published claim of £5.5 million. Was this an appropriate and commensurate quantum, they asked, bearing in mind the wholehearted support I was receiving in Cornwall which I should not put in peril in any way. I replied that this figure was not of my making. Without the Conditional Fee Arrangement I had secured whereby the lawyers take the risk but then have a share of any successful award from the Courts, I would not be able to pursue justice. With the Conditional Fee Arrangement came the reality that my legal team would establish the quantum of our claim and had, quite reasonably, their own interests running in what that sum should be.

Other chums were rallying in kind support each with their own helpful thoughts: don't let your natural optimism and good humour desert you now and particularly when you are under cross examination. You are the ordinary bloke doing your best; the reason you are there is your preparedness to go through all this anguish in your greater desire to see justice and fair play, not just for you, but for all private individuals. You have every confidence in justice and you will not walk away from what Immanuel Kant, the 18th century Prussian philosopher, described as the categorical imperative, a duty to tell the truth, dignity and respect being the right of all individuals. All collusion and untruthful conduct contravenes the categorical imperative. You will not be comfortable under cross examination, but you are there to be heard against all the wrongs that have taken place. Be of good cheer and have your self confidence running high on your own ability to repel constant attacks from one of the best leading Silks in the land whose reputation and good standing has not been built on failing his own client. The last word of advice here came via a call from Rod Hackney. *'Remember, Jonathan, honesty always wins ... so long as you live long enough'*.

Chapter 17

The Best Possible Fudge

And so the day arrived. The skeleton arguments were there and we had spent a happy family weekend in Cornwall. Monday dawned frosty and bright and we departed on the lunchtime train for London and Room One at the Athenaeum where, by dispensation of the Club Secretary we were installed as weekly boarders for the duration of the trial. Just inside the door to Room One was a period mahogany circular table with lamp and a comfortable desk chair. But what mattered most of all was the portrait that hung to the left of the table. It was an image from perhaps the first decades of the 19th century. It was someone I recognised and I looked into his eyes with a delighted knowing. Yes, it was him, the man from Penzance, Fellow and later President of the Royal Society, inventor of the miners' safety lamp and the distinguished founder Chairman of the Athenaeum, none other than my fellow Cornishman, Sir Humphry Davy. I could not have chosen anyone more inspirational to gaze down on me each evening as I prepared for the following day.

We soon settled into a routine and positively set about attempting to create as much comfort and convenience as we could to compensate the demands of each day. The walk across Trafalgar Square to Charing Cross, turning left along the Strand past Somerset House and just beyond the Australian High Commission and St Clement Danes Church fronted by the statue of 'Bomber' Harris, finds you on the steps of the Royal Courts of Justice in about 23 minutes. The weather throughout our London sojourn remained constant and kind. Not once did we need to take a taxi or bus and this morning constitutional set the day, absent the fact that our lungs were more accustomed to air that had travelled three thousand miles to be with us from across the Atlantic Ocean. This walk was soon to enter family folklore, sitting alongside Dad's wartime allotment hedge which saved his life.

We opened in Court 25 of the Royal Courts of Justice on Wednesday 26th November 2003 before Justice Sir Robert Nelson. This had been after two further days of reading in. In his opening remarks the Judge complimented 'the now famously successful Eden Project'

In no time at all it was Day 2, and on this Thursday afternoon at 14.20 I entered the witness box as Plaintiff to commence giving my evidence. Despite the meticulous groundwork, the endless waiting and wondering and all thorough personal focus of mind and emotions, nothing quite prepares you for this moment. The witness box is barely a square metre in plan area and intimidatingly they constructed around me temporary heavy cardboard bookshelves upon which were stacked, I think, 28 volumes of papers which the Court refers to as 'bundles', referenced alphabetically. You remain standing for delivery of your evidence with no more benefit than a timber lectern, just about wide enough to take an opened lever arch file. It was a real deep breaths, and Onward Christian Soldiers moment and as I took the Bible in my hand to swear my oath I purposely fixed eye contact with Sir Robert Nelson unwavering throughout delivery of my oath pledging the truth, the whole truth and nothing but the truth and in emphasising the word 'nothing' my head made an involuntary nod forwards. I could not swear that this unscripted action received a reciprocal movement from the Judge, but I sensed it did. He was watching me as intently as I was him.

The sense of anticipation exerted a strong hold on the atmosphere in Court 25. My thoughts were busied with how this, the moment, had finally arrived. Traditionally the Celts resent authority, but here was the need for utmost deference to procedures and processes. The law of the land shapes and binds us all.

Being of good cheer in answering truthfully about unhappy Eden days and the key moments of trickery and treachery that had led me, finally, to the cruel isolation of the witness box would indeed be a challenge. I was in no doubt from my unsatisfactory mediation experience that I could expect an all out attack launched upon me. The strongest will, the most conscientious preparation, and notwithstanding the most sincere commitment to integrity, anxiety was the prevailing sentiment. I had to be sure not to let this anxiety detach me from my own equanimity.

Deep down we all know our own personal strengths and weaknesses. My mind, after seven years training at the AA, is more of a butterfly flitting from idea to idea. It is more creative than it is disciplined. It does not shake hands warmly with the prospect of being surrounded by some 10,000 documents spanning a decade and being challenged to account at a moment's notice about context, intention and relevance of any and every one of them.

The tricks of the trade of Bernard Livesey QC's calling are many and complex. There are always other agendas running. By any measurement Eden was high profile. Queen's Counsels stand, Judges sit and I was all too aware, beyond the substantive issues, there were people standing with ambitions and expectations to be one day sitting. Bernard Livesey QC was already a Deputy

The elegance of the design is clearly seen when looking upwards inside the biomes.

(Bob Willingham)

High Court Judge, but today, standing, his upright mind was nimble, sure footed and would quickly switch tack and timeline in attempts to wrong foot me.

The opening exchanges are the stuff of legends: quite simply you do not get called to the Bar unless you are good, very good and I was soon rocking against this intellectual power house devoid of any emotion which had been totally squeezed out by mental capacity. I had entered the witness box resolved not to yield to any overbearance to the degree that would prevent or reduce my proper and truthful resistance to his arguments in defence of Druces & Attlee's conduct. Bernard Livesey QC had an entirely different relationship than mine to the intellectual muse Calliope. By the end of the first afternoon I had achieved no more than survival.

It was a long 23 minute walk back to the Club with only the caring, loving reassurance of Victoria as to how I had fared. What is often not understood is that when you take the witness stand you are in Purdah for the duration of your evidence; you are entirely isolated from your legal team, unable to seek their reassurance, unable to question the day's proceedings, to come to any understanding as to why so much focus was given to a particular point, to your mind minor, but clearly of considerable legal magnitude. Those comforting legal minds that have held your hand and been at your shoulder are suddenly not available to you. You have no responding script, no brief to remedy past blips, no teleprompt, no winks and nods; you are on your feet and on your own.

I found myself preparing for the following day under the benign countenance of Sir Humphry Davy, but in truth nothing was going in. We have all experienced the act of reading a piece of paper in an attempt to absorb information and, a few moments later find that any recall of that information has evaporated. I had survived today, how was I going to survive tomorrow?

During the 23 minute walk I concentrated my mind on the many positives in my life. So many people had and were delivering practical and emotional support, on both sides of the River Tamar. Justice is the repair of wrongs that have been done to others and even those who only knew me slightly, or not at all, spoke of the need for fair play and justice for me.

Installed in the witness box at first I was taken aback by the abruptness of the process. There are no new day introductory remarks, there are no reminders of the story so far and the anticipated moment for me to collect my thoughts was not there. I ploughed through a troubled morning in my attempts to trade blow for blow competing inadequately on quick wittedness. Successful QCs soon secure the high ground; they know the question that is coming next and their colour coded tabs on their document files allow them to hop with ease from point to point with Junior Counsel behind them with great swathes of documents laid out ready to be placed one at a time into the hand of the advocate who in turn occasionally thrusts it menacingly in the air as part of the theatre that is the Royal Courts of Justice.

I found my mind inescapably wandering to the game of cricket, madness I know, but that's the way it was. This was an Ashes Test Match; I had to weather the pace attack, to recognise when the spinner came on, to attempt to thump a no ball or a wide to the boundary and to be ever alert to the googly. By mid morning I had fortified myself with a growing awareness that I was digging in, the bails had not been dislodged, the stumps stood firm and true and what I needed was a test match temperament to put dropped catches and near misses to the back of my mind. I might not be scoring a lot of runs, but I was there to defend my wicket and there I would remain.

The afternoon session was both draining and bruising with the odd bodyline ball really hurting but on a Friday stumps are drawn early. I was still in, but in my mind, only just. A brutal weekend followed. The Friday evening train back to Cornwall, I slept all day Saturday and after a Sunday morning walk on the cliffs followed by lunch it was the afternoon train back to London to face more of the same. I was hurting, but the thought occurred to me that the bowling I faced was now more directed at the man, than at the wicket. I had to bring the Judge firmly back to the wicket; somehow I had to wrest the gains from Bernard Livesey and secure, in my own mind and hopefully that of the Judge, that it was Druces & Attlee's conduct that was on trial. What did I need to do? One thing was certain, I had to start with the discipline of not thinking about cricket.

The morning walk was crisp and cold with the air of Christmas not far away. As we passed in front of the National Gallery workmen were erecting an enormous Christmas tree, the annual gift from the people of Norway. The day had not dawned in despondency. And then the most extraordinary thing happened. Whilst we were walking hand in hand across the pedestrian area in front of the National Gallery into my mind and onto my forehead came the picture of a tortoise. How curious. We went past St-Martin-in-the-Fields, turned left at Charing Cross. The tortoise would not go away and suddenly a balloon appeared out of its mouth with the words, '*When did you last see a tortoise trip up?*' I smiled to myself. I will never know whence this apparition came, but if there was somebody, somewhere looking after me, it was from them.

The weekend had given me time to analyse my adversarial exchanges with Bernard Livesey. In answering questions of events up to 10 years previous you need first to recall accurately the sequence of events and the chronology, the actions that were taken and then be prepared to debate the consequences of those actions. Destabilisation comes from being challenged to answer a question suddenly injected out of context to which is attached an assertion that gives an entirely different interpretation as to what actually happened at the time. Bernard Livesey was not present at the time these events took place, I was, but these moments take time to collate your thoughts and truthful reply, time which is purposely denied you by the advocate. By being so time pressured the advocate plies his trade.

I entered the witness box on Monday morning with a new vigour, and a plan. I needed, courteously somehow to disrupt Bernard Livesey's flow and tempo. It was straight into the first question. *'Can I ask you Mr Ball to turn to Bundle G, document 348'.* As on the previous two days I hardly had enough time to find the bundle, open it up, find the page before a detailed question rained down on me. Here goes. *'I think, Mr Livesey'*, I said, *'I deal with this in my Witness Statement – could you please refer me to the relevant paragraph for me to refresh my memory as to context.'* I ignored his protests and repeated my request which had his Junior Counsel Hugh Evans in a tizzy thumbing through my 180 page and 660 paragraph Statement. Having been thus informed I then referred to my own Witness Statement, looked at the paragraph before and following to satisfy myself as to context, briefly scanned the document to which I had been referred and then looked up, thanked Mr Livesey and asked if he wouldn't mind repeating the question. If looks could kill, I was dead, but they can't and I wasn't. Thus the rhythm and pace of the day changed. This was no mischief, no attempt to pervert, this was nothing on my part beyond the need to be in my own time so ensuring I would discharge my absolute obligation for the truth and the whole truth.

After a while, this brought forth vehement protest from Bernard Livesey to Sir Robert Nelson whose comments were kindly, but enquiring to me and I replied that the majority of the events under this judicial review process had taken place eight or nine years previously and I stood before him to answer truthfully to the best of my ability. This was not a memory test.

I maintained as much eye contact as possible with the Judge and sensed a growing awareness from him as to how much all this meant to me as an individual, how long the journey to this witness box had been and how, indeed, in society's eyes the legal profession was also on trial. I won the moment and with it a memorable comment in the Judgment,

> *" ... that at times Mr Ball clung to his Witness Statement as if it were a life raft ... I am however entirely satisfied he was seeking to tell me the truth ... his memory for events some of which were nine years ago*

was less than perfect … his cautiousness and reliance on his witness statement was not due to any desire to obstruct but a desire to give accurate answers …"

And so having entered the witness box the previous Thursday at 14.20, at ten minutes to four the following Thursday we came to what appeared to be an innocuous exchange. I had turned to the Judge to give my reply and then turning back to face Bernard Livesey I found he had sat down. It was over.

Whilst remaining in purdah I had made way during the first part of the week for two other witnesses called in my support. Firstly Ian Hay Davison, whose commanding aura was to be commented upon in the Judgment (RCJ. No.03/TLQ/0035 paras.139 &240), impressively strengthened the Plaintiff case in systematically nailing Druces & Attlee's scope of retainer, hammering home the causational link between their defective conduct and my loss, particularly leaving the Judge in absolutely no doubt that the Eden Trustees wished at all times to negotiate a fair, even generous settlement with the Co Founders (Ian was the only witness who had served as an Eden Trustee to be called during the trial). When it came to quantum he thumped home the most persuasive arguments in support of what reward should have been properly due to me. It became clear Bernard Livesey's pursuit of this cross examination would unlikely be serving his clients' best interests.

The cross examination by Bernard Livesey of Tim Jones, Chairman of the Devon & Cornwall Business Council was similarly unprofitable for him. At the relevant time, Tim Jones had no equal in breadth of knowledge, understanding, experience and authority in the matter of private sector commercial activity in Devon and Cornwall and in particular its interface with the various grant regimes, notably the European Regional Development Fund (ERDF). His intimate knowledge had been brought to bear in securing Eden's multi million pound European funding assistance, a key component of the match funding matrix that liberated the Millennium Commission award. He not only knew every inch of the European funding landscape, but as a Chartered Surveyor of significant standing in the South West his understanding of how complex projects were brought to fruition far exceeded the knowledge that any other witness would bring to the trial.

He had certainly given me incomparably better advice than Druces & Attlee as to how I protected my co-founder position from Day One in a way that was consistent with commercial practice including the concept of an equity stake. This was also defining evidence totally refuting Evelyn Thurlby's arguments to me in my darkest days, when she was trying to nail the lid down on my Eden future, that the ERDF would not permit the co founders to have any equity. On the contrary, Tim Jones said he would never have accepted the exclusion of equity on behalf of ERDF as its principal private sector representative at the time in this decision making process. In his Judgment

Justice Nelson made clear he found this evidence the more compelling. (RCJ. No.03/TLQ/0035 para.138)

And so the case for the Plaintiff drew to its close and it was with considerable relief that I settled down to focus my attention and critical eye on those witnesses who would be defending the way Druces & Attlee had conducted themselves throughout this troubled Project and indeed the degree to which they had contributed to Eden's troubles.

The opening of the case for the Defence found me reminding myself of the need for continuing vigilance, a thought which competed with a feeling of release from the unrelenting pressure that sits with the Plaintiff whilst his case is heard. As the Defence erected its guard, so I could lay down mine. My concentration could wander without penalty. Pity Victoria who surely by this time must have gone well beyond that proverbially sound saying that her head could only absorb that which her bottom could endure sitting in the public gallery on the unpadded benches that make no concession to comfort. Always more disciplined of mind than me, steadfastly by my side, through a period of our lives together that had been more for the worse than for the better and certainly more for the poorer than the richer, now displaying her fabulous skills at maintaining all semblance of normal family life. This commendable capacity was for all to see, maintaining her intent watch and guard of proceedings but also attending to the frantic preparations that always surround our family Christmases in Cornwall. This year there would be no specially designed Christmas card and we had not had the opportunity of falling back on the RNLI and buying our cards from Bude Lifeboat Station (we hadn't been anywhere near the place).

She had a plan. Our pattern was to spend our lunchtimes al fresco, reflecting on the morning having purchased Prêt à Manger snacks and fresh fruit and watching the ice skaters enjoying their lunch break in the courtyard of Somerset House, always returning to the Royal Courts of Justice with 10 minutes to spare. On this day whilst I returned to Court 25 she disappeared with the cheque book and I noticed her scribbling intently during the afternoon. I wondered what had been so important of the afternoon's proceedings – whatever it was it had certainly passed me by. To my delight I found she had been writing our family Christmas cards. This year would be a one off for the Ball family and yes, you've guessed, it was a handsome image of the Royal Courts of Justice. To each Christmas greetings Victoria had added, 'please note, change of address!'

First to take the witness stand was the lead Druces & Attlee Partner, Toby Stroh and despite all my heartache, all the concentration of effort in his contribution to the plotting of my downfall, I had a feeling of compassion for a man who had brought upon himself such overwhelming circumstances that rendered him pitiable. These circumstances had not left him as capable, as

Jonathan and Victoria on the steps of the Royal Courts of Justice. The third and final hearing lasted from Monday 20th November 2003 to Thursday 18th December 2003, prompting the Ball family Christmas card for that year being an image of the Royal Courts of Justice and to each greeting Victoria added, "Please note change of address!"
(Western Morning News)

he ought to have done, of extracting himself from his parlous professional predicament. What part, if any, my erstwhile partner Tim Smit had played in bringing this tragic fall from grace for Toby Stroh will likely never be known. Indeed Tim Smit was subpoenaed to appear on behalf of the Defence at trial and was never called. It can only be concluded that the Defendant's legal team deemed the risk of some horrendous disclosure under cross examination was far too great. The Judge was to comment more than once that Tim had not been called by the Defence to the witness box, this notwithstanding that Tim Smit's name appears in the Judgment 328 times.

My QC Michael Kent having established that Druces & Attlee owed me a retainer duty as their client then skilfully brought Toby's cross examination and all in the Court room to a crescendo by quoting from the letter of March 1998 written by Toby to the Eden Trustees confirming,

"I have never acted for Jonathan Ball in his personal capacity, or at all either in connection with the Eden Project or any other."

A stunned silence fell upon the Court room. It was a pace attack delivery that had removed the middle stump and sent the bails sailing high into the air. I attempted to look into Toby's eyes which were averting every gaze. In the long silence he looked at the ceiling, he looked at the distant Court room wall, he looked to his feet but not into any of the eyes all focused upon him. The hush was broken by the Judge in the most solemn tones, *'Are you able to explain this to me?'* Toby replied, *'Those words are a mistake and they should not be there ...'* The Judge agreed; his expressive displeasure palpable.

The day had been witness to the most excruciating moments for Toby, surely ranking amongst the worst days of his life. From this exposure the pall of professional shame, on his face was written whole chapters of torment. At the conclusion of the session I left the Court Room in company with Ronnie Murning with me expressing some sympathy for Toby Stroh. *'Hang on,'* said Ronnie, with all his Glaswegian forcefulness *'Never forget, he and his firm Druces & Attlee would have had you and your family fall off the end of the world'*.

Both Toby and his Druces & Attlee Partner Richard Monkcom were to be subjected to the most penetrating examination that laid bare contemptible professional conduct towards me.

Whilst the professional misdemeanours paraded were of serious issue, moments of levity made a welcome appearance for all and did not diminish the gravity of the professional misconduct. We were treated to key moments in Eden's evolution with communications that both sides would refer to as 'the fog is clearing' and even more engagingly 'the best possible fudge'. On the important second application to the Millennium Commission Toby Stroh had advised it was impossible for the project structure to be set out in any sort of detail in our application and what we were therefore looking for was 'the best possible fudge' to satisfy the Millennium Commission. Any professional at some time or another has committed to paper firm professional advice capable of returning to haunt them. In this case I would find my very future hanging on these words, my interpretation having been that my intellectual property was not in any way exposed or threatened by this advice, but these words allowed an entirely different construction and meaning to be placed upon them by others.

When it was all over and we had returned to Cornwall one of Victoria's first actions was to empty the local delicatessen of its shelf full of this well known local confectionery and we sent a bag, prominently labelled The Best Possible Fudge (Cornish) to each member of our legal team.

Chapter   18

The Reason Why

Much misery was to come the way of both Toby Stroh and Richard Monkcom before they were released with their own reputations and that of their firm severely tarnished. The Judge reserved the most harsh criticism for the fact that Druces & Attlee failed properly to protect the co-founder's rights, jumping ship to acting for the Trustees and then in turn advising the Trustees that the rights that we, the co-founders, were asking for were past consideration. The facts confirmed my bargaining position had dramatically worsened in consequence of my rights not being properly reserved before the Trust was created. Druces & Attlee's failure to give me proper advice as a co-founder and their advice to the Eden Trustees that our consequent legal position was such that the Eden Trustees were in difficulty in the ways they wished to reward us, brought forth the most stinging rebuke from the Judge. There were the Trustees, remaining anxious properly to reward us, being told by Druces & Attlee, now their legal advisers, they were unable to do so. Meanwhile, Druces & Attlee's negligent advice to me had first placed me in my dire circumstances. The Judge rolled up the condemnation of this conduct describing it as 'particularly unmeritorious'. Ouch! (RCJ 17.06.2004. No. 03/TLQ/0035 paragraph 223.)

As to the evidence placed before Mr Justice Nelson in respect of the Millennium Commission, issues many and complex were paraded not only by Jerry Michell, but additionally by Steven Boxall an Assistant Programme Manager within the Millennium Commission who also prepared a Witness Statement for the Defendants. Their evidence was countered by my witness Eric Sorensen who had been Chief Executive and their boss at the Millennium Commission from March 1997 to March 1998 and I was grateful indeed for the measure of balance he was able to bring to their unsubstantiated assertions. Much argument raged about what would or would not have been acceptable to the Millennium Commission, and what evidence for the Defendants was being advanced as being after the event, ex post facto in construction. From our side how it was indisputable the Millennium Commission had approved the Eden Project on the basis of our submission of January 1997 incorporating the provision of Tim Smit and myself owning a company in which all intellectual property rights were vested, which in turn were to be licensed to the Eden Trust on terms to be agreed. Steven Boxall was now saying if the Millennium Commission had seen any proposal such as this they would have rejected it.

This is not what I had understood from swapping my experiences some time before with my equivalent co-creator of the much publicised Earth Centre at Doncaster, one of the first to receive Millennium Flagship project status. Sadly, the Earth Centre had gone pear shaped with a not dissimilar tale to tell as that of the Cardiff Bay Opera House fiasco when it came to Millennium Commission conduct. Also called Jonathan he had been, in his words, '*beaten up by the Millennium Commission*', and removed as the Earth Centre's Chief Officer as a condition of the Millennium Commission continuing their grant, but this Jonathan had secured recognition of his intellectual property by placing it in the head company in exchange for a non controlling, but substantial, equity stake.

The evidence for the Defence now being presented by representatives of the Millennium Commission was, in my view, a disgrace. Here were public officials holding power over my circumstances who were implicated in the decision to withhold the forensic audit from me, from my MP and from the High Court, now contradicting all previous protestations of impartiality and taking sides against me on behalf of Druces & Attlee.

In his final judgment Mr Justice Nelson concluded that at the material time the Millennium Commission did not have a clear and certain policy as to how to deal with co-founder rewards. However, when giving evidence, its representatives displayed the strongest imaginable reluctance to accept that either equity or intellectual property rights could be allowed to the co-founders. Under cross examination they suggested that they saw proper project expenditure as relating only to that which subsequently added value to the Project, but not to the original idea whence all value had flowed. *There we have our conflict,*' commented Mr Justice Nelson. Private individuals should not receive a return on public money, they said. Set against this, however, was the need for those individuals and private investors to have commercial terms in order to secure the private investment funding necessary in the first place. This was a prerequisite to any Millennium Commission award being given and its own purpose for existence fulfilled. There was a moment, effectively, where our ideas had been nationalised without proper consideration or to employ the word used at the time '*expropriated.*'

I continue to wonder what drove key personnel at the Millennium Commission to act in the way they did, in my opinion against the most fundamental principles of natural justice. The explanation probably lies within the wider political context of the Eden story, in that Eden was a conspicuous success among Millennium projects and that anything which

The author drinking in the essence of Eden, 2014.
(Bob Willingham)

threatened its pre-eminence had to be resisted or simply buried. Perhaps this imperative was best appreciated by the short-lived Secretaries of State who came and went in rapid succession and whose priority was to protect the Eden brand. Civil servants are constitutionally obliged to carry out the policy directions of their political masters and to advise the same and are not, therefore, autonomous, but in recent years this principle has been developed into a culture of unthinking compliance which seeps down through public bodies and into an expectation of those who deal with them. There, it seems to me, are the unfortunate conditions under which career civil servants now work and balanced fastidious neutrality is not an option; this could at least serve as instigation for the stance taken by the Millennium Commission and for the behaviour of intelligent and conscientious public servants whose probity should be one of the cornerstones of any democracy.

The reproachful conversations within my legal team against this volunteering of evidence against me were justified. The perceived interest of the Millennium Commission and ultimately Her Majesty's Government, appeared to sit above any justice for me. Having finally receiving such resounding vindication by way of Mr Justice Nelson's Judgment, it is perhaps ungracious of me to talk here of my own sense of injustice, but the Millennium Commission's evidence on behalf of the Defendants was inevitably given significant weight by the Judge to my considerable disadvantage, impacting as it did on the sum awarded in damages. Michael Kent's first overview had been clear. Such evidence regardless of its questionable veracity or the circumstances surrounding its presentation, and its ability to be properly cross examined, created for me the greatest risk of not securing a commensurate and equitable award. Furthermore, any significant reduction based on this evidence would increase the risk of my not beating the Defendant's payments into court, leaving my family and me to face the life threatening legal bill the Defendant's team would present in such circumstances. Believe me when I say it is hard to reconcile these things in your head when your family is faced with this magnitude of threats directly resulting from what was no more than a public spirited initiative. It's a fine line indeed between receiving the thanks of a grateful nation and having hell and damnation falling on your head.

Why would anyone go out on a limb and take huge risks for the glory of their nation having read my story was a theme taken up by Paul Tyler, now Lord Tyler of Linkinhorne in a conversation with me soon after Tim Smit was invested with his Honorary Knighthood during the 10th Anniversary celebrations marking Eden's success. Paul told me he was a historian before he was a politician and could not resist musing on what he considered an historical comparison with Sir Francis Drake. He narrowly avoided being hanged as a pirate after various unsuccessful and probably very devious unofficial raids on the Spaniards. His Monarch, Queen Elizabeth, was not amused. However, in 1580 when he returned in glory, laden with plunder the Queen decreed that all the records of his voyages should be kept secret 'on pain of death'. Her Majesty's half share in his cargo 'surpassed the rest of the Crown's income for that entire year' and early in 1581 she knighted him. But perhaps the last word here should go to Lord Crickhowell, former Secretary of State for Wales and Chairman of the Cardiff Bay Opera House Trust whose book 'Opera House Lottery' chronicled the cruel abandonment of Zaha Hadid's internationally acclaimed designs and his own unhappy experiences.

> *"The Millennium Commission's approach, as will be painfully familiar to many who have had responsibility in the public sector, seems to have been based on the old-fashioned Civil Service view that the avoidance of blame is even more important than the avoidance of risk. For an organisation also obsessed with the belief that any risks that did exist should be borne by others, this had a paralysing effect ... . Problems (were) not there to be solved but are put to the bottom of the pile in the hopes they will go away."*

After the Millennium Commission witnesses it was the turn of Evelyn Thurlby. Her Statement opened by saying she was currently Chief Operating Officer of the National Botanic Gardens of Wales, another Millennium flagship Project a position she had secured on her departure as Eden's Chief Executive Officer. By the time she found herself in the witness box this job also was no longer hers. In her Statement she stated,

> *"... apart from general PR 'glad handing' and networking, I was not aware of Jonathan Ball doing anything at all during those early stages. As I have said, I very seldom saw him and was not aware he had any practical input into the Project at all."*

Clearly it had slipped her mind that I had been struck off the circulation list of all project information and that, in response to my protest of being excluded from meetings she had replied '*I call the meetings, I decide who attends*'. It was as much my hard earned personal funds risked equally with Tim's that had directly resulted in her well paid Eden appointment.

Evelyn and I had been at loggerheads about my role and my rights from the very outset. There were highly contentious issues between us and my natural pursuit of these rights (which had already been lost to me by Druces & Attlee's negligence) was clearly not likely to win me new friends, commented Mr Justice Nelson.

In those days memories were conveniently short when it suited. In the Millennium Commission Agreement with the Eden Trust I had been enshrined along with Tim Smit and Sir Alcon Copisarow as having the status of key personnel who were to remain with the project. Under examination Evelyn confirmed,

> "*Jonathan requested the role of Corporate Affairs Director, and it was my opinion, and the Trustees agreed because they had to agree all appointments, that that was not an appropriate role for him at that time.*"

However, when asked '*what if my position had been protected*' she accepted my Executive position would have been secured or she and the Trustees would have needed to pay me out fully and allow me to get on with the rest of my life.

As I listened it suddenly became clear to me that something curious was happening. The tenor of Evelyn's evidence was parting company with the atmosphere engendered by her Witness Statement. As she stood there pondering the flotsam and jetsam of Druces & Attlee's ebb tide that surrounded her, the flood tide of final justice coming my way must have appeared as a tsunami.

Her cross examination and re-examination concluded, and she was just stepping down from the witness box, when Mr Justice Nelson interrupted saying he needed to detain her and requested she reinstate her position. The Judge put it to Evelyn Thurlby that her relationship with me had become '*very fraught*' due to my '*increasing anxiety and insistence over what might compendiously be called 'his birthright'* and suggested that her relationship with me and her view of me was such that, whatever merits I may or may not have had, they would not have seemed very apparent to Evelyn in February 1998. Mr Justice Nelson went on,

> "*... it is not a criticism of you, it is just a comment on a question to you, because it seems to arise from your [Witness] Statement that by February 1998, he [Ball] was not the sort of person who was going to be number one in the job application list.*"

It was abundantly clear the Judge had shared my curiosity about the difference between her Witness Statement and her evidence in Court. I don't think there was one person in the Court Room who was prepared for what was to come next: after a moment's silence she replied to the Judge,

" ... when I joined the Eden Project and started working quite a lot on it, which was the summer of 1997, I worked very closely with Tim Smit and I was told [by him] that, at that point, Jonathan was being manoeuvred out of the Project."

The thoughts and minds of everyone in the Court room snapped to attention. Certainly my gasp was audible and it wasn't the only one hanging in the silence which was finally broken by Mr Justice Nelson.

"No further questions thank you Ms Thurlby."

And so, in that single moment there it was finally, penetratingly all laid bare. Tim Smit's treachery and betrayal aided and abetted by her and others' subordinate complicity and Druces & Attlee's compliant assistance, with the Millennium Commission glaringly found wanting, was the explanation as to why we had all spent the last three weeks in Court room 25 in the Royal Courts of Justice.

And why was such compelling evidence elicited by the Judge at the end of the trial? Was it a moment of impulse or was it pre meditated? Was it finally Evelyn's time chosen for retribution against the man with the engaging smile, but the steely eyes who had so ruthlessly assumed her seat in the Wendy Hut at the Watering Lane nurseries? In terminating her own Eden journey, with it went her happiness and professional respect, casualties of collision with Tim's Eden chaos and, with it like others, her effective erasure from Eden's Hansard. How fickle of fate in the final moment to unite Evelyn and me in Tim's attempted airbrushing of Eden's history. Certainly this final evidence from the witness box seemed to confirm beyond all possible doubt the wisdom of the Defendants' legal team in not calling the subpoenaed Tim Smit into the witness box for incisive cross examination. Whatever else there was between the legally gagged Evelyn, Tim and the gatepost, for the purposes of the Royal Courts of Justice that's where it would remain.

But, to the shrewdest and best knowing of observers, were there deeper shades of reason hanging here in her reckoning? For me, Evelyn's timely revelation had delivered crystal chandelier clarity and illumination. She had willingly responded to destiny's cruel and mischievous hand beckoning her here to give her own witness to events on behalf of the Defence. Her own sense of duty beamed untarnished by the past folly, now glaringly apparent to all. Just as I had been too deaf to hear, so Evelyn had been too blind to see until it was too late, the crocodile's teeth had snapped her up showing neither mercy nor shame. Her own honour was surely well served in this, her testimony, given not as an excuse for her conduct, but as an explanation. In so doing she was sending her own signal that at least she had not abandoned the hapless, condemned Toby in the way others had perhaps betrayed them both.

On our last night in London, I sat down to write my thoughts beneath the portrait of Sir Humphry Davy. Perhaps one day I might be writing a book and an aide mémoire as to my feelings and those points uppermost in my mind would be helpful.

I first turned to my diary. It was nine years, two months, three weeks and two days since Tim Smit and I had shaken hands at Heligan on our 50/50 TIMCO ambition, sharing all risks in our campaign of equal misery. It was six years and two months since I appointed Field Fisher Waterhouse and assumed the legal costs burden of getting to this moment. It was three years to the month since the loss of the Jonathan Ball Practice, a Practice of 27 years standing together with loss of the disposal value of a prominent practice with the expectation, as with any professional in private practice, to it contributing a significant element to any pension. My professional years from the ages of 47 to 56, at the peak of my professional and financial capacity, had been lost to Eden.

It was six years and two months since, resulting from Druces & Attlee's negligence, I had been effectively sidelined from the Eden Project against my will. I had been left with nothing but an offer to pay back my expenses when cash flow permitted, together with an arbitrary payment for the time I had spent. From that time I had to fight tooth and nail in order to get back to the financial position I was in before I first started work on the project. Throughout my negotiations and subsequent litigation with the Eden Trust and Eden Project Limited they were being advised by the very solicitors Druces & Attlee who had been instructed to advise on the protection of my position in the first place.

On Thursday 18th December 2003 with the closing submissions heard, suddenly it was all over. Judgment was reserved and we would hear as soon as the Judge was able. All stand, the Judge departs and everyone in the body of the Court is left looking at each other. Both Queen's Counsels drop their professional countenance, the apparatus of this legal stage disappears, the drama already acted out. The relationship as professional colleagues, rather than foes, resumes; there is no residual hostility, that which was said in pursuit of their client's interest, has all been said. I purposely moved into conversation mode. Michael Kent looking at Bernard Livesey and then at me brought the RNLI into conversation suggesting that if Mr Livesey was a sailing man he should steer clear of the Atlantic coast of North Cornwall as if he were to be in trouble he doubted whether I would be launching the lifeboat on service to his rescue. 'Oh yes I would' I replied, and we all shared a parting smile.

We had to endure a pared down Christmas and New Year without the

Judgment being handed down, without knowing and, lurking in the back of my mind, the unthinkable prospect of having won all the battles only to lose the war by our Judgment Award not beating the Defendant's payment into court. As you approach a High Court trial, the Defence makes what is termed a 'Payment into Court'. This is a sum of money they judge sufficient to entice the Plaintiff to accept as due settlement for his grievances, thus avoiding the terrors of trial. In not accepting such Payment and proceeding to trial, the Plaintiff has not only to win his case, but his Judicial Award has to beat this Payment into Court. The consequence of not doing so is the Plaintiff's exposure to the entire legal costs of the defence. The Judge, of course, is not party to the amount of the Payment into Court.

Spring 2014. Bulb Mania, exciting, refreshing, inspiring. (Bob Willingham)

The evidence delivered by Jerry Michell and Steven Boxall had significant negative impact on the quantum of my settlement. It would all hang on the balance of weight Mr Justice Nelson placed upon this Michell and Boxall evidence on behalf of the Millennium Commission. If we did not beat the Payment into Court, we were dead. It would be the last Christmas we would be having in our family home of 18 years, a home that had been lovingly decorated for Christmas by Jemima and Morwenna to await our return from London. Here was a dark thought that neither came to the front of my mind, nor was voiced to anyone throughout the festive season. Whatever the outcome I had done all I could. Honour was satisfied.

2004   The first week of 2004 hung heavy with positive expectation. Back in Calliope's time the first month of the year, January, was called Januarius after Janus the god of doorways, beginnings, endings and time. He is often depicted as having two heads, facing in opposite directions; one head surveys the past year while the other looks forward to the new. For me in January 2004, the retrospection of all that had gone before, together with the prospect and hopes of all that lay ahead, was Janus personified.

I threw myself back into the Great Atlantic Way positives with a gusto that was neither dimmed nor dented by the news filtering through from Duncan that Mr Justice Nelson was sitting on other matters in the Court of Appeal. This would necessarily delay our Judgment. The waiting days were back with us again. As it turned out they were not waiting days, but waiting weeks and months and a great deal of water was yet to flow under Nanny Moore's bridge overlooked by my office window in Bude before we were to raise our right elbows in yippees of celebration.

Interestingly the phone started ringing once again from people seeking my advice. These ranged from individuals calling from my vacated haunt of Shit Creek through to distant Regional Development Agencies wanting to pick my brains on how projects the scale and significance of Eden come about. One such conversation was eventually to lead me to Bedford. Following my initiation of the project this in turn was to have happy consequences for Ronnie Murning. Having resigned from Eden at the height of the troubles he then agreed to return on his own terms as everyone knew the Project could not do without him. This had added to certain tensions along the way, Ronnie is not deferential by temperament and there is no one less likely to genuflect at the altar of Tim Smit than Ronnie. With Eden delivered to time and to budget, a whole new experience for the Millennium Commission, Ronnie went on to become one of the creators of a set of project ideas called NIRAH, the National Institute for Research into Aquatic Habitats, an Eden with fish, taking with him the newly knighted Nicholas Grimshaw whose firm, led by Jolyon Brewis, created amazing design proposals for revitalizing the redundant brick pits for which Bedford is renowned.

Ronnie was never to forgive Tim nor forget what he considered to be betrayal of the integrity of belief. He was one of the few to receive a valuable Gold Pass to the Eden Project for his inestimable contribution. He returned to London and that same evening symbolically gave his lifetime pass away to a man he met down the pub, and has never returned to Eden.

It had become our custom to get together with Clive and Jane in celebration of big birthdays and big wedding anniversaries. Clive and I had been born within a week of one another and we had all been married around the same time in 1974. We came together for 30th wedding anniversary celebrations, on this occasion their wedding date, not ours, at the end of May on the Isles of Scilly. Circumstances happily conspired that the same day we came together in warm friendship to celebrate with friends whose generosity at key moments had ensured our financial survival, Larry and Duncan were desperately trying to get hold of us with the news the Judgment had been handed down.

The wait had been worthwhile. We had won, and won handsomely.

Druces & Attlee had been found to have been negligent in their advice; that there was a clear conflict of interest between the Eden Trust and Tim and I as co founders to whom they retained a duty; that in the course of advising the Eden Trust Druces & Attlee acted against my interests and that in giving advice and acting for the Eden Trust in the negotiations by me in pursuing my claim, Druces & Attlee had been in possession of confidential information, relevant to my strength in negotiation and by continuing to act for the Eden Trust in those circumstances had breached their fiduciary duty to me.

I was awarded damages including interest of £1.865m together with a contribution of £1.775m towards my gigantic legal costs. Having paid my entire legal team's costs and having discharged the accumulated debts of a decade, having regard for the prolonged absence of livelihood and loss of professional practice and pension, my financial reward for the innovation and risks taken would be measured by many, myself included, as modest. But who, in these circumstances would use depth of pocket as the final measurement of reward. My reward was Eden, a world project for Cornwall, together with the total and irrefutable vindication of the stand I had taken against overwhelming odds that so very nearly rendered to naught my entire professional career and for so long had put in such perilous circumstances the lives of all those nearest and dearest to me.

Legal Judgment is reinstatement, it is conclusive, the truth established by positive intervention rooted in a devotion to fairness and equity. For me, it brought closure, and with it the start of the rest of my life. I was entirely content, finally, that justice in our land is substantially free from influence of politics or Parliament albeit I had been left questioning this along the way. It is the business of Government to see the rights and privileges of an individual are not infringed or violated. I doubt I will be moved in my own view that the actions of those civil servants in volunteering themselves to the defence of Druces & Attlee were self-serving actions that ran contrary to equity in both civil and moral law and to levels of conduct we may expect and demand from our civil servants. It should be remembered their boss CEO Mike O'Connor had refused my legal team and my MP access to the records they were charged with administering on behalf of the public, and had refused to make available to the Courts the forensic audit. Equity enjoins on Government as well as individuals. When not kept under proper control men will ever hurry to cross the line of right and reason.

And what of Druces & Attlee? The business of a lawyer is to define and confirm that which is legal or illegal and such advice is the basis of a lawyer's reward. The legal profession sits there between you and me and the big, wide world. They are independent of commercial interests and are there to protect our own interests and to keep our confidences. They are our first port of call for most of the big events in our lives, protecting our families, buying our homes and are there for advice at all key moments in our progress as we make our way in the world. They operate under strict professional codes of conduct.

I felt that, by their actions, found to be wholly unjustified in the Royal Courts of Justice, Druces & Attlee had cast aside all probity and propriety and proper professional conduct and had placed their own interests (including their financial interests) above mine, notwithstanding that I had been their client. In the elegant language of the High Court the description of their conduct as being 'particularly unmeritorious' is severe censure indeed. However, despite my protests to those charged with the regulatory conduct of solicitors, as far as I am aware no further censure was given and the Partners who had fallen so short of expected professional standards were back at their desks the following week. The question pops into my mind that had we been talking of a small firm of provincial lawyers their professional body would have looked to withdrawing practising certificates on the grounds that the legal profession had been brought into disrepute, but not a City of London law firm with direct connection to a former Prime Minister of Britain and whose provenance stretches back to the 18th century.

And what of my co-founder Tim Smit? It is surely a truism that one man's Messiah Smit is another man's Tyrant Tim; some would say unblushingly perverse in visiting chaos on other team members around him for his own ends, destroying along the way the happiness of anyone who seeks to serve the project's ends before the interests of its self appointed leader. He remains as charged by this, my story, of disturbing and disrupting all attempts at good governance, proper regulation and public finance accounting during Eden's evolution until such time as it suited his purpose and his own ends had been served. For the many Eden supporters and fellow travellers along Eden's journey this story serves as 'the fog is clearing' moment by way of securing a balance of understanding. It is for you to decide where the line between right and wrong should be drawn and what means are, and were, justified in securing Eden's humanitarian ends.

In order to compete in the global world Cornwall needs such as Eden as a symbol of our times, something that captures the spirit of the age. Eden has surely delivered handsomely on the original Mission Statement Tim and I brought together in that autumn of 1994:

> *'To create under one roof a range of natural habitats found on planet Earth ... An international resource designed for research, education and public enjoyment to herald the new Millennium, bequeathing a gift of incalculable value to those who will follow us... our hope for and belief in the future.'*

Eden provides Cornwall with its defining piece of world class architecture with which it connects to the global world. It is a flagship leading Cornwall's economic well being into the future, providing so many jobs, so many opportunities and so much prestige flowing to the far South West.

The world now knows that the forces of history were at work and something really important happened at the end of the longest country lane in Britain at the turn of the Millennium. For Cornwall the world had changed and our Mission Statement somehow captured the moment. For all these reasons, despite the incredible and painful journey that was my Eden, I am joyful. The manifestation of my vision and ambitions for Cornwall has been achieved and it is for this reason I bear Tim Smit no malice, no ill will. For me Eden tells a wonderful story with wonderful architecture to inspire you to fight for your grandchildren's future. The way the Eden story has been told these past ten years is truly a testament to Tim's fabulous skills in articulating the issues and concerns of the moment and, in a sense, through Eden's success, Tim has achieved his personal ambition, to become a fashion icon for our times

And what of the Millennium Commission and Eden? It was certainly thus that in presenting our Mission Statement to the world both Tim and I were taking on colossal personal risks. We responded in good faith, to the exhortation from the Secretary of State Peter Brooke... 'to look to the glory of our nation...' It was our choice. Whether, in my own case, subsequent Secretaries of State chairing the Millennium Commission reciprocated or transgressed this good faith is for you to decide.

Critics of New Labour's time have much to ponder as to why the Millennium Commission allowed Eden's legal and governance model to proceed knowing it to be defective. Without check or restraint Millennium Commission funds flowed to Eden in defiance of their own conditions precedent. How, and why, were so many cowed into silence and submission? Why did the Millennium Commission not direct the process and rectify the inadequacies made so abundantly clear to them in timely fashion? The Millennium Commission instituted their own forensic audit, but perhaps, by then, they were already, themselves, too mired in the process. The only possible interpretation can surely be that the forensic audit embraced the seeds of the Millennium Commission's own destruction. Did they commission this work at the public expense, knowing it would never see the light of day?

In these circumstances there are well known procedures for company/Government body/professional body interrogation and these well known procedures should surely have been adopted. What were the uncomfortable truths? Was there indeed misfeasance or even worse, malfeasance? Who knows what letter sits somewhere gathering dust as insurance against these thoughts I now share.

At the end of the Eden journey my last conversation with Paul Tyler, now Lord Tyler of Linkinhorne, delivered his verdict on the way the government of the day handled the unfolding events:

"... there is always a dilemma when something enterprising, but risky, is afoot in an area like Cornwall, well away from the centre of power.

Alexander on a pilgrimage to Hawker's Hut with his grandfather ... 'British by birth, Cornish by the grace of God!' Composite Photograph by Bob Willingham. (JB archive)

Central Government tries to micro-manage when really they should stand back and just ensure the basic essentials are in place: proper accountability, transparency and business integrity. All the evidence I saw confirmed my impression that in the case of Eden they lost the plot and then turned a blind eye because it was so blatantly the only real success story of the whole Millennium project."

The KPMG forensic audit commissioned in the name of Chris Smith MP, Secretary of State, denied to the High Court and to my MP acting on behalf of his constituent, and paid for by you and me, never saw the light of day. I have gone through life with my fear of regret always being far greater than my fear of failure ... of not having done that which I thought right or achievable with all the effort I could summon. I believe history will not record the Millennium Commission kindly, at a macro level for the debacle of the Millennium Dome and the vast sums of public money squandered there and elsewhere, and at the micro level for the wide-ranging inglorious stories such as my own that I have bumped into along the way, where decency was denied. But it matters not. In my eyes of all the Projects great and small that received Millennium Commission support, Eden shines out as a project for our times as being proof positive there is nothing more powerful in this life than an idea whose time has come.

And what of Cornwall and the future? In this past decade Eden has become as characteristic to Cornwall as Elgar's music is to Edwardian England. I hope if you have not already done so you will one day pay Eden a visit. Reserve your most elegant thoughts for your time there and release them to echo round the cavernous enclosures where the magical interplay of light, plants, architecture and engineering will paint images of lasting pleasure in your memory. Who knows, you may suddenly be standing there 'with eyes that feel and hands that see'.

Please be in no doubt I rejoice at Eden's continuing success. Eden is leaving a giant Gulliver footprint on Lilliputian Cornwall's future. Its positive legacy is assured. Eden makes Cornwall feel good about the future, and so it should.

As I come to share my final thoughts with you, I reflect that these events have consumed more than half my adult and professional life. You may be wondering why after 20 long years since Tim and I first shook hands and 13 years since Eden received its first visitor to stand in awe and wonder, I am now sharing my story with you. My motivation lies with none other than that eccentric Victorian cleric who spent his long, lonely hours on the cliffs at Morwenstow gazing out upon the western Ocean from his evocative hut constructed of broken ships' timbers, the Reverend Robert Stephen Hawker. From his hand came Trelawny, the undisputed anthem for Cornwall, the Celtic nation, and my answer to you lies in the final lines of the refrain:

'And Shall Trelawny live?
And Shall Trelawny die?
Here's 20,000 Cornishmen shall know the reason why!

End

Afterword

It was inevitable that my story was on a collision course with those who would argue the merits of the saying, least said soonest mended, but this is not a story of an individual who fell victim to unprofitable speculation on his own account. It speaks primarily of the management and conduct of public bodies and of the political imperatives of Government who dictate implementation policy handed down to civil servants charged with delivery of the will of their political masters. Independence of other interests and integrity of mind are the bulwarks that straddle a line so fine and yet so defining it must never be smudged. Those civil servants charged with the execution of these policies on our behalf have a precious duty of care that surely starts with the question being asked, in implementing the will of the State, my employer: am I denying or violating the demonstrable and legitimate rights of an individual?

In this memoir I genuinely believe we have a tale of cock up rather than conspiracy but alas we then had conspiracy to cover up cock up. All written codes of conduct are in place to express and protect underlying first principles, be they for the practising professions or anyone employed by the State or assuming public office, thus ensuring and enshrining the practical application of wisdom and prudence. In this regard my Eden story is told entirely in sorrow rather than in anger. Individuals who inadvertently strayed across the line found themselves in an entanglement placing them in personal difficulty in the discharge of their professional obligations or public duty.

I have taken the view that the public interest is not best served by the concealment of uncomfortable truths within the public realm. The pursuit of truth always threatens someone. As individuals we all have free will, we all make our choices in life.

Leading Individuals in the Narrative

Family:

Victoria Ball — Jonathan's wife
Jemima and Morwenna — Jonathan and Victoria's daughters

Cornwall:

Michael Galsworthy — High Sheriff of Cornwall 1994, Chairman Millennium Committee in Cornwall
Viscount Falmouth, (George Boscawen,) — The Tregothnan Estate and Goonvean and Restowrack China Clay Co.
Hon. Evelyn Boscawen
Henry Boettinger — The Springs of Inspiration
Paul Tyler MP — Member Parliament for Cornwall North
Tim Jones — Devon & Cornwall Business Council
John Nelson — The Lost Gardens of Heligan
Mike Jane — The author's bank manager

Eden Project Limited (EPL):

Tim Smit — Project Co Founder
Jonathan Ball — Project Co Founder
Ronnie Murning — Project Director
Philip Macmillan Browse — Horticultural advisor and EPL Director
Peter Thoday — Horticultural advisor and EPL Director
Evelyn Thurlby, — CEO 1997-1999
Dr Ken Hill — Chairman, EPL
Gaynor Coley — Finance Director
Richard Sandbrook — Director, EPL

Design Team

Nicholas Grimshaw — Architects
Anthony Hunt Ass. — Engineers
Arup Associates — Environmental & Transport Consultants

Arup Economics
Davis Langdon — Quantity Surveyors
McAlpines JV — Contractors, Land Use Consultants Landscape

The Eden Trustees:
Founding Trustees

Dr Alcon Copisarow — Chairman
Dr Alan Donald
Dr Richard Carew Pole
Dr Ralph Riley
Ian Hay Davison

Second Generation Trustees

Sir Ronnie Hampel — Chairman
Sir Ghilean Prance — RBG Kew

Lawyers:

Bruces & Attlee (co-founders,EPL, Eden Trust,Lost Garden of Helegan, Tim Smit)
Field Fisher Waterhouse (Jonathan Ball)
McDermott Will & Emery (Jonathan Ball)

Secretaries of State:
Chairman Millennium Commission

The Rt Hon Peter Brooke, MP
(The Rt.Hon Steven Dorrell MP)
The Rt Hon Chris Smith MP
The Rt Hon Tessa Jowell MP

The Millennium Commission:

Jennifer Page — Chief Executive
Mike O'Connor — Chief Executive
Steven Porter
Jerry Michell
Steve Boxall

High Court judges, Royal Courts of Justice

Mr Justice Laddie 11.04.2001
Mr Justice Burton 12.12.2001
Mr Justice Nelson 24.11.2003- 18th December 2003

Royal Institute of British Architects

Lord Rodgers of Quarrybank
Rod Hackney PPRIBA
Dr Frank Duffy   PPRIBA

Acknowledgements

Having read thus far you will appreciate the pure scale of the debt of gratitude I owe to so many.

Firstly, to dear Dad, now 35 years in his grave, for his Solomonistic wisdom which forms part of my story, and Mum, God Bless her, a few months away from 101, the longest love I have ever known. Her advice to me was that happiness comes from going through life as a giver rather than taker.

To my wife, best chum and soul mate of 40 years, Victoria, the mother and grandmother of our loving and much loved family, along with our daughters Jemima and Morwenna, all unquestioning and unconditional in their faith and support through years of tumult for us all, holding on tightly to the roller coaster that we neither welcomed nor understood.

To my colleagues at the Jonathan Ball Practice since its inception, especially the team whose Eden conceptual contributions were considerable. So cruel, as the Project was to be the seed of the Practice's own demise. And of course, lest we forget, the clients of the Practice, out of whom came substantial offers of financial support to Eden and, most importantly, its location in Bodelva.

I cherish all those happy relationships with colleagues on our early Eden journey together, the first generation Eden Trustees who so defined the essence and secured the political endorsement by pledging their substantial reputations. To the many rank and file from the early days, their wholehearted commitment to the vision and who held onto their integrity of belief when others around them were losing theirs; and in several instances parting company with their own Eden future in consequence.

To the London chums in large part defined by the Athenaeum, Pall Mall, a Club whose membership these past 190 years can be characterised by the substantial contributions made to society in science and medicine, engineering, literature and the liberal arts. The Athenaeum Strollers whose collective contributions to Eden's gestation and forward progress helped establish an unstoppable intellectual power house in securing political support and intellectual rigour.

Within these ranks the inestimable Mike Shaw, lately Curtis Brown, who initiated and shepherded my nascent literary ambitions. Surely we will never forget one of our early meetings at his offices in Haymarket witnessing, aghast, the collapse of the first Twin Tower. And his warning that writing my book at that time would deliver short term profit, but at the likely expense of Eden's own survival: sage advice that has delayed this book's publication for more than a decade, to a time when I firmly believe no harm to its future can flow from these pages.

To all my fellow members within these portals who have pledged their friendship, support and influence to Eden's cause and then to our survival, and the Athenaeum staff - loyal, discreet, and ever caring who, with the chums, saw us through many dark London days.

I have more than paid my dues in support of the legal profession in Britain. Take a bow Hayley Stallard of Field Fisher Waterhouse who first established a legal framework to secure my future and Larry Cohen with Duncan Curley from McDermott Will and Emery together with their supporting teams, Counsel and Queens Counsels who ensured we finally prevailed.

The support I received from the professional press and the media at national and particularly regional level, delivered a better public understanding of the injustices along the journey and I will be ever grateful for their generous support, crusading when Eden needed it most and sympathetic in championing a sense of fair play when Eden's Cornish Co-founder was being denied legitimate expectation.

Since inception there has been a core team of close friends there to raise the right elbow at times of celebration and to drop everything to be at our side in moments of crisis, in particular Tim Jones, Devon & Cornwall Business Council, who effectively became my campaign manager to see me through torrid times. My loyal Bude friends who have shared my dream since the very beginning and of course those in the narrative mentioned in Christian name only, Clive and Jane, Tony and dear Zoo.

And finally my inner sanctum friends who have unstintingly given their time and advice to get me over the finish line with this book: William Murray of Wordsearch, Terry Woodger, Jim Sloman in Sydney, Jamie Donald, Robert Godber, Stephen Brooker, Bruce Hunter, Cameron Doley lawyer and friend, Senior Partner Carter-Ruck who has steered us through complex legal intricacies, Bob Willingham for his cover design and photographic expertise, and my PA of more than a decade Penelope Hasell whose wit and wisdom has contributed much to the production of this book and for the fun we've had along the way.

For Daniel Nanavati, my publisher who has an elegant and able mind. He is patience personified and ever courteous.

My heartfelt thanks to you, one and all, and to the many more of my tribe whom I have never met but who share my values and my hopes for what Eden can enable for future generations.

Jonathan Ball
1st May 2014

Index

A

B

C

D

E

Lightning Source UK Ltd.
Milton Keynes UK
UKOW06f0809250614

233967UK00005B/13/P